Corporatism and Economic Performance

NEW DIRECTIONS IN MODERN ECONOMICS

Series Editor: Malcolm C. Sawyer,
Professor of Economics, University of Leeds

New Directions in Modern Economics presents a challenge to orthodox economic thinking. It focuses on new ideas emanating from radical traditions including post-Keynesian, Kaleckian, neo-Ricardian and Marxian. The books in the series do not adhere rigidly to any single school of thought but attempt to present a positive alternative to the conventional wisdom.

A list of published titles in this series is printed at the end of this volume.

Corporatism and Economic Performance

A Comparative Analysis of Market Economies

Andrew Henley and Euclid Tsakalotos

University of Kent at Canterbury

Edward Elgar

Published by
Edward Elgar Publishing Limited
Gower House
Croft Road
Aldershot
Hants GU11 3HR
England

Edward Elgar Publishing Company
Old Post Road
Brookfield
Vermont 05036
USA

British Library Cataloguing in Publication Data
Henley, Andrew
 Corporatism and Economic Performance: Comparative Analysis of
 Market Economies. – (New Directions in Modern Economics
 Series)
 I. Title II. Tsakalotos, Euclid III. Series
 330.12

Library of Congress Cataloguing in Publication Data
Henley, Andrew, 1961–
 Corporatism and economic performance: a comparative analysis of
 market economies/Andrew Henley and Euclid Tsakalotos.
   p. cm. — (New directions in modern economics)
  Includes bibliographical references and indexes.
  1. Industrial organization (Economic theory) 2. Efficiency,
 Industrial. 3. Employment (Economic theory) 4. Comparative
 economics. I. Tsakalotos, Euclid, 1960– . II. Title.
 III. Series.
 HD2328.H46 1993
 338.7—dc20   93–28604
                                                                                          CIP

ISBN 1 85278 539 X

Printed in Great Britain at the University Press, Cambridge

Contents

Figures

Tables

Acknowledgements

A number of people gave their time generously and commented on various parts of this book. We are grateful to Malcolm Sawyer, as editor of the **New Directions in Modern Economics** series, for his comments. Heather Gibson and Peter Sanfey at the University of Kent read through most of the book and made particularly incisive comments on Chapters 6 and 3 respectively. We are also indebted to two non-economists who were relatively polite about this contribution coming from economists – Chris Howell commented on Chapters 2, 3 and 4 and Chris Pickvance gave us extensive feedback on Chapter 2. Some of the material in Chapter 5 stems from collaborative work with Francis Green, whose contribution we therefore gratefully acknowledge. We would also like to thank a number of colleagues at the University of Kent who have commented at various stages, especially Alan Carruth, Andy Dickerson, Richard Disney and Howard Gospel. We have also benefited from the insights of participants at various study groups and conferences where we have aired some of the themes of this book, including the 1992 European Association of Labour Economists conference, the ESRC Political Economy and Post-Keynesian study groups and the University of Warwick's Industrial Economics workshop. Finally Sue Henley and Heather Gibson showed their usual high standards of tolerance and support during the writing of this book and to them we give particular thanks.

1. Introduction: An Overview of Economic Performance in Corporatist and Liberal Economies

Institutions matter for economic performance: that is the central message in this book. During the 1970s and 1980s the market-liberal challenge to the post-war economic and social consensus of the mixed economies was that unfettered markets could best promote efficiency and thus improve economic performance. If this is the case then institutions, and not least the corporatist institutions which form the subject of this book, can be seen as 'imperfections' or 'rigidities' which hinder the operation of the free market. This book argues that, on the contrary, such institutions are necessary for the efficient operation of markets because they constitute important mechanisms for reducing the uncertainty and potential for conflict which are inherent in market economies. Appropriate economic institutions can make a difference to economic performance, and institutional divergence is an important explanatory factor for the wide range of economic performance of OECD economies.

The industrialized market economies of the world have experienced a quite considerable diversity of economic performance in the period since 1945. In particular, it is possible to observe a substantial range of experience of adjustment to the economic shocks of the early 1970s, shocks which marked the end of what has been termed the post-war 'golden age' of sustained growth and low unemployment.[1] In comparison with what went before, the 1970s was a decade of rising unemployment, lower rates of economic growth and considerably higher inflation. A greater measure of price stability was generally achieved in the 1980s but at a cost of sustained but slower growth and appallingly high levels of unemployment. However, some countries seemed to weather the crisis of the 1970s and 1980s more easily than others, in that they managed to prevent the rapid growth in unemployment that characterized the experience of most of the world's larger economies. The central theme of this book is that this range of economic experience can, in significant measure, be explained by differences in the institutional framework within which economic policy is formulated and implemented. In particular, in countries where interest groups such as trade unions and employers' federations are strong, corporatist institutional features appear to have enabled a more prolonged achievement of full employment than where such corporatist features were absent.

The notion of corporatism is one that is notoriously difficult to pin down – indeed its definition has generated considerable academic heat in the period of the last twenty years during which interest in corporatism has re-emerged.[2] Our own understanding of corporatism will, in the fuller sense, emerge as the book progresses, and we will attempt to summarize its important characteristics later in this introductory chapter. At this stage it is worthwhile perhaps limiting ourselves to noting some important features of corporatist systems. The most commonly identified of these, recognized by economists and political scientists alike, is that corporatism is characterized by a high degree of centralization in collective bargaining. In some corporatist economies a high level of bargaining coordination may serve as an alternative to high structural centralization. A further feature, discussed more often by political economists and political scientists, is that in corporatism the bargaining relationships between labour and capital, and also that between these two and the state, appear to be long-term and durable. One consequence of this is that the bargaining strategies adopted tend to be longer-term in nature and thus can encompass aspects of economic policy which extend beyond the determination of wages and employment.

THE DIVERSITY OF MACROECONOMIC PERFORMANCE AMONG THE INDUSTRIALIZED ECONOMIES

The diversity of economic performance across the industrialized economies, since the end of the long boom of the 1960s, is a subject on which a great deal has written by economists of all persuasions.[3]

We shall not be able, in one short introductory chapter, to do justice to the many ways in which countries have differed. Instead we concentrate on a few key macroeconomic indicators.

The unprecedented prosperity of the immediate post-war period up to the 1960s has led to the 1960s being identified as the zenith of a post-war Keynesian 'golden age'. Following upon this historically exceptional period of economic prosperity, the divergence of performance across the industrialized economies was by the 1960s comparatively small, by past and future standards. This is because sustained economic prosperity among the world's richest industrialized economies easily spilled over to less rich members of the developed world. This is particularly so since the long boom of the 1950s and 1960s witnessed a massive growth in trade between the industrialized economies.[4]

Table 1.1 provides GDP growth rate averages for the leading nineteen of the twenty-four OECD member states[5] between 1960 and 1990. We divide this thirty-year period into four. The first period from 1960 to 1973 is one of sustained, but progressively overheated growth from the zenith of the 'golden age' to the first OPEC oil shock. The second period from 1974 to 1979 is the 'inter-shock' period between the first and second OPEC oil price increases. In most countries unemployment peaked roughly around 1985 – in some countries the peak came slightly earlier, in others, such as France and Japan, it came slightly later. The decade since 1980 is thus divided in 1985 to roughly capture a distinction between the post-'stagflationary' recession during which unemployment rose dramatically and the (temporary) return to growth and falling unemployment in the latter half of the 1980s. Countries are grouped into four. The first of these comprises current European Community (EC) members and the second the current members of the European Free Trade Area (EFTA). The EFTA group contains the countries usually cited as being strongly corporatist, namely Austria and the three Nordic economies of Norway, Sweden and Finland. Switzerland is the exception, although as we shall later see, despite a very decentralized collective bargaining structure it does have some corporatist features. The English-speaking non-European economies comprise a third group. Japan is left classified on its own both because of its geographical and cultural distance, and because of its institutional differences from the other non-European economies.

Table 1.1 shows very clearly the growth slowdown after 1973 right

Table 1.1 Growth experience across the OECD since 1960

Average rate of real GDP growth	1960–73	1974–79	1980–85	1986–90
European Community				
Belgium	5.0	2.3	1.4	3.2
Denmark	4.5	1.9	2.2	1.5
France	6.2	2.8	1.5	2.9
Germany	4.7	2.4	1.1	3.1
Ireland	4.5	5.0	2.6	4.4
Italy	5.4	3.7	1.9	3.0
Netherlands	5.2	2.7	1.0	2.7
Spain	7.0	2.2	1.4	4.5
UK	3.3	1.5	1.3	3.2
Average	5.1	2.7	1.6	3.2
EFTA				
Austria	5.1	2.9	1.6	3.1
Finland	5.3	3.3	3.3	3.5
Norway	4.3	4.9	3.5	1.6
Sweden	4.2	1.8	1.8	2.1
Switzerland	4.6	−0.3	1.9	2.8
Average	4.7	2.3	2.4	2.6
North America & Australasia				
Australia	5.2	2.6	3.2	2.8
Canada	5.3	4.2	2.7	3.0
New Zealand	3.8	0.8	2.6	0.9
USA	3.8	2.4	2.4	3.0
Average	4.5	2.5	2.7	2.4
Japan	10.1	3.6	3.7	4.6

Source: Calculated from OECD National Accounts, 1960–90

across the industrialized world. Average growth rates fell from between four and five percent per annum in the 1960s to only one or two percent per annum by the early 1980s. If economic growth rates improved slightly on average in the late 1980s that improvement was

Table 1.2 Unemployment experience across the OECD since 1960

Average unemployment rate	1960–73	1974–79	1980–85	1986–90
European Community				
Belgium	2.4	6.3	11.3	9.5
Denmark	1.8	5.5	9.3	8.6
France	2.0	1.9	8.3	9.8
Germany	0.8	3.2	6.0	5.9
Ireland	5.2	7.6	12.6	16.2
Italy	3.9	4.6	6.4	7.8
Netherlands	1.5	5.1	10.1	8.8
Spain	2.5	5.3	16.6	18.7
UK	2.9	5.1	10.5	8.6
Average	2.6	5.2	10.1	10.4
EFTA				
Austria	1.4	1.5	3.0	3.4
Finland	2.0	4.4	5.1	4.3
Norway	1.9	1.8	2.6	3.5
Sweden	1.5	1.5	2.4	1.7
Switzerland	0.1	1.0	1.7	1.9
Average	1.4	2.0	2.9	3.0
North America & Australasia				
Australia	2.1	5.0	7.6	7.2
Canada	5.0	7.2	9.9	8.3
New Zealand	0.2	0.8	3.9	5.6
USA	4.8	6.7	8.0	5.8
Average	3.0	4.9	7.4	6.7
Japan	1.3	1.9	2.4	2.5

Source: Computed from Layard, Nickell and Jackman (1991), Table A3, pp. 526–528

very patchy and, as we now know, rather short-lived.

Table 1.2 gives unemployment averages for the same periods, and shows that, while the growth slowdown is more or less uniform, it is by no means the case that this has been translated in all countries into a rapid departure from full employment. Before 1973 there is a good deal of uniformity in unemployment rates, in comparison with what was to come later. Only Ireland had an average unemployment rate which exceeded five percent of the labour force. It is after 1973 that experience diverged significantly, and we begin to notice the improved performance of the corporatist group. Average unemployment rates doubled in the EC countries and increased by two-thirds in North America and Australasia. Within the EFTA group only Finland recorded an average rate above two percent. In Austria, Sweden and Norway average unemployment effectively remained at the same level enjoyed in the 1960s.

For the EC economies the first half of the 1980s saw a further doubling in average unemployment relative to the 1970s to over ten percent of the workforce, with France and Spain experiencing particularly dramatic rises. Average unemployment outside Europe also rose sharply. The average for the North American and Australasian economies rose to over seven percent. Among the EFTA economies, although unemployment rates rose in the 1980s, the picture was much less bleak. In the case of Switzerland and, to a lesser extent, Austria the burden of employment adjustment in the 1970s was borne by foreign workers who do not appear in unemployment statistics. Nevertheless all of the economies in this group have unemployment averages during the 1980 to 1985 period which are lower than the best-performing EC economy (Germany).

By the second half of the 1980s unemployment had peaked in nearly all the developed economies, although the onset of global economic recession in the early 1990s means that this welcome return to conditions of falling unemployment has proved short-lived. In terms of the average unemployment data in Table 1.2 the late 1980s appears as a period in which unemployment in most countries stabilized. Stabilization in average unemployment occurred in the corporatist EFTA group of countries but at a rate which is only a third of the average rate in the rest of Europe and slightly less than half the average outside Europe (excluding Japan).

Figure 1.1 depicts average unemployment in the EC member countries and the EFTA groups (as defined by present membership) over the period since 1960. It shows very clearly how the latter countries have on average managed to avoid the debilitating growth in unemployment that has followed the end the 'golden age'.

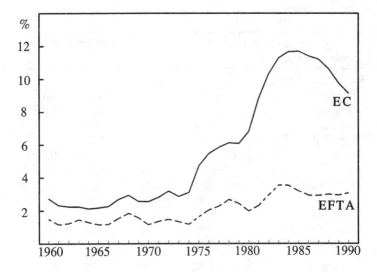

Figure 1.1 Average unemployment in European Community and EFTA countries, 1960–1990

Some may argue that for each of the EFTA economies there are exceptional circumstances which have contributed to their superior performance.[6] We have already mentioned the problem of unobserved unemployment among foreign workers in Switzerland and Austria. To a certain extent this is borne out in Table 1.3, which gives average annual rates of growth of civilian employment since 1960. The table shows that employment growth weakened considerably after 1973 for nearly all economies. Within the EFTA group during the mid-1970s period the contrast between on the one hand falling employment in Austria and Switzerland and on the other sustained employment growth in the Scandinavian economies is very apparent. All three Scandinavian economies managed to achieve higher average employment growth rates in the 1973 to 1979 period than they had between 1960 and 1973. In the case of Norway, where this improvement is most pronounced, this has in good measure resulted from the growth in the offshore oil and gas sector during this period. After 1980 all the EFTA economies maintain growing civilian employment, in contrast to many other

Corporatism and Economic Performance

Table 1.3 Employment growth across the OECD since 1960

Average rate of civilian employment growth	1960–73	1974–79	1980–85	1986–90
European Community				
Belgium	0.47	0.02	−0.66	1.16
Denmark	0.92	0.39	0.58	0.89*
France	0.74	0.35	−0.31	0.73
Germany	0.35	−0.56	0.37	1.45
Ireland	0.07	1.12	−1.05	0.42*
Italy	−0.36	0.90	0.37	0.68
Netherlands	1.01	0.53	0.88	2.37†
Spain	0.53	−0.95	−1.85	3.41
UK	0.40	0.25	−0.56	1.93
Total	0.36	0.08	−0.20	1.53*
EFTA				
Austria	−0.12	−0.53	0.99	1.07
Finland	0.54	0.72	1.30	0.25
Norway	1.28	2.09	1.07	0.11
Sweden	0.81	1.26	0.47	0.96
Switzerland	2.26	−0.90	1.32	1.23
Total	0.89	0.38	0.97	0.82
N. America & Australasia	2.76	0.85	1.70	3.22
Australia	2.86	2.90	1.31	2.30
Canada	2.12	1.69	0.88	−1.81+
New Zealand	1.98	2.55	1.37	1.94
USA	2.10	2.47	1.37	2.41
Total				
Japan	1.38	0.69	0.97	1.48

Source: computed from OECD Labour Statistics, various issues
Notes: * 1985–89, † 1988–90 (series rebased in 1987), + 1987–89 (series rebased in 1986)

European economies. It is only after 1985 that the EC economies on average return to conditions of growing employment. Outside Europe, with the exception of Canada, employment growth has remained

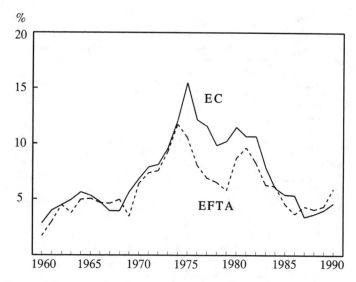

*Figure 1.2 Average inflation rates in European Community and
EFTA countries, 1960–1990*

buoyant since the end of the 'golden age'. So in contrast with most of
the larger European economies the small corporatist economies have
managed to achieve a much greater stability in levels of employment
during the crises of the 1970s and 1980s.

An immediate issue concerns whether these countries have acheived
this superior performance because they have adopted more
expansionary macroeconomic policy, and thus have been more
prepared to tolerate higher inflation. Figure 1.2, which graphs average
inflation rates for the EC and EFTA groups, shows that this is not the
case. Table 1.4 provides the same country-by-country breakdown as in
the earlier tables for average inflation. Before 1973 we see that the
comparative uniformity of economic experience across the OECD is
especially so in terms of average inflation rates. This is perhaps not
surprising as the period in question was one in which the world's
major currencies were still fixed through the Bretton Woods system.
Average inflation rates rise significantly for all countries after 1973
and decline again in the face of macroeconomic restraint and recession

Corporatism and Economic Performance

Table 1.4 Inflation experience across the OECD since 1960

Average inflation rate	1960–73	1974–79	1980–85	1986–90
European Community				
Belgium	3.9	8.1	5.4	3.1
Denmark	6.6	10.1	7.9	4.4
France	5.9	10.6	9.9	3.6
Germany	4.2	4.7	3.4	2.5
Ireland	6.7	14.5	11.9	3.8
Italy	5.2	17.2	15.2	6.4
Netherlands	5.8	7.5	3.8	1.2
Spain	6.6	18.2	11.8	7.2
UK	4.9	16.1	9.0	5.5
Average	5.4	11.9	8.7	4.2
EFTA				
Austria	4.5	6.1	4.9	2.9
Finland	6.5	12.6	8.7	5.7
Norway	5.0	8.2	9.4	2.8
Sweden	4.9	10.7	9.0	7.5
Switzerland	5.2	3.8	4.3	3.4
Average	5.2	8.3	7.3	4.5
North America &				
Australasia	4.6	11.9	8.6	7.1
Australia	3.6	10.1	7.2	3.8
Canada	5.2	14.3	10.9	9.9
New Zealand	3.3	7.6	5.9	3.7
USA	4.2	11.0	8.1	6.1
Average				
Japan	5.9	8.0	1.7	1.0

Source: Computed from Layard, Nickell and Jackman (1991), Table A4, pp. 530–532

in the 1980s. The growth of inflationary pressure is generally attributed to increasingly tight labour markets in the last years of the 1960s, with a specific and substantial boost to inflationary pressure being provided by the oil price shock of 1973. Reduced global demand and falling productivity resulting from these pressures imposed severe constraints on the potential for economic growth among the industrialized economies. The increased interdependency within the global economy ensured that the stagnationary disease of the 1970s was quickly passed between national economies.

What is clear from Table 1.4 is that certain economies were better able to resist this inflationary pressure than others. Germany and Japan stand out as examples from the larger economies, although a number of smaller economies also maintained better than average performance through this decade, such as Belgium and Netherlands within the EC and Austria, Norway and Switzerland outside it. In the EFTA economies where unemployment did not rise rapidly, inflation rates were no higher than average after 1973. The average across the group is, in fact, considerably lower than for the EC and the North America/Australasia groups, although this average conceals a better measure of price stability in Austria and particularly Switzerland than in the Scandinavian economies. The virtuous performance of Austria and Switzerland is due to their economic proximity to Germany and in Austria's case its policy, since 1976, of maintaining a currency peg with the Deutschmark. In general, high inflation in the 1970s was more likely to go hand in hand with a poor unemployment performance than lower unemployment as a cross-country Phillips curve might suggest.

The inflationary economic experience of the 1970s provided the world's industrialized economies with a stern test in so far as a possible return to price stability, low unemployment and sustained growth was to depend on both stable economic management and on successful economic institutional design. As we shall, see these two factors are by no means independent of each other. The degree of success with which different economies passed or failed this test is to be seen in the diversity of economic performance in the 1980s. On average the developed economies have certainly not unequivocally succeeded; if anything they have performed rather poorly in this test. The tables confirm that the 1980s were on average a decade of much higher unemployment and even lower growth, though this was mitigated by some improvement in price stability when compared with what went before. Table 1.5 shows the Okun 'misery' index (the sum of inflation and unemployment rates) for the 1970s as a decade compared to the 1980s. Averaged across all nineteen economies the Okun misery index worsens slightly when compared to the 1970s. Only for seven economies does the Okun index improve as we move from

Table 1.5 Okun index averages for 1970s and 1980s

	Okun index 1970s	Okun index 1980s
European Community		
Belgium	11.98	15.08
Denmark	13.41	15.53
France	12.66	16.38
Germany	7.79	8.96
Ireland	20.44	22.95
Italy	17.88	18.23
Netherlands	11.61	12.24
Spain	18.77	27.59
UK	17.30	17.48
Average	14.62	17.16
EFTA		
Austria	7.57	7.17
Finland	14.51	12.24
Norway	10.00	9.35
Sweden	10.77	10.24
Switzerland	6.01	5.63
Average	9.77	8.93
North America & Australasia		
Australia	14.50	15.79
Canada	14.80	15.14
New Zealand	13.41	15.44
USA	12.72	12.16
Average	13.86	14.63
Japan	9.39	3.88

Note: Okun index is the sum of inflation and unemployment rates
Source: See Tables 1.1 and 1.2

the 1970s to the 1980s. These are Austria, Finland, Japan, Norway, Sweden, Switzerland and the USA. Five of these are the EFTA economies, and of these four comprise the main corporatist economies.

The strategies adopted by the different members of the OECD to bring about a greater degree of price stability in the 1980s have varied considerably. Some countries such as Britain and the USA have espoused a neo-liberal approach which has stressed the importance of reforms to improve labour market flexibility and bring about greater deregulation of economic activity. Corporatist economies, as we shall be discussing in much greater length, have rejected such an approach, maintaining their centralized and coordinated strategies of wage determination in conjunction with a much more consensual approach to the conduct of economic policy.

Such diversity in policy approach has resulted in a wide variation in the observed cost of reduced inflation in terms of increased unemployment. This is illustrated in Figure 1.3 which graphs the 'sacrifice ratio' of higher unemployment for lower inflation for each of the nineteen economies. The vertical axis plots the percentage point reduction in the average annual rate of inflation between the 1970s and the 1980s. The horizontal axis plots the corresponding percentage point

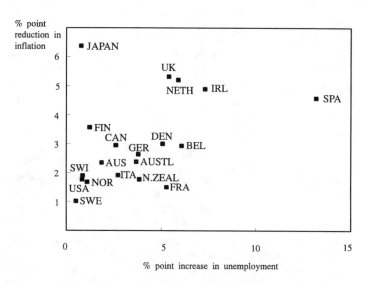

Figure 1.3 'Sacrifice ratio' of reduced inflation for increased unemployment, 1970s to 1980s

increase in average unemployment between the 1970s and 1980s. For countries such as France, Spain, New Zealand and Belgium, the sacrifice ratio has been very high; a two to three percentage point increase in unemployment being required to secure a one point fall in the average inflation rate. At the other extreme for countries such as Japan, Sweden, Finland, Norway, US, Switzerland and Austria each one point reduction in inflation has been achieved at much lower cost; in the extreme case of Japan the sacrifice ratio is as low as 0.13 percentage points of unemployment, and in the other cases between a half and a one percentage point of increased unemployment. An important comparative question which this book attempts to address is, therefore, why the costs of macroeconomic stabilization in the aftermath of the harsh world economic shocks of the 1970s have been so much more severe and longer lasting in some economies compared to others.

THE IMPORTANCE OF CORPORATISM

Corporatism is difficult to define, as already indicated. As we shall discuss in more detail in Chapter 4 the word corporatism has its origins in the 1920s and 1930s and during that time was associated with nationalistic, fascist forms of government. Post-war forms of corporatism, particularly in Scandinavia, derive from very different social-democratic origins, and have been termed, particularly by sociologists, as 'neo-corporatism'. Some, for example Therborn (1992), think that we should abandon altogether the use of the term because it is too vague, and in that it encourages economies to be grouped together may obfuscate other important differences between them. Nevertheless, in our view corporatism as a concept is a useful starting point, especially since corporatist economies do have certain similarities that stand out in contrast to 'liberal' or 'pluralist' economies.

In Britain in the 1980s the word 'corporatist' was hijacked as a term of abuse by those of the 'new right' such as Keith Joseph to describe a process of State control of prices and incomes which was coupled to Keynesian macroeconomic management. The word has been employed disparagingly to characterize a form of economic policy which is concerned with imposing government priorities on economic agents, such as private companies, against the free expression of individual choice. As Gamble (1993) points out, this definition of corporatism is eccentric and is unrelated to how the concept is usually understood in the political science literature. Here the contrast between corporatism and pluralism lies in the way in which interests are represented in the policy-making process. Under corporatism the interests of individuals are collectively represented through particular groups. These are given explicit recognition by the state in its function of reconciling the competing demands on government policy. In return, responsibilities in the process of policy implementation are conferred on these representatives. Under pluralism interest representation is through competitive groups and transitory alliances, with the government fulfilling the function of referee. This distinction, as we shall see, has important and significant consequences for the way in which economic policy is formulated and conducted.

So while corporatism constitutes a useful starting point, it is none the less the case that it is a multidimensional concept. Different corporatist economies will have different dimensions to varying degrees. Thus we cannot begin the book with a full definition of what is entailed in corporatism. Rather, as the remainder of the book progresses, it is intended to shed light on a number of different aspects of corporatist economies especially in so far as they help to understand why these economies appear to have performed rather differently. In the remainder of this chapter we introduce in a rather schematic form some of the themes and complexities which will be developed more comprehensively throughout the book.

At the beginning of this introduction we highlighted two important aspects of corporatism. The first was the structural feature that corporatist economies tend to be defined by their high degree of centralization or coordination in wage determination. Not surprisingly, it is this aspect of corporatism that has most interested economists. However, the previous discussion implies that a sole emphasis on this aspect of corporatism is too narrow. The second aspect was that economies tend to be defined as corporatist if public policy formulation and implementation are conducted through tripartite mechanisms. The corporatist policy agenda may include as a major element the determination of incomes, but will also include much more besides. Corporatist arrangements seek to achieve a consensual framework in which durable, long-term relationships between state, trade unions and business can be fostered. It is this aspect of corporatism which has attracted the interest of political scientists and political economists. In particular, a number of political scientists stress the importance of the role of the state in corporatism as broker between labour and capital. These aspects of corporatism lead to an understanding of it as a branch of the theory of the state.

But we prefer to stress the importance of corporatist arrangements as economic institutions. Institutions are arrangements which, by force of law or by voluntary agreement, restrict the choices or strategies open to groups in the economy. They can influence agents to adopt other strategies, and in so doing promote stability and reduce uncertainty. Corporatist arrangements seek explicitly to alter market outcomes, by establishing a durable process which encourages agents to behave differently from the way they would behave where market forces are less regulated. By seeking the achievement of compromise, corporatism should lead to a rather different distribution of the costs and benefits of economic activity than obtains when the market is left to reward individual effort (Schmitter 1991). Institutions may also be important in that they regulate and coordinate economic relationships which might otherwise be subject to detrimental forms of conflict. While forms of corporatism which existed in the inter-war period might have been enforced through state coercion, in modern democratic societies such arrangements are voluntary, and thus contingent, agreements. They are intended to operate in such a way as to rule out market-liberal responses to economic shocks by coordinating wage restraint in such a way as to avoid the use of unemployment as a labour-disciplining device, and thus as a method for regulating distribution conflict. In corporatist economies there is an intention of the parties concerned to ensure that the burden of adjustment to economic shocks should not fall in an uncoordinated way on particular groups, but should be shared more equally.

A good deal of the economic literature on corporatism has been concerned with investigating empirically the degree of wage responsiveness to economic shocks in corporatist compared to non-corporatist economies. Calmfors and Driffill (1988) reach a much discussed conclusion that both highly centralized (corporatist) and highly decentralized collective bargaining systems may equally deliver a high degree of real wage flexibility, necessary to ensure that adverse shocks do not generate persistent increases in unemployment. In decentralized economies the efficient operation of competitive market forces ensures rapid restoration of equilibrium without serious employment cost. In centralized economies a collective strategy of wage restraint, combined with a heightened sense of macroeconomic conditions possessed by national-level wage bargainers, ensures that shocks can be accomodated with little employment cost. In economies with intermediate degrees of centralization, such as the larger European economies in the 1970s and early 1980s, a lack of coordination between the strategies of powerful bargaining groups means that some will be able to use their bargaining power to protect real wage levels, while the burden of adjustment is borne by others in weaker, lower or non-unionized sectors.

So, in corporatist economies we observe that government, unions and employers have, in the past, mutually articulated a joint commitment to the maintenance of full employment. In short, national or 'peak-level' union bargainers opt for a strategy of short-run wage restraint in order to pursue the objective of long-term growth and employment stability. This is brought about because in corporatist economies the ability to avoid profit squeeze in response to an adverse economic shock enables employers to maintain rates of investment and deliver sought-after future employment stability.

Political economists and political scientists point out that such a cooperative approach between workers and employers, brokered through a state-guaranteed commitment to full employment, is fraught with problems. It is well known in game-theory that cooperative solutions may be unstable, although where the game is repeated cooperative behaviour may have a better chance of emerging. Thus, corporatist compromises are unlikely to be one-off occurrences but rather the result of durable and stable relationships between the parties concerned. We need, therefore, to examine carefully the conditions under which such relationships may emerge and the circumstances under which durability can be preserved.

Pizzorno (1978) describes the relationship under corporatism between capital and labour as one of 'political exchange', where labour exchanges wage restraint in return for greater influence in the policy-making process over factors which affect longer-term capital accumulation. Two particular difficulties may emerge. The first is a problem of 'preference aggregation' where national-level union and employer organizations may experience considerable difficulty in holding together different constituent groups of their respective organizations in the pursuit of a common strategy. So, for example, wage restraint may be much less acceptable to groups of workers who enjoy considerable bargaining power. The second problem is one of an 'interpretation gap' between what is promised at the bargaining table and what is eventually delivered. The benefits that workers would like to receive in return for wage restraint will only accrue in the future and may be eroded by any attempt by capitalists to renege on their investment commitments. On the other hand, the profitability of investments may, under current conditions of wage restraint, be diminished if workers subsequently renege on their part of the agreement (Lancaster 1973).

Any tendency to cheat will undermine the corporatist compromise and so such agreements have been most successful in maintaining low levels of unemployment where the relationship between the parties is a long-term and durable one. In game-theoretic terms cooperation is more likely to emerge where over time the parties become aware that cheating by one player is likely to be punished by subsequent non-cooperation by the other, to the disadvantage of both.

Political scientists outline several factors which may assist the creation of this durable compromise. One is that durability may be enhanced where labour, capital and government benefit from a tradition of regular joint consultation about economic objectives and policy. The process through which the parties reach agreement about shared national economic objectives and a concerted action programme of policy implementation is referred to by Lehmbruch (1984) as the 'concertation' process. Such consultation arrangements characterize policy-making in many countries, particularly in Europe. They are particularly well-developed and established in corporatist ones. A further feature is that corporatist countries tend to be ones which have experienced lengthy, stable government by political parties of a social democratic persuasion. Trade unions may feel a much stronger ideological affinity with a social democratic government and feel a greater sense of security about the government's commitment to, and ability to deliver, low unemployment.

Corporatism may be associated with, in employment terms, less painful adjustment to adverse economic conditions. In the light of what we have said, its existence as an institutional arrangement in some countries may also be motivated by longer-term economic objectives.

It may therefore operate hand in hand with other policies, which together are directed towards the improvement of long-term international competitiveness, through forms of industrial policy and policies aimed at improving the human-capital base of the labour force. The most highly developed form of this type of corporatism is that which was adopted in Sweden through the Rehn–Meidner plan. Here a national uniform wage policy (the 'solidaristic wages policy') was designed to accelerate the decline of less-profitable sectors. The policy was coupled with the industrialized world's most extensive form of 'active labour market policy', designed to retrain displaced workers for employment in nascent sectors of the economy.

The Swedish social democratic commitment to full employment and the 'solidaristic wages policy', with its aim of narrowing wage differentials, in themselves demonstrate the further objective of egalitarianism. As a general observation, therefore, corporatist societies may have maintained lower levels of income inequality, in contrast to the trend towards greater inequality that is apparent in many market-liberal economies since the end of the 'golden age'. Egalitarianism is a feature, particularly, of 'inclusive' forms of corporatism practised in Scandinavia (Pekkarinen *et al.*, 1992). It is manifest in a strong degree of commitment to high levels of social welfare expenditure, in order to protect the least advantaged from the costs of economic adjustment and to ensure that all, be they wage-earners or transfer-recipients, benefit from the proceeds of more stable economic growth.

In the area of macroeconomic policy, in particular, there has been much recent discussion of the inflationary vices of policy-makers in democratic societies, and of the virtues of adopting some self-imposed monetary or exchange rate discipline in order to provide the conditions of price stability under which employment and output growth are more likely to occur. The most frequently advocated institutional reform in this context is the creation of an independent central bank with sole responsibility for the conduct of monetary policy. In corporatist economies macroeconomic policy-making also takes place under self-imposed constraints, but these constraints are rather different in nature and in many ways incompatible with the prescriptions of the new classical macroeconomics literature. The key difference is that market-liberal solutions, which may be highly exclusive in the lack of benefit they confer on the least economically advantaged groups, are ruled out. Macroeconomic strategies are more likely to command general acceptance if they are self-imposed through a democratic and consensual process. So, in our view, it is as important, if not more important, to emphasize the nature and conduct of the economic policy-making process as a vital ingredient of corporatism, as much as the centralized and coordinated structure which underlies bargaining relationships in corporatist economies.

The remainder of the book is structured in the following way. Chapter 2 develops the theme of corporatist arrangements as institutions, by examining in greater detail the role of institutions in uncertain and conflict-prone societies and the function of corporatism as one solution to these problems. Chapter 3 reviews the 'economic' literature on corporatism. It assesses the improved real wage flexibility argument that economies where collective bargaining is highly coordinated or structurally centralized are able to adjust to economic shocks with reduced employment cost. Chapter 4 widens our view of corporatism by addressing the point raised by political economists and political scientists that corporatism should be seen as a vehicle for promoting a relationship of long-term, durable compromise between state, employers and workers. Chapter 5 assesses evidence for the alleged longer-run objectives of corporatism which follow from viewing corporatist arrangements in this way. In Chapter 6 we examine macroeconomic policy in corporatist economies, and contrast the use of macroeconomic policy under corporatism with the prescriptions of new classical macroeconomics for liberal economies.

Finally, in Chapter 7 we conclude by looking to the future and examine the question of whether corporatism is now in terminal decline. We look at the pressures now faced by the corporatist economies and the prospects for maintaining a distinctively social democratic, corporatist mode of public policy in an increasingly integrated world economy. We conclude by arguing that, while the pressures on corporatism are intense, both theory and past empirical evidence point to the enormous benefits that can be achieved where it has been able to operate successfully. It may be difficult to transplant an institutional structure that has developed in economies that are small in size, economically open and which enjoy a high degree of social cohesion. Nevertheless, there are important lessons to be learned from the experience of corporatist economies for those concerned to find institutional reforms through which market economies may achieve sustained full employment through an economically democratic mode of public policy.

NOTES

1. The 'golden age' is a phrase coined by Marglin and Schor (1990) to describe the long post-war economic boom running from the early 1950s to the early 1970s. Armstrong, Glyn and Harrison (1991) use the phrase 'great boom'. While many readers may find much about the world economy during this period that is far from 'golden' or 'great', we use the phrase 'golden age' throughout the book as a convenient shorthand.
2. The origins of the notion of corporatism can be traced back to the late nineteenth century, and particularly to work on the relationship between corporatism and nationalism in the 1930s. Manoilescu (1938) is seen by many writers as the seminal work on the theory of corporatism. It was Manoilescu who made the observation that the twentieth century was the 'century of corporatism', an idea revived by Schmitter (1974).
3. For a particularly influential account, see Bruno and Sachs (1985).
4. Batchelor, Major and Morgan (1980) report that trade in manufactured goods between the industrialized market economies grew nearly ninefold in real terms between 1950 and 1971. Of course this ignores that the fortunes of the less-developed world diverged during the period.
5. The five omitted members are Greece, Portugal and Turkey, for which a reasonably continuous run of data since 1960 is not available, and Iceland and Luxembourg, which are excluded on account of their small size. In addition the three former countries are excluded because in the post-war period they have experienced sustained periods of non-democratic government. This argument may also be applied to Spain, however it is included because since the restoration of democracy in 1974 it has assumed a role as a significant industrialized market economy.
6. See Rowthorn and Glyn (1990) for a more detailed analysis and country-by-country discussion.

2. Institutions and Economic Performance

Economics has usually paid little attention to institutions. Consequently it has not had much to say about the relationship between institutions, institutional change and economic performance. In the light of the wider concerns of social science, this is surprising to say the least. To most social scientists a long and detailed defence of the importance of institutions would scarcely be necessary.

While most social scientists are in agreement about the importance of institutions, there is rather less agreement on how to define them and on what their role is. Thus, the term is used in a wide range of ways. Although this chapter is explicitly about the role and importance of institutions, it is perhaps useful to begin with a working definition. Institutions are best understood as rules or arrangements which limit the choices or strategies available to individuals or groups.[1] These can be regulations, with the backing of law, or voluntary restrictions on behaviour without legal backing. Furthermore, these constraints can be formal or informal.[2] Institutions can influence economic behaviour in particular directions, not least because other directions are ruled out.

An examination of why economists have traditionally neglected institutions and why this has been changing in more recent times, combined with the insights from other social and political scientists, can serve a useful purpose. It provides the framework for the more specific focus of the following chapters, where we concentrate on corporatist institutions, and on the different views that exist over exactly what role such institutions play and on what effect that role has on economic performance.

INSTITUTIONS AND NEOCLASSICAL THEORY

Two reasons can be given for the neglect of institutions within much of mainstream economics. The first has to do with the nature of the neoclassical world assumed in the economic modelling of Walras, Marshall and Edgeworth. Their basic building-block is the rational self-interested individual, who works out his or her optimum response to a set of price signals. Here exchange relations have pride of place because individuals do not combine in a social production process and so are linked only through their meeting to buy and sell in the market place (Rowthorn 1980). Market phenomena have primary importance in any consideration of the nature of society. The privileged methodological standpoint of neoclassical economics is a theory which is built *a priori* on the axioms of rationality and the logic of individual choice.

However, it has been recognized that there is a tension between such *a priori* theorizing and the claim of economics to be an 'empirical science' (Allsopp and Helm 1985). Lange (1935) long ago argued that the market model can exist under various socio-economic frameworks – market economies need not be capitalist ones. To the extent that orthodox economics confines itself to be a theory of distribution of scarce resources between different uses, then it does not need any sociological or institutional data. In this sense, some may even go so far as to agree with Lange that economics is not really a social science at all. For the most part, then, institutions, and other influences such as specific aspects of culture or history, are given little attention in economic analysis. Instead it seeks to test hypotheses which are of more universal applicability (Hirsch *et al.* 1990). So it is not surprising that, to many economists, theory has seemed relatively autonomous from developments in the real world.[3] This stance is also enhanced within economics by the dominant epistemological tradition of positivism. This tradition suggests that the validity of a model's assumptions is less important than its capacity for successful prediction. Such a view is not likely to provide much scope for a serious consideration of institutions.

Beyond this tension between neoclassical economics and empirical reality, the search for intellectual autarky is a second explanation for the neglect of institutions. As we will go on to discuss, a proper understanding of the role of institutions must draw insight from various academic disciplines. Yet economists have often been very sceptical about crossing intellectual borders. The distrust of political economy by some economists is indicative of this. Hahn's view is particularly representative:

As a theoretical economist I share the distrust of grand theorizing and in fact believe it cannot be done... when the political economist is not being purely descriptive, he provides murky, often barely comprehensible theories which cannot be used to answer any of the important questions of the subject. (Hahn 1985, p. 4)

This attitude tends to prejudge what are the important questions of economics. What is more important is to determine how much abstraction is desirable and what important variables and exogenous factors should appear in any theoretical model (Marglin 1990).

For political economists, such as Goldthorpe, this search for autarky in part explains the difficulty that orthodox economists have found in coming to terms with the end of sustained growth in the 1950s and 1960s. He argues that the introduction of such *ad hoc* notions as worker militancy and behaviour enforced by social pressure, in the works of such economists as Hicks and Solow, indicates an acceptance of the inadequacy of the reigning neoclassical paradigm. A search to preserve intellectual autarky, in the face of having to explain such previously unobserved phenonoma as simultaneously rising unemployment and inflation, means that unexplained residual categories have had to grow in size (Goldthorpe 1984).

Whatever the causes of the divergence of experience of economies in the 1970s and 1980s, mainstream economics has not, to any great extent, accorded to the diversity of institutional arrangements a central explanatory role. Of course, there are many schools within economics for which this neglect of institutional diversity is not the case, and some of these will be discussed in what follows. However, even within the mainstream there is a growing literature which has begun to take institutions far more seriously. Much of the analysis here, as we shall see, stems from the reassessment of the importance of the role of information in economics.[4] This has considerably enlarged the scope of economic analysis and enjoys wide applicability in such diverse areas as the economics of industry and the theory of the firm; the role of financial regulation and institutions, and the relationship between finance and industry; and, of even more importance given the concerns in this book, the economics of the labour market. We shall be returning to these developments shortly.

However, any revival of interest in institutions within economics still sits uneasily beside the tradition of contrasting an ideal view of how the market is supposed to operate with the rigidities that exist in the real world. The importance of equilibrium notions in neoclassical economics (Bleaney 1985) implies the general vision that it is 'imperfections' in the real world which prevent the achievement of full employment. The implication of this is that the removal of such imperfections is the appropriate policy response (Sawyer 1989). Of course, many influential general equilibrium theorists, such as Arrow and Hahn, have been well aware of the dangers of descriptively interpreting the implications of the high theory of neoclassical economics.[5]

But in the 1970s and 1980s, the rise of monetarism, and later new classical economics, as well as the prominence of neo-liberalism within society at large, has indeed suggested that the general equilibrium model is taken descriptively. An example is in the 'Eurosclerosis' explanation for the declining performance of European economies in the 1970s and 1980s (Giersch 1985, Lindbeck 1985). This explanation emphasizes 'imperfections' which provide for inflexibility in the market mechanism. These include the welfare state, restrictions on hiring and firing, protectionist industrial policy, legal restrictions enhancing the power of trade unions and so on. It is argued that the appropriate policy response to these is to undo them by emphasizing supply-side reforms to facilitate market clearing and the achievement of full employment. In the context of the labour market, it is implicitly assumed that individual employers can by their own actions bring about the necessary adaptation to change once those forces which create inflexibility have been removed. In other words, it is also assumed that the principles of competitive equilibrium are adequate for understanding the economic performance of modern capitalist economies. If economic performance is disappointing then measures should be taken to ensure that the real world becomes more like the market economy of the textbooks.

There is a sharp distinction between the ideal of competitive equilibrium and the allegedly second-best nature of the real world. Our own view is that this distinction misses much of what is important in understanding how modern capitalist economies function and leads to a particularly negative and impoverished view of the role of institutions in explaining economic performance. The dominant metaphor for competitive equilibrium within economics is that of the Walrasian system. To highlight the essentials of the system, Walras used the analogy of an auctioneer who invites all economic agents to reach agreement about all their trading decisions (both present and future). The auctioneer begins by quoting a set of prices for all commodities and asks all individuals to state their demand and supply for these commodities at this set of prices. These original prices are unlikely to equate supply and demand in all markets. The auctioneer keeps changing the prices until demand does equal supply for every commodity. Only when equilibrium prices are found does the auctioneer allow trade to take place, and this trade happens instantaneously for all goods for all time.[6] The above is a metaphor and is not meant to be taken literally, but it does suggest a world of isolated atomistic individuals whose only social interaction is through the market. Agents in this system meet only briefly to conduct the trades organized by the auctioneer. There is therefore no incentive to develop long-term trading relationships.

The neglect of long-term relationships is a characteristic shared by the Austrian school of economics which is, otherwise, critical of the Walrasian metaphor. In particular, Austrians are sceptical about the usefulness of equilibrium notions, preferring to see market competition as a process where learning and discovery take place. Prices act as signals, especially for possibilities previously undiscovered. But their emphasis on exchange relations of little durability is one which is shared with neoclassical economists.

The Walrasian metaphor is not a good one for understanding modern capitalist economies. To see why this is the case we will, in the next couple of sections, be drawing from a number of academic disciplines including more recent economics literature. There are a number of common themes that arise.

One is the importance of information and uncertainty in economic activity. The Walrasian metaphor presumes perfect information. Because of this it is severely out of step with how markets are experienced in a real economy, where market transactions operate through a web of institutions. These include the legal basis of contract law and the framework of property rights; the state, regulatory bodies, employers' and workers' organizations and so on. The latter cannot be seen merely as 'imperfections' in the working of the market. Indeed, most of the time markets only work because of the existence of such institutions.[7] In other words, institutions have an important role in making market exchange possible by, among other things, providing information and reducing uncertainty. Another theme is that the

Walrasian metaphor ignores the possibility of conflict in market processes. Real economies have to accommodate such pressures in one way or another. This focuses attention on the fact that the coordination of society and economic activity cannot rely on the market alone. Both these themes are of importance because corporatist institutions play a critical role in both reducing the uncertainty faced by economic agents, or groups, and in providing a framework for mediating conflict. In large part this aspect of corporatism is vital to understanding the apparently superior economic performance of a number of corporatist economies.

The literature on which we draw to shed light on these themes is very disparate. This is not surprising given that various traditions have different epistemological foundations and different concerns. For some the narrowness of the Walrasian conception of neoclassical economics may be so important that relaxing it opens up a Pandora's Box (Hirsch *et al.* 1990). For others a serious concern for institutions can be incorporated into neoclassical economics (North 1990). However, an arbitration between neoclassical economists and political economists, 'new' and 'old' institutionalists etc. is not the subject of this chapter. The approach adopted here is more eclectic, trying to bring together the insights from various traditions. How institutions are important, what role they play, and through what mechanisms and processes they operate is highly contested. The differences between the various traditions is important, but we shall approach these as they specifically relate to corporatism in subsequent chapters.

INFORMATION, UNCERTAINTY AND INSTITUTIONS

Within the economics literature institutions have been introduced into the analysis of markets by examining the implications of removing the assumption of costless information from the Walrasian economy.[8] One important approach has concentrated on transactions costs and its origins can be traced to the seminal contributions of Coase (1937, 1960). Coase was particularly interested in why production and exchange activities are internalized within firms and why they are not always coordinated through the market. His answer relied on the existence of costs in using the price mechanism, especially the costs of finding out information about prices and the costs of negotiating, renegotiating and monitoring a myriad of contracts. However, firms cannot totally replace the market since they too are associated with supervision and management costs. Therefore, an equilibrium is reached when no more is to be gained from further superseding the market – that is where the marginal cost of supervising an additional internal managerial relationship just equates to the marginal reduction in transactions costs from not using the market. Coase's work implies that institutions cannot be ignored when transactions are costly. The efficiency of competitive equilibrium relies on the assumption of perfect information and no transactions costs. In such a world institutions would be unimportant, or, more precisely, any institutional arrangement would be as good as any other. Those transactions which rational, optimizing agents would undertake in a Walrasian world may not occur if transactions costs exist.

The concept of transactions costs can be rather nebulous and a rigorous definition is almost impossible (Hodgson 1988). In general, transactions costs have been seen to cover a wide 'spectrum of institutional costs' including those of information, of negotiation, of drawing up and enforcing contracts, of delineating and policing property rights, of monitoring performance and of changing institutional arrangements (Cheung 1987). North (1990) discusses the fact that most exchanges entail not homogeneous goods but those with many attributes. For example, the service of a doctor includes his or her consulting manner, his or her willingness to spend time with the client and so on. North points out that the value of a market exchange is the sum of the values of the different attributes contained within the good or service. The definition and measurement of these attributes is resource consuming for the agents concerned. Because it is costly to measure and monitor these attributes, it is possible that one or other party may try to underprovide what was agreed contractually. Therefore of equal importance is the problem of enforcing the performance of agents. The problem of enforcement leads to what Bowles and Gintis (1993) have termed 'contested exchange' because 'unlike the transactions of Walrasian economies, the benefit the parties derive from the transaction depends on their capacities to enforce competing claims' (op. cit., p. 85).[9]

The work of Coase has been taken up by Williamson (1975, 1985).

Williamson suggests that hierarchical relationships within institutions can be explained by a search for economizing on transactions costs. Powell provides a useful summary of Williamson's approach:

> transactions that involve uncertainty about their outcome, that recur frequently and require substantial 'transaction-specific investments' – of money, time or energy that cannot be easily transferred – are more likely to take place within hierarchically organized firms. Exchanges that are straightforward, non-repetitive and require no transaction-specific investments will take place across a market interface. Hence, transactions are moved out of markets and into hierarchies as knowledge specific to the transaction (asset specificity) builds up. (Powell 1991, p. 265)

According to Williamson, the attractiveness of hierarchy in given circumstances rests on two further problems. The first is bounded rationality, a term associated with the work of H. A. Simon, which arises because there are significant cognitive limits operating on economic actors given the enormous complexity of economic problems. The second is opportunism. This is defined as self-interest-seeking, and Williamson takes it as a given behavioural assumption. Hierarchy can be seen as a response to both bounded rationality and opportunism, since it internalizes these problems within the firm's 'governance structure' (Powell, op. cit.).

The transactions costs approach is a diversified one with many differences of emphasis. Matthews (1986) argues that Williamson's stress on opportunism is too narrow. Errors in organizing and monitoring transactions may occur. For example, the calculation of a bill may turn out to be incorrect but this need not imply dishonesty on the part of a supplier. Others have argued that 'bounded rationality' refers not only to the lack of information in any context, but also to the computational capacity of economic actors (Hodgson 1989). Such a conceptualization of bounded rationality may be particularly important in understanding why institutions are important, since it highlights the necessity of regularized patterns of human relationship (North, op. cit.). The institutional arrangements which facilitate this will exist to reduce the uncertainties that occur in human interaction.

North also argues that Williamson does not sufficiently examine the implications of the need to enforce contracts. Institutional change and economic performance are, to a considerable extent, related by the extent to which contracts can be enforced between agents at low cost. As we shall see, Williamson's approach has also been criticized as being too limited, especially in its sharp distinction between the domain of the market and the domain of hierarchy (organizations). However, the importance of the transactions cost approach is registered by the fact that it has spawned a very large literature in a number of areas of economics, such as the theory of the firm and industrial organization, public choice theory, and in economic history (Clarke and McGuiness 1987, Reid 1987). Some of this work is often referred to as the New Institutional Economics.[10] By focusing on the themes of information and uncertainty the transactions costs approach has shown that economists cannot ignore institutions.

The rigid distinction between market and hierarchy has been challenged by those who see markets themselves as being dependent on institutions (Hodgson 1988, Grahl and Teague 1990).[11] The type of institution which may be necessary to underpin a market is a function in part of the scale of the information problem confronted by various markets. Grahl and Teague draw a useful distinction between centralized and decentralized exchange. The standard example of centralized exchange is a commodity market for some homogeneous product such as an agricultural product or a mineral. The problems of information here are typically not acute and it is this which even makes possible the existence of futures trading. This form of exchange comes closest to our Walrasian metaphor and not surprisingly some arrangement is necessary to mimic the Walrasian auctioneer. Thus, even in centralized commodity markets there is a need for some form of 'external social support' such as a clearing house or financial centre with 'rules of procedures and specialist intermediaries' (Grahl and Teague 1990, p. 47).

But most markets, such as those for labour and consumer goods, are not, and cannot be, so centralized. The informational problems concerning the nature of the good (which may be non-homogenous and have many attributes), prices, possible trading partners, etc. are far more acute in these markets. The scale of the information problem is indicated by the fact that it is not possible even to envisage the use of futures trading in consumer goods and labour. Grahl and Teague argue that decentralized exchange in particular needs 'external social support'. This can take the form of social relations 'which mitigate the uncertainty and lack of information which would otherwise paralyze economic life' (op. cit., p. 49). It may also take the form of social structures such as 'networks of associated producers which can distribute information on prices and costs; regulatory bodies, private and public, which can reduce uncertainty about the nature of the product to be sold and the quality which should be expected' (op. cit., p. 49). We shall discuss examples of such social relations and structures shortly.

However, we first need to consider the nature of this uncertainty. Economists have employed game theory to shed light on the issue of uncertainty and the role of institutions. Game theory, by examining the logic of decision-making given certain assumptions about the environment, the cooperative or non-cooperative behaviour of other players and so on, is a powerful tool for examining decision-making under conditions of uncertainty and interaction.

The literature on game theory is vast and it is beyond our scope here to give full justice to its achievements.[12] In any case some of the major results are well-known. Possibly the most well-known form of non-cooperative game is the prisoners' dilemma, illustrated in Figure 2.1. This shows that non-cooperative actions may be sub-optimal, that there are consequently gains from cooperation and finally that such cooperation may be difficult to achieve in practice because of the incentive to cheat. The game envisages two prisoners arrested on suspicion of a serious crime (for example theft), and placed in separate rooms for interrogation. The police have sufficient evidence to convict both of a lesser crime (for example receipt of stolen goods). Conviction of the lesser crime carries a sentence of (say) two years imprisonment and of the serious crime a sentence of (say) five years imprisonment. In order to obtain a confession the police devise a scheme allowing a sentence of only one year for a prisoner who confesses and offers evidence against his partner. In this case the partner will receive a ten-year sentence. Figure 2.1 illustrates the 'pay-offs' to each player in terms of reduced years of freedom, for each combination of two choices open to each ('confess' or 'not confess'). A widely accepted solution concept in game theory is that of the Nash equilibrium, where each player selects the choice which maximizes his pay-off (minimizes the prison sentence in this case) regardless of what the other player does. In the prisoners' dilemma that is to confess, in order to avoid the possibility of being jailed for ten years, in this example. Thus, both prisoners receive sentences of five years each, and fail to achieve the cooperative outcome of two years each.

Many game theorists, from different academic disciplines, have

	(A, B)	Prisoner B	
		Confess	Not Confess
Prisoner A	Confess	(-2, -2)	(-1, -10)
	Not Confess	(-10, -1)	(-5, -5)

Figure 2.1 Prisoners' dilemma game

looked for those conditions which would promote cooperative activity. One condition that would allow cooperation is the ability to make binding pre-commitments. In the prisoners' dilemma this is ruled out, in part, because the prisoners are kept in separate cells. More generally, it is also ruled out because there is no way that one player can prevent the other from reneging on any arrangement to remain silent in order to reduce his sentence. A further condition might be that if the game is repeated rather than single-shot (strictly speaking it may be necessary that it goes on for ever), then the players will become well informed about each other's past actions. In the case of a game with several players, cooperation may be more likely where that number is not too many. Axelrod (1984), for instance, shows the efficacy of a 'tit for tat' strategy – this involves cooperating in the first instance and reversing this to a cheating strategy if the other side cheated in the previous round. In a game lasting a long time a cooperative approach could develop from such a strategy, since both players will learn that cheating will be punished by their opponent in the next stage of the game. Schofield has concluded that:

> The theoretical problems underlying cooperation can be stated thus: what is the minimal amount that one agent must know in a given milieu about the beliefs and wants of other agents to be able to form coherent notions about their behaviour and for this knowledge to be communicated to others. It seems to me that this problem is at the heart of any analysis of community, convention and cooperation. (Quoted in North 1990, p. 15).

Schotter (1981) argues that in repeated games the players may develop certain socially accepted rules of thumb and conventions of behaviour, which in turn may be passed on to following generations of players. Indeed, the work of Schotter is important for our purposes in that it explicitly confronts that neo-liberal tendency to conceptualize institutions or norms as 'imperfections'. For those like Schotter and Hodgson this is deeply mistaken and ignores the fact that institutions, by providing information, not least concerning the intentions of other economic actors, actually expand the opportunity sets available to economic agents.[13]

Some institutionalist economists such as Hodgson have reached similar conclusions not through game theory but through the long tradition, associated with the work of Frank Knight, which stems from the insights of the distinction between risk and uncertainty. A future event can be described as risky if we can calculate an objective probability of it occurring, that is a probability that is calculated on past experience. On the other hand, if there is no past history of the event, or if such history is meagre, then an objective probability cannot be calculated and the future event can be described as uncertain. For Keynes (1936) such a distinction played a crucial role in his analysis of investment and the way financial institutions operated. Some have called this form of uncertainty radical or real uncertainty. The distinction has fundamental implications for neoclassical economics and its methodology.[14] What is important for our purposes is its implications for the role of institutions. Where the future is risky and objective probabilities cannot be calculated:

> rules, norms and institutions play a functional role in providing a basis for decision-making, expectation and belief. Without these 'rigidities', without social routine and habit to reproduce them, and without institutionally conditioned conceptual frameworks, an uncertain world would present a chaos of sense data in which it would be impossible for the agent to make sensible decisions and act. (Hodgson 1988, p. 205)

This nexus of information, uncertainty and institutions can be brought into sharper focus by a look at the formal and informal constraints that operate on the labour market. Given our interest in corporatist institutions, this is of great importance here. Because the employment relationship is often a durable one, and because workers may formulate and adopt strategies to achieve their own objectives, the labour market is most unlikely to operate in a way that means wages adjust instantly to Walrasian excess demand. Furthermore, these characteristics indicate the usefulness of an analysis of uncertainty and institutions in a game-theoretic context.

Robert Solow, in a book revealingly entitled *The Labour Market as a Social Institution* (1990), has employed game theory to show that informal constraints, such as social conventions or norms, can help us in understanding certain puzzles. One is why workers do not undercut wages during high unemployment as they are presumed to do in simple textbook accounts. Solow presents a small game-theoretic model of whether an unemployed worker should undercut the current wage level.[15] If the worker decides to offer to work below the existing wage, he or she will benefit immediately since the wage offer will be above the level of unemployment benefit. If the worker decides not to undercut then he or she receives that level of benefit. In a one-shot game the worker in this example would try to undercut. In a repeated game undercutting may lead to 'tit for tat' retaliation by other workers which will push down the wage even further. A rational worker, under certain conditions, which Solow examines, may therefore decide not to undercut fearing that a 'reversion to Hobbesian competition' may damage his or her future long-term pay-off. Solow makes it clear that he intends this as a metaphor and that workers do not at every moment make such rational calculations. In reality social norms are somehow established which constrain workers and that 'once established they draw their force from shared values and social approbation and disapprobation, not from calculation' (Solow op. cit., p. 49).

In some cases social norms or conventions can be so important that it may be appropriate to label them ideologies. Later, in our discussion of corporatism, we shall refer to the importance of ideas or ideologies such as the social democratic consensus, the notion of social harmony in the social teaching of catholicism, the commitment to a solidaristic wages policy or egalitarianism, and the commitment to full employment. These often accompany corporatist institutions and can be seen as forces, or constraints, which, for good or for ill, structure economic activity. For this reason they can have an important role in determining economic performance.

Sociologists, business organization specialists and others have argued that the distinction in Williamson between markets on the one hand and hierarchy on the other is, in many cases, too sharp (Perrow 1990, Powell 1991, Bradach and Eccles 1991). Within hierarchical structures firms may employ many market-type mechanisms, such as shadow prices for intra-firm exchanges and divisional profit criteria for internal investment. Firms may also develop relationships with other firms which extend deeper than market relations. These relationships have been labelled networks, or, within economics, 'relational contracts'. Hirsch *et al.* (1990) describe them as durable relationships of trust and mutual dependency. Their existence suggests that between markets and firms there may exist a third ideal-type decision structure which is based on informal social relations, one which Boulding (1968) describes as the 'integrative mechanism'.

A typical example of a network is usually a group of firms in a specific industry which have many ties, both formal and informal. Dore (1983) has argued that the relative success of Japanese firms has relied on 'obligated relational contracting'. Such arrangments differ from formalized contractual arrangements by being conditioned through 'duty, trust, and give-and-take, in the context of long-term trading relations' (Hodgson 1988, p. 210). Kay (1993) argues that long-run relations may be crucial to the competitive advantage of firms and therefore their ultimate success. For Kay the 'architecture' of corporate advantage may lie in the links that a firm develops with its workers, customers or suppliers. However the 'ability to make relational contracts effectively depends on the environment in which the company is placed. It is easier to make relational contracts when the relational style is the norm, safer to do it with someone who has made many other relational contracts.'[16] And clearly the 'environment' will depend on the institutional framework.

It is argued that such lasting relationships can achieve a number of objectives. They may allow reduced costs of exchange and production, by allowing firms to learn about the behaviour of other agents. They may make for a degree of mutual control over each other, and may enhance relationships with other economic agents both as a way of extending those relationships and as a way of providing mutual defence against hostile forces (Johansons and Mattson 1991, Kay 1993).[17] In each of these the communication of information is important, and this information will not be adequately communicated through a hierarchy or through price. Powell (1991) points out that in matters such as those relating to technological ethos and production style, the value of information is not easily quantified. It cannot, therefore, be easily traded in a market or communicated through a corporate hierachy. Within durable 'relational contracts', where there is no expectation on the part of agents of an immediate *quid pro quo*, such information, and the skills associated with it, may be more effectively transmitted.

A detailed account of networks and firm organization is beyond the scope of this book. Indeed, much of the literature in this area is rather sanguine in its conclusions with respect to the efficacy of networks. In many cases it could be argued that industrial networks are rather 'conservative' in their implications – for instance, allowing large firms to transfer risk from their own establishments to independent small subcontractors, or facilitating implicit collusion against potential competition. It is often assumed in the literature that there is an implicit egalitarianism about inter-network relationships. This is difficult to sustain in practice, without considerable empirical research.

But two themes of the network literature are of particular relevance for corporatist institutions and will be developed in Chapter 4. They are the roles of long-run relations and of trust.[18] The existence of long-run trust relationships may, in an uncertain world, promote stability. Some networks may enable the attention of economic actors to be focused on the long run and beyond the immediate insistence of an equivalence of benefits in any exchange. Whether such trust relationships imply an equivalence of benefits is the subject of debate in the literature. However, the importance of trust lies in the reduction of uncertainty and the promotion of relationships and trades which may not otherwise have been possible: 'trust reduces complex realities far more quickly and economically than prediction, authority or bargaining' (Powell 1991, p. 273).

Long-run trust relationships may have a role to play in the economic performance not just of individual firms and industries but also of the national economy. Soskice (1991) argues that some of the most successful economies have what he terms 'flexibly coordinated systems'. He defines these as 'characterised by relatively long-term and high-trust relations with and between institutions, and at micro as well as macro levels' (op. cit., p. 48). This presents an interesting attempt to integrate the economics of markets and institutional analysis – institutions have an important role in making market exchanges possible through providing information, reducing uncertainty and allowing long-term and trust relationships to develop. In Soskice's view all are important for international competitiveness. However, as he stresses, these institutions do not replace the market. Rather, they are reliant on it to ensure that economic agents remain aware of the strength of the competitive environment.

For Soskice flexibly coordinated systems incorporate a number of features including a high level of provision of infrastructural services, such as R&D, marketing, training etc. *Short-term* profitability is not necessarily seen as a primary objective. Stable longer-term relationships are of greater importance, so, for example, such systems entail a tacit long-term contract with labour. The most developed example of this is to be found in the Japanese 'life-time' employment contract. Soskice's argument is that such systems are able to avoid the short-termism from which other more liberal economies suffer. Thus he concludes that flexibly coordinated economies have a 'thinking' capacity, in that they are better suited to facilitate communication between business, finance, labour representatives and government.

While we have stressed that economic activity cannot take place without institutions there is nothing to say that those institutions will necessarily be efficient. North (op. cit.), in an approach which is much more individualistic than that of Soskice, concentrates on the incentive structure facing entrepreneurs or firms. He points out that institutions will affect the direction in which knowledge and skills are acquired. This in turn will be decisive for the long-run development of a society since human capital investment in both workers and entrepreneurs will generate productivity increase and therefore economic growth. Thus, it is important to study exactly how particular institutions affect economic performance. Furthermore, the way in which various institutions interact with each other will also have an important bearing on economic performance. This can be seen from Soskice's 'flexibly coordinated systems'.

To summarize, the Walrasian metaphor is not an appropriate one for understanding modern economies. In the presence of uncertainty, institutions, defined as a set of informal or formal constraints, can perform a positive role. They are not merely imperfections or rigidities. They have a role to play in facilitating and structuring economic activity. Furthermore, in seeking to overcome informational problems, economic actors are brought together in long-lasting trust relationships and not just by fleeting moments of exchange. In the words of Grahl and Teague (1990, p. 47): 'whereas flexibility is built into full-information markets, decentralized exchange requires a degree of inertia and internal rigidity to make it possible'.

This approach is clearly relevant to corporatist institutions. Under corporatism long-run trust relationships can be fostered, and these can have significant effects at all levels: between firms and within firms, between employers and workers. They will also affect economies as a whole by fostering long-term relationships between the state, employers' organizations and trade unions. However, to see why these sorts of relationships are so significant we need to examine a further limitation of the Walrasian metaphor – namely the assumption that economic actors can undertake exchange relationships without conflict.

CONFLICT, INSTITUTIONS AND THE COORDINATION OF ECONOMIC ACTIVITY

The emphasis on market relations and equilibrium in the Walrasian neoclassical world need not logically entail social harmony. However the neoclassical theory of the late nineteenth century, from which much of modern economics is derived, does suggest that any conflict can in principle be eliminated. The notion of general equilibrium implies that macroeconomic bliss will automatically follow from prices achieving their equilibrium values. Macroeconomic disequilibrium can thus be solved by appropriate adjustments to relative prices, and those adjustments will not lead to social friction of any kind. Recurrent phenomena such as unemployment or output recessions can be regarded as deviations from equilibrium, resulting from market imperfections or incomplete market adjustment. These problems are regarded as neither intrinsic nor functional to the capitalist economy (Rowthorn 1980).

We are hardly the first to notice that this seems to be severely at odds with the experience of modern economies. A fundamental problem is the assumption that market outcomes are generally accepted by all agents and that those outcomes are not in themselves a source of dissent and conflict (Goldthorpe 1987). From the market-liberal perspective social conflict and an opposition to market outcomes would seem irrational. Economic agents are best served by the operation of the market (Mullard 1992). However, as Goldthorpe argues, those who do not accept that market outcomes are fair or do not treat them as unavoidable will work to reverse them through organizing 'against the market'. It is difficult to see why this is in any sense an irrational response. How such activity is accommodated, through what institutions and with what implications for economic performance constitutes, in our view, a major motivation for considering corporatist arrangements.

Once the possibility of conflict in capitalist economies is allowed, the market imperfection view of unemployment can be replaced with one of unemployment functioning to control wage inflation and enforce labour discipline.[19] As Sawyer (1992) argues, the reduction of unemployment requires the development of institutions and policy instruments which would perform these functions instead. Successful corporatist institutions may perform just such a role.

A number of schools of thought, including Marxists and Kaleckians, place the sources of order and disorder at the centre of their analysis of capitalist economies. For instance, the 'new political economy' approach argues that the capitalist economy is inherently unstable and that this instability cannot be corrected by the intelligent manipulation of a few economic instruments. One concern of the 'new political economy' is to understand the perceived failure of mainstream economics to explain the decline of the post-war golden age of economic growth and the increasingly divergent experience of capitalist economies since the early 1970s (Goldthorpe 1984). A similar approach can be detected in the so-called paradigm of economic sociology,[20] where again there is much discussion of the divergent experience of capitalist economies and the perceived inability of neoclassical economics to explain this.

The same concerns are, of course, shared by a number of schools within economics. One obvious example is the institutionalist tradition associated with Veblen, Commons and others, which has influenced many other economists not strictly known as institutionalists, such as Galbraith and even Williamson.[21] Institutional economics has always demonstrated the importance of the power of different groups in the economy and of the organization and control of the economy as a system. One of the major themes of institutional economics is that the formation and operation of institutions should be seen as both the cause and consequence of the power structure in an economy and of the way in which individuals and groups behave. They influence the way in which economic opportunities are formed, in contrast to neoclassical economics which investigates choices from given sets of opportunities. Institutions thus reflect the way in which economic activity is organized and controlled (Samuels 1987).

The 'radical political economy' tradition also stresses the instability of capitalist economies (Sawyer 1989). It sees full employment equilibria as rather fleeting and exceptional occurrences. Sawyer distinguishes this approach from those of orthodox Keynesian and monetarist economists which regard full employment as normal and unemployment as the exceptional occurrence to be explained. Radical political economy aims to integrate political and economic factors into a framework which can explain long-term historical changes in capitalist economies. Abstraction is not rejected but there is a concern that such abstraction should not be so sparse 'that it has next to nothing to say about concrete problems' (Marglin 1990, pp. 25–26).

A final example of an approach which explicitly takes into account order and conflict within capitalist economies is that of the Regulation school, associated with Aglietta (1982), Boyer (1987, 1992) and Lipietz (1986).[22] Dunford summarizes the concept of regulation as one which:

> is used to denote a specific local and historical collection of structural forms or institutional arrangements within which individual and collective behaviour unfolds and a particular configuration of market adjustments through which privately made decisions are coordinated and which give rise to elements of regularity in economic life. ... A mode of regulation therefore defines the rules of the game. In addition, it allows a dynamic adaptation of production and social demand and, in capitalist societies, guides and stabilizes the process of accumulation. (Dunford 1990, p. 306)

Within the regulation approach institutions play a critical role, in that they are seen as the codification of social relations. For modern capitalist economies four types of institutions are seen as particularly important: the monetary system and monetary mechanisms; institutions which regulate the wage relation; institutions which define modes of competition within the capitalist sector and its relationship with non-capitalist sectors; and the state itself (Dunford, op. cit.). Glyn *et al.* (1990) discuss all four factors in their account of the deteriorating economic performance of the world economy since the 1970s.

Once more we are less concerned, in the present context, with the individual contributions of the above approaches and the differences between them, than with the general principle that the reaction of societies to the problem of conflict and the possibility of disorder has important implications for economic performance. In the previous section we discussed the importance of coordination mechanisms whose function is to order and structure economic activity, such as market or hierarchy and other arrangements, for instance networks. At the level of the national economy the market, the state and community have traditionally been seen as the key sources of order.

To this list political scientists such as Streeck and Schmitter, who are important writers on corporatism, have proposed that we add associations. Associations are described as 'organizations defined by their common purpose of defending and promoting functionally defined interests' (Streeck and Schmitter 1991, p. 231). Those interests may be class-, sectorally or professionally based. Associations may in particular be those entities which in certain circumstances will not accept market outcomes and therefore organize 'against the market'. Such associations, or interest groups, are a particularly important aspect of the corporatist institutional landscape.

Olson (1965, 1982) has made a seminal contribution to understanding how interest groups impinge on the degree of order and disorder in a society and on economic performance. Olson's view is that interest groups do not have a particularly benign effect on economic performance, although there are, as we shall see, some caveats to this general conclusion. In particular, interest groups have a tendency to outstay their welcome – there is a form of inertia which prevents such groups from withering away even if they lose much of their original support and the rationale for their existence. So Olson argues that shocks, of whatever kind, which dislodge such entrenched interests can be very beneficial to economic performance. Such shocks could be likened to a process of creative destruction at the macroeconomic level. The obvious examples where a 'shock' has had beneficial effects on economic performance are the cases of Germany and Japan in the aftermath of the Second World War.[23]

One of Olson's important caveats is that the objectives of encompassing organizations may extend beyond the politics of income distribution into a concern for economic growth. As we shall see in later chapters, a recognition of this possibility is the starting point for much of the theoretical work on corporatism. Encompassing organizations may be large enough to have a discernible effect on the size of the economic 'pie'. Thus, they will not be indifferent to factors which could promote growth and long-term development. Nevertheless, Olson's overall view of interest groups is a sceptical one. However, as

Streeck and Schmitter (1991) point out, Olson does not allow this scepticism to justify reliance on any simple market-liberal strategy. This is in contrast to public-choice theorists, who share with Olson a distrust of the power of interest groups, but use their potential for disruptive influence to argue in favour of economic liberalism.[24]

For writers on corporatism, an appropriate institutional framework for organized interests is of paramount importance and will be an important determinant of economic performance, if anti-democratic solutions to curbing the power of interest groups are ruled out. Streeck and Schmitter argue that an associative model of order can never be *the* coordinating mechanism of modern societies – it will always have to be integrated with a consideration of market relationships, state intervention and so on. So, while some refer to corporatism as a 'middle way', extant corporatist economies remain firmly market-based. Within market economies, encompassing associations can provide a response to some of the problems discussed earlier in this chapter. With respect to the question of order Streeck and Schmitter (1991) argue that what they call private interest government – that is 'self-"government" of categories of social actors defined by a collective self-regarding interest' – can play a useful role since 'an attempt is made to make associative, self-interested collective action contribute to the achievement of public policy objectives' (op. cit., p. 235).

The reason why private-interest government may, in certain cases, more effectively achieve policy objectives than state intervention is that associations may be better able to enforce any decisions they take. Such enforcement may command greater legitimacy because the constraints that those decisions impose on individual agents are more likely to be seen as in some way self-imposed.[25] Furthermore, private-interest government can work to reduce uncertainty in a number of areas, particularly concerning the preferences of other associations and about likely economic outcomes. Thus associations can, under appropriate circumstances, both reduce uncertainty and promote order.

However, the ability of private-interest self-government to achieve economic policy objectives and contribute to improved economic performance relies on the institutional framework. That framework will lay down game rules which will, in turn, determine what strategies associations adopt in particular circumstances. It is difficult to model these in abstract, so we now turn in the rest of the book to an examination of how specific groups, in particular employers' associations and trade unions, behave in the specific context of a corporatist institutional environment.

CONCLUSION

Institutions have a fundamental social importance and permeate the whole of economic life. In particular we have stressed the possibility that institutions can promote stability and structure in economic decision-making by reducing uncertainty and by providing game rules for organized interests or associations. Thus, we have stressed the inadequacy of the typical position of market-liberal economics that the ideal of the market can be counterpoised with the institutional 'rigidities' of the real world. The role of institutions should be seen in a more positive light than this. Of course, nothing we have said implies that any existing institutional framework will necessarily be efficient or optimal. The effect of any institutional framework on economic performance can scarcely be analysed in the abstract.

The importance of institutions is brought out in many academic disciplines and schools of thought. Not surprisingly, we have glossed over important methodological controversies such as those concerning methodological individualism and the concept of equilibrium (Hodgson 1988, North 1990, Zukin and DiMaggio 1990). To some, this synthesis may seem too eclectic or too agnostic. Our defence is twofold. Firstly, methodology is not a primary concern of the present book and up to a point important insights can usefully be drawn from various schools without laying open too many contradictions. Secondly, and of more importance, is the point that important issues or controversies can best be illustrated by a detailed examination of specific institutions.

In what follows, we concentrate on corporatist institutions: on precisely what role such institutions play and with what consequences for economic performance. Even within this narrower purview there are controversies and disagreements – for example, are corporatist institutions best seen as an aid to short-term macroeconomic management and as a solution to narrow labour market coordination problems of the prisoners' dilemma type or are they motivated by longer-term economic and political concerns? An examination of corporatist institutions in some detail can shed light not just on their impact on economic performance but may also reveal insights into the relationship between institutions and economics in general.

NOTES

1. Our definition is close to that of North (1990, pp. 3–4): 'institutions are the rules of the game in society or, more formally, are the humanly devised constraints that shape human interaction ... in the jargon of the economist, institutions define and limit the set of choices of individuals'.
2. Informal constraints, such as norms, are crucial in much of the sociological literature where the essence of institutions is patterned behaviour. This patterning derives from norms and values which change relatively slowly and which reflect such factors as history and culture.
3. An extreme example here is George Stigler who has suggested that 'whether a fact or development is significant depends primarily on its relevance to current economic theory' (quoted in Lazonick 1991, p. 6).
4. Two seminal articles here which have initiated a huge literature are Akerlof (1970) and Grossman and Stiglitz (1976). For a survey of the importance of information in economic analysis, see Stiglitz (1985). This literature examines the implications for market outcomes of imperfect information which is costly to gather. Akerlof (1970), for example, shows that the market outcome will be inefficient because trades that would take place with full information now no longer occur. Grossman and Stiglitz (1976) also present evidence of inefficiency. In an efficient market the price should convey all the information available about the good or asset in question. If markets are efficient, then there is thus no need to gather information (a costly exercise). But of course, if no one gathers information then the price cannot reflect it. Thus the fact that information is costly means that markets can never be fully efficient.
5. For example, Hahn writes of general equilibrium theory that 'one of the mysteries which future historians of thought will surely wish to unravel is how it came about that the Arrow–Debreu model came to be taken descriptively; that is, as sufficient in itself for the study and perhaps control of actual economies. Having spent most of my life as an economist on this theory I confess that such an interpretation never occurred to me' (Hahn 1984, p. 308).
6. According to our opening definition the auctioneer can be viewed as an institution, in that he limits economic activity until equilibrium prices are established.
7. In the sociological tradition this idea dates back to at least Durkheim, who argued that no actor had an incentive to reach any agreement or make any transaction with someone else without the belief that such a contract would be upheld. This is turn depends on a 'precontractual' consensus of shared values. Markets, in short, cannot exist on their own and thus need a pre-existing social cement.
8. There are other theoretical considerations which also suggest that the Walrasian metaphor should not be used descriptively. Chief amongst these is the problem of stability – that is, that even if a set of prices which clears all markets exists, thereby arriving at a general equilibrium, no one has shown, even at the level of theory, how this comes about (Hahn 1984).
9. This endogeneous enforcement problem is treated in economics as one of finding the optimal incentives under conditions of moral hazard and adverse selection. Bowles and Gintis (1993) provide a very good account of some of the radical implications of this approach.

10. This literature is distinguished from neo-institutionalists who see themselves as a development of the institutionalist school associated with Veblen, Commons and others (Hodgson 1989). We shall discuss these later.

11. On the idea of markets being themselves institutions, see Hall (1986) and Block (1990). Within this political science literature, the argument develops from Polanyi's insight that since labour is not a commodity, and does not behave like a commodity, it cannot be regulated by a pure market system.

12. For further discussion see, for example, Friedman (1986).

13. See Hodgson (1988, pp. 191–192). Hodgson, as well as showing the power of game theory, also discusses some of the limitations of the approach.

14. On this issue see Hodgson (1988, Chapters 8 and 9).

15. Solow makes clear that he is not interested in explaining why unemployment occurs, but why it persists. The model and discussion can be found in Solow (1990, Chapter 2).

16. See J. Kay, 'The unwritten code of lasting business', *Financial Times*, 29 March 1993.

17. Lorenz (1991) has studied small to medium-sized industrial firms around Lyons which have developed a network of subcontractors and main firms. This network was particularly successful in the introduction of new technology. He also argues that trust relationships were compatible with strong competition and that for the companies long-run mutual cooperation was more important than short-term profit

18. For Hodgson trust relationships imply a radical critique of neoclassical economics since preferences can no longer be taken as exogenous: 'Trust is ... not best explained as a phenomenon resulting simply from the rational calculation of costs and benefits by given individuals. In any social order based on a degree of trust, the regime affects the preferences, goals and behaviour of the individuals concerned' (Hodgson 1989, p. 254).

19. See Sawyer (1992) on this theme.

20. See, for instance, the collection of articles in Zukin and DiMaggio (1990).

21. For a discussion of institutional economics, 'new' and 'old', see Hodgson (1988, 1989) and Solo (1989). This approach can be seen in both the *Journal of Economics Issues* and the *Review of Political Economy*.

22. For an excellent review of the Regulation school, see Dunford (1990).

23. For an empirical investigation of various versions of the Olson hypothesis, see Quiggin (1992). Of course the Olson hypothesis has been hotly debated. For instance, Lazonick (1991) explicitly counters Olson's view on the decline of the British economy and argues that Britain actually suffered from not having sufficient collective organizations to maintain international competitive advantage. Interestingly, with respect to some of the earlier arguments of this chapter, Lazonick is also critical of the implicit market counter-factual in Olson's analysis: 'It is also the case that the centrality of collective business organisation to US and Japanese industrial successes in the first half of the twentieth century is devastating to the standard neoclassical view of the world – a view that correlates market coordination with economic success' (Lazonick, op. cit., p. 320).

24. A discussion of public-choice theory and corporatism is taken up in Chapter 6.

25. See Streeck and Schmitter (1991, pp. 238–239). We develop this theme in the final section of Chapter 6.

3. Corporatism, Labour Market Institutions and Unemployment

Within mainstream economics certain labour economists have for a long time shown a concern for the importance of institutions in explaining wage-setting behaviour, a tradition that originates with the work of the 'founding fathers' of modern labour economics in the 1940s and 1950s and even earlier, for example Taylor and Pierson (1957), Kerr (1950, 1954) and Slichter (1954). In the 1960s and 1970s much of this interest was directed towards assessing the consequences of institutions related explicitly to the promotion of wage restraint and incomes policies, for example Ullman and Flanagan (1971) and Fallick and Elliott (1981). It is perhaps the generally pessimistic tone of the conclusions of much of this later work that has led to the discrediting of overt forms of income restraint, and a renewal of the search for types of institutional arrangement which may prove beneficial to the achievement of the macroeconomic objectives of price stability and low unemployment. This search has led to a now considerable literature on wage-setting and corporatism.

However, as we shall see, the focus in both theoretical and applied areas has been on very specific aspects of corporatism as an arrangement. One view, very simply stated, is that corporatism as practised in the small open European economies outside the EC has been able to impart a rather different form of wage-setting behaviour. In unemployment terms this behaviour has generated less painful short-run adjustment to past macroeconomic shocks when compared to the larger European economies, and offers a better prospect of effective remedy for currently high levels of European unemployment. Thus, the purpose of this chapter is to review the theoretical arguments for such a conclusion and to review the large volume of applied research which attempts to shed light on it.

CORPORATISM AND WAGE-SETTING: THEORETICAL CONSIDERATIONS

There has emerged a common basis to much of the economic analysis of unemployment. Movements in the level of unemployment are seen as an equilibrating device reconciling the conflicting claims of workers and employers over the distribution of income. At this equilibrium point the prevailing level of unemployment will serve to regulate claims in order to establish stable, though not necessarily low, inflation, given no change in the vast array of environmental and institutional factors that determine those claims. This level of unemployment is termed the non-accelerating inflation rate of unemployment (NAIRU) and has been popularized in the model of Layard and Nickell (1986) – see also Layard, Nickell and Jackman (1991). This concept is supported by a vast literature on the mechanics of the wage-determination process and specifically on how the level of unemployment influences the real wage demands of workers (see Nickell 1990, Layard, Nickell and Jackman 1991 and Bean 1992, for surveys). The overall approach is more general than those theories which are based on Walrasian perfectly competitive foundations (such as Natural Rate theories) since it specifically encompasses the existence of imperfect competition and thus the existence of an economic rent over which conflict between workers and capital can exist. It can therefore encompass consideration of the nature of the choices and strategies open to the players concerned.

These recent theories of wage-determination have focused on the microeconomic foundations for the relationship between the real wage and the level of unemployment. In general, the approach of these theories is institutionalist in the sense of the previous chapter in that they are game-theoretic or incorporate consideration of various informational aspects of the relationships between the players in the labour market. So they include theories about the union–firm bargaining process (Oswald 1985), efficiency wage theories of various forms (Akerlof and Yellen 1987), and theories about labour market inflexibility such as insider–outsider models (Lindbeck and Snower 1989). The starting point for these developments has been the observation that real wage levels have in many larger European economies appeared quite unresponsive to the rising and subsequently stubbornly high unemployment of the 1970s and 1980s.

The theoretical framework adopted here considers a situation where equilibrium unemployment and stable inflation occur where unemployment adjusts to bring the wage aspirations of workers into line with the 'feasible' real wage that employers are prepared to pay. We assume that workers (or their union representatives) have a 'target' or 'bargained' real wage which will depend on the level of unemployment. Higher levels of employment will act to moderate the wage claims of workers. So we can specify the relationship between the bargained real wage, w^B, and labour market conditions under collective bargaining – we follow closely the approach of Carlin and Soskice (1990):

$$w^B = f(U) \tag{3.1}$$

where U is the unemployment rate, with unemployment equal to the difference between the size of the labour force and employment. Assuming that $dw^B/dU < 0$, this describes a downward-sloping relationship between the bargained real wage and the level of unemployment. In other words, falling unemployment imparts to trades unions the perception that they can push for higher real wages. We need to derive the form of the function $f(.)$ which will encapsulate conditions governing the nature of the bargaining process (for instance, whether workers and employers bargain over wages alone, or wage and employment jointly) and the nature of worker preferences. Specifically for the latter we will be concerned with the extent to which workers directly perceive a threat to their employment opportunities from extracting a higher nominal wage from their employer.

Taking the case where workers are unionized, the most simplistic representation of the union–firm wage-setting process is the case where the union bargains to achieve a real wage (and implicitly a level of employment) to maximize the utility of a representative member, and the firm selects the profit-maximizing level of employment consistent with that real wage – the so-called *monopoly* union model (i.e. the firm does not bargain over the wage). The representative union member's utility will be a weighted average of the union-set wage level if he or she gets a job at that real wage and the alternative income if he or she fails to obtain a job (given by the level of unemployment benefit). The weights will be the probability of obtaining a job offer, $1 - U$, and the probability of unemployment, U, respectively. The rate at which the employer lays off additional workers in response to the union expressing a preference for a higher real wage will be determined by the wage elasticity of demand for labour. Thus, Carlin and Soskice (op. cit., p. 391) show that under such circumstances and at a given level of aggregate demand, the relationship between the bargained real wage and the rate of unemployment for a risk-neutral union is:

$$w^B = b \left(1 - 1/(\eta U)\right)^{-1} \tag{3.2}$$

where b is the level of state-provided unemployment benefit and η is the absolute value of the wage elasticity of demand for labour. A full derivation and statement of underlying assumptions is given in the Appendix to this chapter. Equation 3.2 provides an inverse non-linear relationship between the bargained real wage and the unemployment rate, illustrated as the bargained real wage curve in Figure 3.1. It shows that this relationship with the rate of unemployment (and

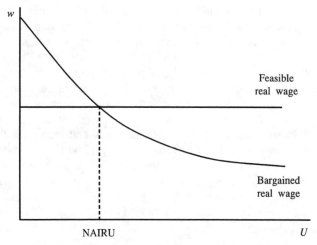

Figure 3.1   Equilibrium unemployment in the Layard-Nickell model

assuming a fixed labour force, the level of employment) is steeper (i.e. a more negative slope) the higher the employment–real wage elasticity.

A more realistic and more commonly adopted representation of the union–firm relationship allows for bargaining over the real wage level. This is known as *right-to-manage* bargaining (Nickell and Andrews 1983) since the union and the firm strike a bargain over the real wage, but the firm retains the right to set a level of employment following the bargain that is consistent with profit maximization.[1] Here the relationship between the bargained real wage and employment is broadly similar to the monopoly union case. The union may be forced to accept a lower level of overall utility compared to the monopoly union case, since it may not have sufficient strength to take effective industrial action to impose its utility-maximizing real wage on the firm. Thus, the relationship between wage and unemployment is additionally conditioned by the union's bargaining strength (greater bargaining strength implies higher real wage). Since the bargained real wage is constrained to lie on the firm's labour demand curve, which is in turn derived from product market conditions, the bargaining solution will depend on two further factors influencing the conditions under which the demand for labour is derived. It is conditioned by the product market price elasticity of demand (higher product price elasticity implies a bargained real wage curve which is lower and further to the left) and also by the output elasticity of employment (higher elasticity implies a bargained real wage curve which is lower and further to left; see Carlin and Soskice op. cit. pp. 392–397).

As already indicated, the assumption that unemployment acts to reconcile claims over the surplus or quasi-rent means that equilibrium in wage-setting has to be established by the additional consideration of price-setting by firms under conditions of imperfect competition. Real wages form an important part of costs, and under imperfectly competitive conditions the price level in aggregate will depend on a mark-up on costs. Conversely, if firms face particular product market conditions and thus are able to impose a particular cost mark-up then there will exist for employers a real wage level that is consistent with those price-setting conditions. This is termed the *price-determined real wage* by Carlin and Soskice, and the *feasible real wage* by Layard and Nickell.

To consider how this feasible real wage is determined we shall first consider the case of monopoly in the product market. Here the relationship between price and marginal cost is given by the Lerner condition. Profit maximization by firms implies that labour is utilized according to the marginal productivity condition such that the wage equals marginal cost (*MC*) times the marginal product of labour (*MPL*). Thus:

$$P = 1/(1 - 1/\varepsilon) \, MC = 1/(1 - 1/\varepsilon) \, (W/MPL) \qquad (3.3)$$

where ε is the absolute value of the price elasticity of demand for output. Equation 3.3 simply states that the lower the product price elasticity of demand the greater the extent to which the firm can raise price above cost without suffering a reduction in total profits from lost sales, and so the greater its profit mark-up. Rearrangement of equation 3.3 gives an expression for the real product wage (the real wage in terms of product price):

$$W/P = 1/(1 - 1/\varepsilon)MPL \qquad (3.4)$$

and in the Layard–Nickell formulation *MPL* is determined by a further specification of production technology.

Relaxing the assumption of monopoly, it can be shown that under imperfectly competitive conditions the size of the profit mark-up of price over marginal cost will be greater the more concentrated the structure of industry in question and the greater the extent to which firms in that industry collude over price-fixing (Cowling and Waterson 1976, Waterson 1984). Thus Kalecki (1938) describes the mark-up of price over marginal cost as capturing the 'degree of monopoly'. Under general but precisely unspecified conditions of imperfect competition we can denote the mark-up as μ and rewrite equation 3.4 as:

$$W^P = \mu \, MPL \qquad (3.5)$$

where W^P is the price-determined real wage. μ may vary anti-cyclically (Rotemberg and Saloner 1986, Bils 1987) or pro-cyclically (Cowling 1983), however for present purposes we will assume that it remains independent of demand conditions.[2] This allows us to show the price-determined real wage as independent of the level of unemployment and so it is determined by a horizontal curve in Figure 3.1.

The competing-claims equilibrium rate of unemployment or NAIRU is thus determined by the joint solution of equations 3.1 and 3.5, and this is illustrated in Figure 3.1. Equilibrium will depend on a number of factors affecting the positions of both curves and the slope of the bargained real wage curve. These factors will include the way in which price expectations are formulated, the nature of production technology and cost conditions, the extent to which industrial structure is concentrated or firms collude over price-setting, and the strength of the trade union bargainers. Factors which affect production conditions are not easily illustrated diagrammatically since both curves are affected. On the other hand, an increase in the market power of firms (i.e. higher industrial concentration), for example, will shift the feasible real wage curve down so increasing the NAIRU. Similarly an increase in the bargaining power of unions will shift the bargained real wage curve up and to the right so increasing the NAIRU.[3] The contribution of these factors to the rise in unemployment since the end of the post-war 'golden age' has been extensively investigated by, for example, Layard and Nickell (1986) on the UK, and Bean, Layard and Nickell (1986), and Layard, Nickell and Jackman (1991) on comparisons across OECD countries.

The sensitivity of workers' real wage demands to changes in unemployment is given by the slope of the bargained real wage curve. It is the question of what determines this sensitivity that is pertinent to the question of the role of corporatism. Corporatism will also influence the horizontal position of the bargained real wage curve. As we shall see, it can be demonstrated that under conditions of intermediate-level bargaining centralization, or coordination, the curve will be, *ceteris paribus*, higher and further to the right than under either high-level centralization or coordination or decentralization. Therefore, *ceteris paribus*, the NAIRU will be higher under intermediate-level centralization compared to either of the other two scenarios.

We consider first the decentralized case, where collective bargaining proceeds at a low level, typically at the enterprise or plant level between a single employer and workplace trade union representatives. If the union demands a sizeable real wage then under such circumstances any bargained wage increases will, assuming some degree of imperfect competition, be passed swiftly into higher product prices. Because the price of the product may contribute negligibly to the aggregate price level, workers in the firm will have obtained a significant improvement in their real consumption wage, that is their wage net of income tax expressed in terms of the aggregate economy-wide price level. However, the consequence of that real wage increase will be to reduce the market competitiveness of the firm in question. In the context of the Chamberlinian model of imperfect competition the single firm's demand curve will be much more price elastic than that for the industry as a whole, at a particular price level. Thus, if the firm in question raises its price it will experience a considerable reduction in product demand and so will have a rather high wage elasticity of demand for labour, η. Consequently it will reduce its employment level sharply. Demand for the output of other employers, who have not conceded the same wage demand, will increase, allowing them to hire the displaced workers.

The importance of external product demand conditions will thus impinge on the wage demands of firm- or plant-specific union organizations. If the workers care about employment levels (although, as we shall see, they may not necessarily do so) they will be forced to take account of the employment consequences of a substantial real wage increase, and so may exercise moderation in formulating wage demands. So wage bargainers will not be very powerful. Their bargained real wage curve will be steep in the area of the equilibrium because any increase in unemployment will quickly force them to moderate their wage demands. It will be relatively further down and to the left because of the high product price elasticity. This is illustrated in Figure 3.2, panel A. The diagram shows that with such a bargained real wage curve the equilibrium level of unemployment (NAIRU$_1$) will be fairly low. Of course in the most decentralized, competitive economies unions may be very weak or even nonexistent, and the threat of bankruptcy may mean that competitive firms are in no position to pass on wage increases into higher prices. Therefore employers will be able to impose wage levels at external competitive levels.

If we consider the effect of an adverse shock to the economy, which reduces the level of real demand in the economy, this has the effect of shifting the feasible real wage curve down from FRW$_1$ to FRW$_2$. So with the bargained real wage curve described a new equilibrium can be established at a lower real wage with only a slight increase in the NAIRU. More generally during conditions of high unemployment decentralized bargaining may allow considerable downward real wage flexibility as currently employed workers find themselves forced to

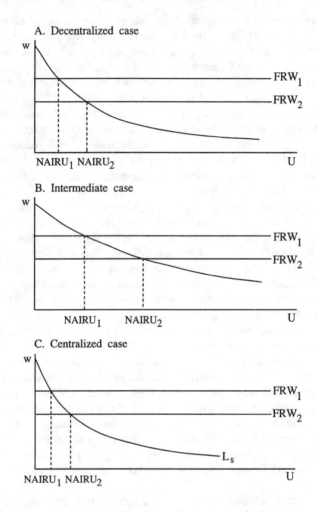

Figure 3.2   Effects of a reduction in the feasible real wage under different bargaining scenarios

compete with the unemployed for their jobs.

Whether economies of this type exist in practice is a matter of empirical investigation. Even in decentralized structures the nature of union preferences may be such as to place little weight on the employment consequences of wage-setting behaviour. This will be particularly so where unions behave according to the so-called *median voter* model (Oswald 1987, Disney and Gospel 1989). A key consequence of this model is that lay-offs are determined according to a known rule, typically 'last-in, first-out'. For marginal (i.e. below fifty percent) reductions in employment union members with median or above job tenure will feel that their jobs are secure. So they will press hard to preserve a particular real wage, regardless of the effects on product competitiveness and on the level of unemployment.

With collective bargaining at the industry-level, such a lack of attention to external economic conditions may also hold, although this again is a matter for empirical investigation. Here union bargaining strength and representation may be quite strong, because the firm-specific skills workers possess are very valuable to firms. Thus the costs to the firm of rapid labour turnover will be high. So wage-setting may proceed with little attention to external economic conditions. At the industry level the effect on the aggregate price level of firms passing on higher wages into prices will remain slight, and workers will feel little impact of bargained wage increases on their real consumption wage. Assume all firms in the industry face the same wage increase together and raise prices simultaneously. If total industry demand is reasonably price-inelastic, the effects on industry output and employment will be thought to be less severe than in the decentralized case, because at the level of the industry compared to the individual firm ε is lower. This lower perceived product price elasticity will mean that the bargained real wage curve is higher and further to the right, so that the equilibrium NAIRU is higher, as illustrated in panel B of Figure 3.2. Workers will think that a given increase in real wages can be achieved, assuming firms can be persuaded to allow the feasible real wage to rise, without a serious reduction in employment at the industry level. They will anticipate some reduction in employment resulting from the real wage concession made to workers. However, in aggregate the total reduction will be considerably greater than the sum total anticipated in this way for each industry, since a reduction in output and increase in price in one industry will have spill-over effects into other sectors. These occur as higher output prices in some sectors feed through to higher materials costs in other sectors further down the production sequence. Consequently economies with intermediate levels of collective bargaining centralization coupled with strong or moderately strong trade unions may experience particularly poor employment and inflation performance. This arises because of poor economy-wide coordination of economic adjustment. In the case of an adverse economic shock which reduces the feasible real wage, the new bargained equilibrium will entail a rather larger rise in the NAIRU (see Figure 3.2, panel B). This is because in the area of equilibrium the bargained real wage curve is flatter than in the decentralized case, as workers are less concerned about the impact of unemployment on their wage demands. In general terms we can say that intermediate centralization entails a form of coordination failure in which the inability of wage bargainers to ascertain the economy-wide consequences of their actions results in a sub-optimal outcome. In practice this may result in such behaviour as 'leap-frogging' where different powerful groups in the labour market seek to preserve their position in the wage distribution by bidding up real wage claims as they observe wage concessions made elsewhere.

In the present context the role of well-developed corporatist arrangements is to reconnect wage setters to external economic conditions, by accurately informing workers about the economy-wide levels of η and ε. If unions wish to maximize the utility of their employed members they will choose the real wage that will maximize employment. They will recognize that the only real wage consistent with equilibrium is the FRW and so will bargain for that. At that real wage labour will be supplied according to the underlying labour supply curve (see Figure 3.2, panel C). Consequently the equilibrium level of unemployment in the centralized case will be very low. In equilibrium any remaining unemployment is voluntary in that it represents those workers who are not prepared to supply labour at the prevailing real wage level. If an adverse economic shock occurs wage-setters will correctly work out the economy-wide implications at the current real wage level in terms of increased unemployment. The bargained real wage curve will be steep, reflecting unions' realism about the aggregate implications of higher wages on employment, and so the increase in the NAIRU will be slight. The increase in equilibrium unemployment will represent those workers who are now additionally unwilling to work at the lower real wage. Other workers will recognize that the economic shock has had the effect of reducing the economy-wide feasible real wage. These workers will take that new lower real wage level as given.

In the case of intermediate bargaining centralization, trade unions will establish the effect on their particular sector or industry in isolation but will not immediately become aware of second-round effects on employment in that sector or industry, until the impact of other bargains elsewhere in the economy works through. More favourable adjustment to a nominal shock, such as an oil price increase, will occur under centralized, corporatist conditions. Here workers will correctly establish the employment effects of a wage demand designed to restore their real wage to the pre-shock level, whereas with less centralization trade unions will, at least initially, underestimate the true employment consequences of an increase in nominal wages to restore the real consumption wage. This reflects the observation by Calmfors (1987) that greater centralization of collective bargaining serves to internalize an externality.

Therefore, under well-developed corporatist conditions, with highly centralized or highly coordinated bargaining and with powerful peak employer and labour organizations, more rapid (in the sense that it takes workers less time to recognize any adverse movements in the feasible real wage) and less painful adjustment to adverse economic shocks can be achieved through real wage flexibility. Whereas under decentralization real wage flexibility is achieved through the operation of supply and demand in competitive labour markets because trades unions are weak, under corporatism it is achieved because those corporatist institutions draw the attention of powerful employee wage bargainers to the potential macroeconomic consequences of the use of maximum bargaining strength by subgroups of workers. Under intermediate forms of labour market arrangement the existence of poorly coordinated monopolistic power in the labour market fails to result in the successful operation of either adjustment mechanism. This leads to a prediction that there exists a 'hump-shaped' relationship between the degree of bargaining centralization and coordination and unemployment performance (illustrated in Figure 3.3).

The existence of such a hump-shape was first pointed out in a seminal paper by Calmfors and Driffill (1988). Their argument is similar to the one discussed above. The model they present suggests a monotonic relationship between the degree of wage moderation and bargaining centralization. Moderation in wage claims is greatest at the highest level of centralization because under these circumstances

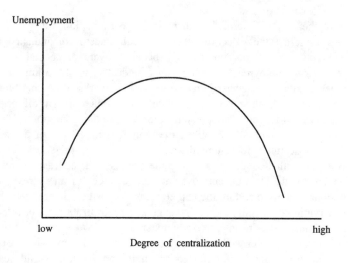

Figure 3.3   Unemployment and centralization – the Calmfors–Driffill hump

workers fully recognize the economy-wide implications of their behaviour. Operating in the opposite direction to this is the effect that the more trade unions combine as bargainers, as centralization gets higher, the greater their market power and thus their ability to raise wages above the competitive level by restricting the supply of labour to the economy. The combination of these two effects working in opposite directions produces the hump-shape in Figure 3.4. If we consider the employers' side of the bargaining process as well, a similar argument may apply – that greater coordination between employers may facilitate easier coordination of price increases across the board. This further reinforces the existence of the hump. The point about price-setting power, of both unions and firms, arguably increasing with centralization suggests that there is a risk that corporatism, as a form of producer combination, may entirely negate the benefits of greater bargaining coordination, because it entails increased monopoly power. Under such circumstances corporatism might degenerate into a form of collusion 'against' consumers. This serves to illustrate that an understanding of the operation of corporatism in its successful forms requires a consideration of issues beyond the labour market. We shall turn to these in the next chapter; however, it is worth pointing out at this stage that successful corporatist economies have been those where such monopolistic behaviour has been ruled out by their small, open nature. Price-setting is severely constrained by the pressure of international competition – indeed, that pressure has focused the attention of wage bargainers on the importance of effective means of achieving wage restraint.

Calmfors and Driffill discuss a further reason for the superior unemployment performance under bargaining centralization, namely the

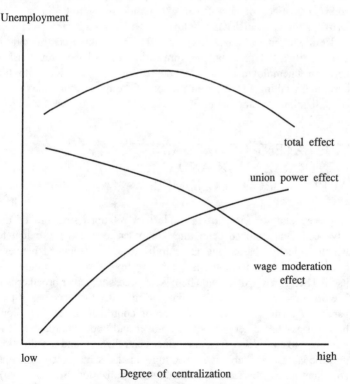

Figure 3.4 Union power and wage moderation effects

internalization of what they term the *fiscal externality* resulting from the financing of unemployment benefit. When bargaining at a centralized level, a union is more likely to realize that a large post-tax real wage increase will eventually be reduced since additional unemployment will incur increased state expenditures on unemployment benefit and thus higher taxes. Only if unemployment benefits are financed from profits taxes alone will this not be the case. Where benefits are income tax financed the exercise of maximum bargaining strength will be partially self-defeating, and this fact is more likely to be recognized where bargaining is highly centralized. Pohjola (1992) states that this is the 'most convincing argument found so far' (p. 65) for the claimed success of corporatism. In fact, the additional effect of this fiscal externality will, in Calmfors and Driffill's view, mean that unemployment will, *ceteris paribus*, be lower under maximum centralization compared to maximum decentralization. This justifies the fact that they draw the hump-shaped relationship between unemployment and the degree of centralization with the correlation falling further from the top of the hump at the maximum centralization extreme (as in Figure 3.3).

THE EXTENT OF BARGAINING CENTRALIZATION AND COORDINATION ACROSS OECD ECONOMIES

A survey and summary of the industrial relations structure of the advanced industrialized economies, in order to assess the extent to which collective bargaining is centralized and coordinated between both employers and unions, is a task worthy of several volumes in itself. Therefore the discussion here is, of necessity, rather broad brush. We organize our discussion by considering firstly the *structure* of pay bargaining, and secondly the degree of coordination (or collusion) between pay bargainers on both employer and trade union sides. It is important to consider coordination since centralization and coordination may be *de facto* alternatives, resulting in the same outcome. High coordination may be a substitute for high centralization (Soskice 1990), although it may work less effectively. To continue a framework borrowed from the industrial organization literature, we consider coordination as an aspect of the *conduct* of pay bargaining.

Bargaining structures, as they exist in the industrialized world, are diverse. While we can identify in a sizeable number of countries a trend towards greater decentralization, the extent of change in those structures over the last decade does not suggest to any extent growing convergence between countries. Table 3.1 summarizes the principal levels at which wage negotiations are conducted across the main OECD economies. The table also includes the rankings by degree of centralization calculated by Bruno and Sachs (1985) and Calmfors and Driffill (1988).

Within the EC it seems that bargaining parties in many countries remain committed to multi-employer industry-level bargaining arrangements in contrast to the progressive decentralization towards the local, plant or firm level that is apparent in the UK, and that has always been the case in North America. Only in Belgium, Italy and very recently in Greece (Kritsantonis 1992) does a similar trend towards greater company- or establishment-level bargaining appear to have taken place in the 1970s and 1980s. In Belgium the 1986 private sector central collective agreement over pay seems to have reversed this trend, representing a return to national inter-industry agreements (Vilrokx and Van Leemput 1992). In most other EC members a commitment to industry-level or sectoral-level bargaining remains. Those EC economies where pay bargaining is currently rather decentralized comprise the UK, Spain and Portugal. In the latter two there have been moves recently to bring about a greater degree of centralization (IRRR 1990, Martinez Lucio 1992); in the Portuguese case at the employers' behest (Barreto 1992).

Outside of the EC, in the corporatist Scandinavian economies, a growth in plant- and enterprise-level bargaining has occurred, albeit from a highly centralized level, in response to worsening economic performance. This is so especially in Sweden. For some time writers have examined the phenomenon of 'wage drift' in the Scandinavian context.[4] Wage drift refers to wage increases which are agreed at a plant or firm level in addition to the centrally negotiated rate. In particular there is concern that such wage drift may undermine the intent of centralized negotiation by allowing private sector wages to be determined by local or sectoral market conditions. Recent evidence (Holden 1989, 1990, Holmlund and Skedinger 1990) suggests that, while wage drift does occur in the Scandinavian economies in response

Table 3.1 Degree of bargaining centralization in OECD economies

	Economy level	Industry/sector level	Plant/enterprise level
EC:			
Belgium (9,8)	mainly	some in mid 1980s	
Denmark (7,4)	in some years, esp. in 1960s	principal level	
France (13,11)		yes	
Germany (2,6)	implicit coordination of sector bargains	yes	
Greece	bargaining over minimum wage level		growing since 1988
Ireland	pre-1970 and 1990	coordinated sector bargains in 70s and 80s	some secondary bargaining
Italy (14,13)	1975–86	pre-1975 and post-1986	
Netherlands (3,7)	some implicit coordination of sector bargains	yes	
Portugal		main sectors	preferred by unions in large companies
Spain		main sectors	growing in 1980s
UK (12,12)		declining	growing in 1980s

Table 3.1   (continued)

Non-EC Europe:

Austria (1,1)	coordination of industry agreements		
Finland (8,5)	yes		secondary bargaining but anticipated in central agreements
Norway (4=,2)	yes		secondary plant bargains
Sweden (4=,2)	yes		secondary plant bargains, growing pressure for decentralization
Switzer-land (6,15)	coordination of lower level bargains	some	mainly

Non-Europe:

Canada (16,17)			almost all bargains
USA (17,16)			almost all bargains
Japan (10,14)	coordination through Shunto		mainly firm level
Austr-alia (15,10)	norms set by National IR Commission	main level	some secondary firm-level bargains
New Zealand (11,9)	compulsory arbitration until 1984	main level	some secondary firm-level bargains

Note: The numbers in brackets are the Bruno–Sachs and Calmfors–Driffill rankings by degree of centralization respectively; 1 = most centralized, 17 = least centralized.

to variations in excess labour demand, it does not result in an offsetting effect such that the central bargain has no impact in those sectors where there is secondary lower-level bargaining.

The important contrast within Europe is still between the more decentralized, and predominantly industrial or sectoral bargaining of the members of the EC and the highly centralized small economies outside the EC, namely Austria, Norway, Sweden and Finland. The exception to this rule is Switzerland where collective bargaining has traditionally taken place at a very decentralized local, plant-based level. As we shall discuss shortly, the Swiss case is also exceptional because, despite experiencing a very atomistic collective bargaining structure, there are reasons for believing that the conduct of pay bargaining is quite highly coordinated. In this respect Japan is similar in that pay bargaining is predominantly conducted at the firm level but, as we shall also discuss shortly, bargaining is synchronized.

Australia is particularly difficult to categorize in terms of degree of bargaining centralization. It is exceptional in that for most of the post-war period it has had in place a centralized system of compulsory arbitration. Over the last twenty years the level of wage bargaining has switched between decentralization and centralization and back again on more than one occasion (Archer 1992). Moves towards centralized setting have generally been motivated by the imposition of incomes policies, and thus, if they are to be viewed as attempts at corporatism, they bear more resemblance to 1970s British 'crisis corporatism' than to corporatism as manifest in Scandinavia. Centralization was in effect imposed after 1983 through the 'Accord' between the governing Australian Labour Party and the Australian Council of Trades Unions, although since 1987 this has been weakened by allowing lower-level productivity bargaining. The industrial relations system in New Zealand was traditionally rather similar to that in Australia, however here compulsory arbitration was ended in 1984, and it has not pursued the tripartist policies of Australia since.

Apart from obvious factors such as variations in collective agreement coverage, and in trade union structure (whether industry- or craft-based or fragmented along political and ideological divisions) and strength, the determinants of the level at which bargaining is conducted are closely tied to the degree of coordination amongst employers and employees. A high degree of coordination of pay bargaining is a further hallmark of pay bargaining in Scandinavia and in Austria.

Within the EC a high degree of coordination between pay bargainers, which is effective at a national level, is a feature only in Denmark and The Netherlands. Even in these cases central negotiations have aimed at providing a framework for lower-level bargaining and have not always been successful, for example in The Netherlands. However, the level at which union and employer representatives meet to conduct bargaining activity should not be confused with the level of bargaining coordination. Soskice (1990) argues that the focus of Calmfors and Driffill on bargaining centralization results in a underestimation of the degree of corporatism in Germany and Switzerland, where sector- and plant-level bargaining is implicitly coordinated by the activities of powerful employers' organizations. Outside Europe the same argument also applies to the Japanese case. Indeed, in Japan and Switzerland coordination is high despite rather weak trade union movements. Thus Lehmbruch (1984) characterizes Japan as 'concertation without labour'. Coordination, or more precisely synchronization, in pay bargaining has been traditionally achieved through the Shunto, or Spring Offensive. Elsewhere, within the EC, coordination is, at best, only effective between bargainers within the same industry, or if it is in operation at the national level it has been limited in scope, as in the controversial and now dissolved national wage indexation arrangements in Italy.

Coordination of bargaining in Australia, to the extent that is exists, has been achieved through outside control, working through the compulsory arbitration process. Centralization of bargaining in Australia since the early 1980s has proceeded through state intervention rather than effective coordination. Employers in particular have played little role in the 'Accord' process. In North America there is no coordination of bargaining.

The degree of trade union representation also varies greatly across the advanced industrial world. Table 3.2 reports union densities, measured with the employed labour force as denominator. They vary within the EC from under twenty percent (France) to over eighty percent (Denmark). For those EC members who are included in Table 3.2, only Germany records an increase in density since 1970. However, since the mid-1980s here too density has been in decline. In the highly corporatist economies outside the EC, namely Austria, Norway and Sweden, density is stable, if not increasing.

However, levels of union density may be a very poor indicator of the level of bargaining coordination on the supply-side of the labour

Table 3.2 Union membership in OECD countries

	Union density % of civilian employment		
	1970	1980	1988
European:			
Austria	59.8	53.8	45.7
Belgium	46.0	56.5	53.0
Denmark	60.0	76.5	73.2
Finland	51.4	69.8	71.3[f]
France	22.3	19.0	12.0
Germany	33.0	37.0	33.8
Ireland	53.1	63.4	52.4[g]
Italy	36.3	49.3	39.6
Netherlands	37.0	35.3	25.0
Norway	50.6	56.9	57.1
Portugal[a]	59.0[c]	58.8[d]	30.0
Spain	–	22.0[e]	16.0[h]
Sweden	67.7	80.0	85.3
Switzerland	30.7	30.7	26.0[g]
UK	44.8	50.7	41.5
Non-European:			
Canada[a]	31.1	35.1	34.6
USA	30.0[a]	23.0	16.4[f]
Japan[a]	35.1	31.1	26.8
Australia	50.2	49.0	42.0
New Zealand[b]	46.2	55.0	42.1[i]

Notes:
1. Data refer to total employed membership except: [a] union recorded membership [b] private sector employed
2. Years as indicated except: [c] 1969   [d] 1979–84   [e] 1981   [f] 1989   [g] 1987   [h] 1985   [i] 1990
Source: OECD (1991)

market. Certainly in France a low level of unionization is associated with a highly fragmented labour movement. But in the UK, where density is at moderately high levels, the single peak association, the Trades Union Congress, has rarely, if ever, attempted to coordinate bargaining. Visser (1990) distinguishes between vertical and horizontal integration in national European trade union structures. (His study does not include consideration of the other non-European OECD countries.) The horizontal dimension attempts to capture the degree of cohesion and unity between trade unions, and the vertical the extent to which central union associations command authority over constituent member unions. Figure 3.5 shows the cross-tabulation of Visser's estimates of the two dimensions for the main European economies for the period 1970 to 1985. Table 3.3 summarizes the degree of representation coordination for trade unions in both horizontal and vertical directions, along with the degree of employer coordination.

Two principal features emerge. Firstly, the levels of both dimensions of union movement integration of the main EC economies tend, with

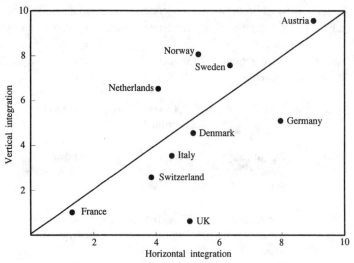

Figure 3.5 Horizontal and vertical integration in European trade union organizations

Corporatism and Economic Performance

Table 3.3 Representational coordination in OECD countries

| | Trade unions | | Employers |
	Horizontal	Vertical	
EC:			
Belgium	3 federations, politically fragmented	weak	several groups, central mandate weak
Denmark	3 federations, moderate	moderate	strong in manufacturing
France	4 federations, politically fragmented	weak	moderate, 3 groupings by firm size
Germany	strong, single federation	strong, due to clear sectoral structure	strong employer's association
Greece	one federation, moderate	weak, esp. in private sector	weak, low coverage
Ireland	single federation	moderate	single federation
Italy	3 federations, moderate	moderately high	one federation, regional strength
Netherlands	2 federations, moderate	moderately high	several peak associations, fair coordination
Portugal	2 federations	not very coordinated	reorganized in 1975, 3 sector-level groupings
Spain	2 politically divided federations	very weak	founded in 1977, growth promoted by State
UK	one federation, but does not negotiate	TUC has no authority over member unions	weak, single federation

Table 3.3 (continued)

Non-EC Europe:

Austria	very strong	very strong	strong, single federation
Finland	strong, single manual federation	strong	3 strong, sector-level groupings
Norway	strong	strong	single federation
Sweden	traditionally strong, but growing stress between white and blue collar	strong	single federation
Switzer-land	4 federations, fairly weak	weak	strong and coordinated

Non-Europe:

Canada	single federation covering 70 percent of unions	weak	not involved in bargaining
USA	AFL-CIO is single confederation but does not bargain	weak	not involved in bargaining
Japan	several weak confederations	weak	quite high
Austr-alia	moderately powerful single confederation	not very strong	weak, similar to UK
New Zealand	single confederation	not very strong	weak, similar to UK

the exception of Germany, to be rather low. Levels of integration in the non-EC economies tend to be higher. Secondly, in Figure 3.5, although the points seem to be scattered along the upward sloping diagonal, the main EC economies are below the diagonal, with rather higher levels of horizontal integration than vertical integration. The Netherlands is the only EC exception. The non-EC highly corporatist economies tend to be above the diagonal. So among the present EC members the degree of supply-side bargaining coordination in the labour market appears to be low, particularly in the important vertical dimension. This dimension provides the level of effective peak labour organization representation necessary for the success of corporatist arrangements, and the avoidance of the prisoners' dilemma outcome associated with more fragmented bargaining arrangements.

The degree of coordination on the employers' side is, in contrast to that of the trade unions, rather better in some parts of Europe and also in Japan. In the Swiss case employers are much better coordinated, through an effective national federation, than are trade unions, which are fragmented along religious and political lines. Thus Soskice (1990) argues that there is a high degree of implicit pay bargaining coordination in Switzerland through the commitment of the employers' federation to the arbitration system. Similarly Soskice argues that the degree of corporatism may be understated in Germany and The Netherlands if the considerable degree of inter-industry employer coordination is ignored (on Germany, see also Sisson 1987). Highly coordinated employers' federations are an important feature of the industrial relations background in Austria and the Scandinavian countries. In the case of Sweden the employers' federation, SAF, has recently been very insistent on withdrawal from national-level bargaining. Decentralization has also occurred as a result of pressure from the trade union side.[5] In the UK the benefits in terms of reduced inflationary pressure of greater 'synchronization' have been the subject of discussion by the employers' organization, although they have shown considerable scepticism towards calls from certain TUC member unions for greater centralization and coordination of bargaining.

CORPORATISM, WAGE-SETTING AND UNEMPLOYMENT: A REVIEW OF THE EMPIRICAL EVIDENCE

The empirical evidence on the macroeconomic effectiveness of corporatist labour market arrangements falls into descriptive or correlative evidence and evidence from econometric modelling. Several authors have attempted to correlate observed changes in unemployment and other macroeconomic indicators, particularly relating to the crisis period of the mid-1970s and early 1980s, to indices of corporatism and rankings of countries according to the extent of corporatist arrangements. Econometric modelling evidence builds from this first approach by attempting to specify models, of varying complexity, of the wage-setting–employment process. Two broad methodologies have been adopted. The first involves the estimation of a single-equation augmented Phillips curve and the second entails the estimation of a wage equation specified as part of a more complete model of the wage–price–employment determination process. The advantage of the latter is that it allows the investigation of a wider range of influences on wage-setting. But this is at the cost of imposing a more far-reaching model structure which may or may not be generally applicable to a range of countries which, as we have seen in the previous section, enjoy somewhat different collective bargaining arrangements. The former methodology focuses explicitly on wage adjustment mechanisms which is the important issue under consideration here.

We discuss first the evidence from simple correlations of macroeconomic indicators and measures of corporatism. Because of the difficulty in maintaining a common model of the wage-setting process across many countries, a number of authors (Calmfors and Driffill, 1988, *inter alia*) are inclined to place greater weight on this descriptive methodology than on econometric evidence. Table 3.4 reports summary results from Calmfors and Driffill (1988) for their grouping of countries into centralized, intermediate and decentralized categories.[6] Because the rise in unemployment in Switzerland was largely 'exported' through the repatriation of guest-workers, they report alternative averages for the decentralized group which include and exclude Switzerland. Since precisely the same point also applies to Austria (Guger 1992), we have in addition included averages for the centralized group which exclude Austria. The table shows firstly that on average economic performance is best (or 'misery' least) in the centralized economies and that the transition to the post-1974 oil price shock period has been least painful for this group. The monotonic relationship between centralization and 'misery' is shown by the Okun index averages, which add inflation and unemployment rates together.

Table 3.4   Macroeconomic performance averages for countries grouped by degree of centralization

	Unemployment		Employment		Okun Index	
	level	change	level	change	level	change
Centralized						
1	4.0	+2.3	72.5	+2.7	13.0	+6.1
2	4.4	+2.7	74.1	+3.8	14.2	+6.9
Inter-mediate	6.1	+4.8	60.9	−3.2	14.5	+8.7
Decentralized						
1	5.8	+2.9	65.8	−1.1	15.2	+7.7
2	6.7	+3.3	64.6	−0.5	17.0	+9.0

Notes:
   Level: 1974–85 average; Change: 1974–85 average minus 1963–73 average
   Employment is the percentage of population between 15 and 64 in work; the Okun
      index is the sum of the unemployment and inflation rates.
   Country groups:
   Centralized 1   Austria, Denmark, Finland, Norway, Sweden
   Centralized 2   as above excluding Austria
   Intermediate   Australia, Belgium, Germany, Netherlands, New Zealand
   Decentralized 1 Canada, France, Italy, Japan, Switzerland, UK, US
   Decentralized 2 as above except Switzerland
Source: Calmfors and Driffill (1988)

This illustrates that, while decentralized countries may have achieved similar unemployment levels to centralized ones, this has been at the expense of higher inflation. Bruno and Sachs (1985) demonstrate this monotonic relation between centralization and performance shown by the Okun index. They find a strong negative correlation between an index of centralization and an alternative, closely related 'misery index', defined as average inflation, 1973–79, over the 1965–73 average plus average real GNP growth, 1973–79, over the 1965–1973 average.

A second feature shown in the table, and identified by Calmfors and Driffill, is that the intermediate group of countries appears to have responded to economic crisis least well. Calmfors and Driffill go on to assess more closely the existence of the hump-shape implied by this second observation. They demonstrate significant correlation between these various indicators and a reworked centralization ranking, where the countries with the highest and the lowest centralization are ranked one and the countries with the second highest and second lowest centralization are ranked two, etc., with the intermediate countries having the lowest ranking.

We now turn to cross-country econometric analyses of the wage-setting process. As already mentioned, these divide into Phillips curve-type models and structural aggregate labour market models. Several studies (McCallum 1986, Bruno and Sachs 1985) suggest that highly corporatist economies, along with other star performers, notably Japan, appeared in the post oil-shock period to inhabit a considerably flatter Phillips curve than the bulk of OECD states. So, for example, McCallum finds that for the corporatist economies a two point reduction in the unemployment rate over the 1974–83 period could have been achieved at an average cost of a one percentage point increase in the inflation rate. For non-corporatist economies the sacrifice would have been five percentage points.

There is in the work of Bruno and Sachs an alternative explanation for poor supply-shock adjustment of certain OECD economies. As discussed above, they initially point to a monotonic relationship between 'misery' and corporatism. This is borne out by a cross-country model of the inflation–output sacrifice. They show that the cost of a one percentage point increase in average GNP growth between 1965–1973 and 1973–1979 would have been an eight percentage point increase in inflation in the least corporatist economies (such as, according to their index, the UK or US) but only a two percentage point increase in the most corporatist economies (such as Austria, Norway and Sweden). They extend their simple relationship between the 'misery' index and corporatism, discussed above, to include an index of nominal wage responsiveness. The latter is drawn from the evidence of estimated wage equations for a limited number of countries (providing results not dissimilar to other comparative work on inflation transmission, including Sachs 1979, Branson and Rotemberg 1980, and the more recent work discussed below) and a consideration of wage contracting arrangements in each country. The index shows that nominal wage responsiveness to prices is much lower in North America than elsewhere. This is because in North America there is little synchronization of wage-setting and because nominal wage contracts are typically of long duration. Their extended relationship leads to the conclusion that the most successful adjustment to the 1970s supply shocks took place in countries with either a high level of corporatism or a lowish nominal wage responsiveness, or both. Countries which are badly positioned, in their account, on both scores are the UK, Australia and New Zealand, while Austria, Germany, Norway and Sweden are the most favourably positioned. The United States and Canada, despite being highly decentralized, may have performed better because of their low nominal wage rigidity.

The main problem with the Bruno–Sachs analysis is that an independent index of nominal wage rigidity is constructed from their interpretation of wage-setting arrangements in individual countries. These arrangements will in fact be inextricably bound up with the factors that determine the extent of corporatism and thus they fail to shed light on what determines what. Other authors provide time series econometric estimates of the degree of wage flexibility in each country in turn, in order to assess its impact on the rise in unemployment. Some of these have attempted to attribute the differences in flexibility to the presence or otherwise of corporatism. From within a Phillips curve framework wage flexibility has been investigated by Grubb, Jackman and Layard (1983) and Grubb (1986). Country-by-country time series wage equations have been estimated by a number of authors including Coe and Gagliardi (1985), Newell and Symons (1985, 1987), Bean, Layard and Nickell (1986), Alogoskoufis and Manning (1988) and Layard, Nickell and Jackman (1991). In addition to these studies, a number of others have focused specifically on comparisons between the corporatist economies of Scandinavia (see Calmfors and Nymoen 1990 for a survey, and the contributions in Calmfors 1990). Estimating equations are typically derived from a model of the union–firm bargaining process, such as that presented earlier in the chapter, coupled to a structural specification of production technology, tax and benefit effects and open economy effects. Two further studies have undertaken a limited international comparison using data disaggregated to the industry level (Pissarides and Moghadam, 1990 and Holmlund and Zetterberg 1991). The literature as a whole allows inter-country comparisons of several aspects of labour market flexibility. We deal with each of these different approaches in turn.

Firstly we consider inter-country variations in the extent of nominal wage flexibility. The concept can be understood by considering a time-series Phillips curve representation of the form used by Bruno and Sachs (see Bean 1992, p. 29):

$$\Delta(w-p)_t = -\gamma_0 \Delta^2 p_t - \gamma_1 U_t + \varepsilon_t \qquad (3.6)$$

where w is the nominal wage level in logs, p is the consumer price level in logs,[7] U is the rate of unemployment and ε is a random error term. Δ is the time difference operator and t is the time subscript. Nominal flexibility is captured through the coefficient γ_0. If γ_0 is equal to zero then rising inflation has no effect on the real wage level because nominal wage-setting keeps pace with price inflation to allow real wages to remain constant. Under these circumstances nominal wages are highly flexible. High nominal flexibility means that inflationary pressure is rapidly transmitted through to wage-setting and thus to unemployment. In contrast if γ_0 is above zero then an increase in inflation will reduce the real wage because workers are unable to secure nominal wage adjustments sufficient to keep pace with rising consumer prices. Estimates of the extent of nominal wage flexibility for each OECD country are provided by Grubb *et al.* (1983) and Layard *et al.* (1991). In these empirical implementations the definition is more complicated in that equation (3.6) is considered simultaneously with the determination of the price–real wage mark-up (i.e. the feasible real wage). These studies find that nominal wages are least flexible in North America, because the long-term nature of labour contracts ensures that the linkage between wage claims and inflation at any point in time is weak. Within Europe wages exhibit rather less nominal rigidity. Table 3.5 summarizes average nominal wage flexibility estimates for EC, non-EC European and non-European countries from both studies. The absence of nominal flexibility in North America

Table 3.5 Average wage rigidity across the OECD

	EC	Non-EC Europe	US/CA/ AL/NZ	Japan
Nominal rigidity				
Grubb *et al.*	0.55	0.33	1.24	0.18
Layard *et al.*	0.31	0.53	0.62	0.05
Real rigidity				
Grubb *et al.*	1.25	0.61	0.75	0.13
Layard *et al.*	0.40	0.14	0.48	0.06

Notes:
   The numbers are simple average of reported coefficients from the different comparative studies.
   EC countries: Belgium, Denmark, France, Germany, Ireland, Italy, The Netherlands, Spain, UK
   Non-EC Europe countries: Austria, Finland, Norway, Sweden and Switzerland
Sources: Computed from results reported in Grubb, Jackman and Layard (1983), and Layard, Nickell and Jackman (1991)

helps to explain the rather better performance of the economies on the decentralized side of the Calmfors–Driffill hump. However, the presence of levels of flexibility in the corporatist economies which are not too dissimilar from levels in the intermediate European economies suggests that we need to look for additional empirical explanations through which nominal flexibility is overcome in those countries on the centralized side of the hump.

The same two studies also provide cross-country estimates of the degree of real wage flexibility, and here the distinction between corporatist countries and the rest is more clear-cut. Real wage flexibility measures the extent to which unemployment will rise following a given rise in real wages, holding price inflation constant (and thus requires the additional estimation of a pricing equation alongside equation (3.6)). In other words, it captures the severity with which the actions of wage bargainers will impinge on employment prospects, assuming the presence of a government not prepared to accommodate the inflationary effects of upward pressure on wages through expansionary fiscal or monetary policies. Averages for country groupings are also provided in Table 3.5. The most corporatist countries, who are in the non-EC Europe group, generally display the highest degree of real wage flexibility. This is consistent with the argument that in corporatist economies if unions push for higher wages then they will have already taken into account the macroeconomic implications of their actions. So they will only push for real wage increases where productivity improvements warrant them. Real wage increases will therefore have little impact on employment levels. In non-corporatist economies real wage increases will be poorly coordinated across the economy with bargainers taking little account of macroeconomic conditions. Such wage increases may not have been justified by productivity gains and will result in employers responding with lay-offs. The two different studies show some disagreement about many of the other countries but in both cases Australia and the UK appear to have the least flexibility.

These two studies and a number of further studies (Newell and Symons 1985, Grubb 1986, Bean, Layard and Nickell 1986, and Alogoskoufis and Manning 1988) also provide estimates of the overall short-run responsiveness of real wage-setting to changes in unemployment. In the case of these further studies this is not done in the context of a theoretical framework which allows separation of real and nominal influences on real wages. This responsiveness is captured by the size of the γ_1 parameter in equation (3.6), and, if we think of equation (3.6) as representing the bargained real wage curve of Figure 3.1, then γ_1 measures the slope of that curve. Table 3.6 summarizes the results of these studies for each country group. The numbers in the table are interpretable as the short-run (i.e. within the first year) percentage-point reduction in real wage growth resulting from a one percentage-point increase in unemployment. The table suggests some variation in the size of the responses between the different studies. This is inevitable given differing model structures and specifications and differing data. However, in the more corporatist economies, which predominate in the non-EC Europe group, real wage setting is much more responsive to changes in external economic conditions. This much larger short-run impact on wage-setting helps to ensure that the effects of aggregate demand shocks are more short-lived, allowing levels of employment to be more quickly restored.

A further conclusion to emerge from this literature concerns the responsiveness of real product wages (wages deflated by the output price deflator) to changes in what is known as the 'wedge'. The wedge

Table 3.6 Real wage responsiveness to changes in unemployment in OECD countries

	EC	Non-EC Europe	US/CA/ AL/NZ	Japan
Grubb *et al.*	0.99*	2.69	0.77	8.09
Newell & Symons	0.45#	0.99	0.24++	3.22
Grubb	1.20*	3.02	1.32	4.13
Bean *et al.*	1.64+	9.86	1.17	41.00
Alogoskoufis & Manning	1.43*	4.95	0.91**	14.72
Layard *et al.*	0.97*	1.50	0.77	6.40

Notes:
  The numbers are simple averages of reported coefficients from the different comparative studies.
  EC countries:
  * Belgium, Denmark, France, Germany, Ireland, Italy, The Netherlands, Spain, UK
  + Belgium, Denmark, France, Germany, Ireland, Italy, The Netherlands, UK
  # Belgium, France, Germany, Italy, The Netherlands, UK
  Non-EC Europe countries: Austria, Finland, Norway, Sweden and Switzerland
  ++ US/CA/AL; ** US only
Sources: Computed from results reported in Grubb, Jackman and Layard (1983), Newell and Symons (1985), Grubb (1986), Bean, Layard and Nickell (1986), Alogoskoufis and Manning (1988), and Layard, Nickell and Jackman (1991)

measures the difference between the real wage cost to the employer and the real take-home wage. So any increase in direct tax rates or in employer labour taxes will widen the wedge. A number of the studies (Bean *et al.* 1986, Newell and Symons 1987, and Layard *et al.* 1991) have found that more corporatist countries appear to exhibit a lower responsiveness of real product wages to increases in this wedge. Thus, if direct taxes rise or consumer prices rise faster than producer prices there will be less pressure on the part of employee wage bargainers to push for nominal wage increases to compensate for the resulting fall in the real post-tax consumption wage level. As Calmfors and Driffill (1988) point out, one feature of the 1970s crisis period in most OECD economies was the dramatic rise in the wedge, due to the oil price shocks and rising tax rates in response to growing government budget deficits. This experience was thus potentially less inflationary in the corporatist economies. We shall discuss in greater detail in Chapters 4 and 5 the reasons why this flexibility is desirable in corporatist economies and why they are better able to achieve such flexibility.

A final finding of interest to the present discussion is that unemployment hysteresis has been found to be rather lower in the 1970s and 1980s in the corporatist economies by the two studies that explicitly investigate it (Alogoskoufis and Manning 1988, and Layard *et al.* 1991). Unemployment hysteresis refers to the extent to which the current level of unemployment is dependent on the past history of unemployment, or more precisely that the equilibrium rate of unemployment is dependent on the actual rate of unemployment. In other words, once an adverse economic shock has driven unemployment up, a high level of hysteresis means that the processes through which that pool of unemployed workers exerts downward pressure on real wage growth are weak. Consequently unemployment is rather slow to return to its original equilibrium rate. Conversely, the equilibrium rate can be viewed as non-constant, rising as unemployment rises. Averages for unemployment persistence, measured by the size of the coefficient on lagged unemployment in unemployment regressions, for the three groups of countries are presented in Table 3.7.

The observation that hysteresis is less prevalent in corporatist economies provides supporting evidence for the conclusion that in more corporatist economies wage-setting is more responsive to external economic conditions. However, it is not clear whether this implies that of themselves labour markets work better under corporatism, or that in corporatist countries there exists a greater political will to direct government effort into active labour market policies which seek to remove quickly workers from the register of unemployed. More direct evidence on the responsiveness of wage-setting to external economic conditions across the different types of countries is provided by Pissarides and Moghadam (1990) and Holmlund and Zetterberg (1991). Pissarides and Moghadam model the determinants of relative hourly

Table 3.7 Average unemployment persistence in the EC and non-EC Europe

	EC	Non-EC Europe	US/CA/ AL/NZ	Japan
Alogoskoufis & Manning	0.95	0.63	0.48**	0.91
Layard *et al.*	0.73	0.42	0.58	0.46

Notes and sources: see Table 3.6.

earnings for a number of separate industrial sectors in Sweden, Finland, UK and USA. Relative wages in the USA are much more responsive to economic variables such as sectoral relative productivity and economy-wide cyclical performance than in the other three countries. In all four countries sectoral conditions have a significant influence on relative wages in around one-quarter or one-third of industries. Holmlund and Zetterberg find rather less uniformity in this respect. They model the wage-setting process in Norway, Sweden, Finland, Germany and the USA using disaggregated industry-level data, in order to test for 'insider–outsider' effects. Their main conclusion is that wages in the United States exhibit rather less dependence on wage levels outside the industry in question, compared to the other countries. Furthermore, price and productivity conditions within a particular industry exert substantial influence on industry wage levels in the United States. This influence is only modest in Germany and negligible in the three Scandinavian countries. Their conclusion places a considerable qualification on the Calmfors–Driffill hump story in that they suggest that decentralized collective bargaining in practice bears little resemblance to the competitive neoclassical labour market, and in fact may operate to enhance the ability of trade unions to share in product market quasi-rents. Indeed the US experience suggests that such rent-sharing may be important even without formal bargaining, a phenomenon described by Okun as the 'invisible handshake' (Okun 1981, p. 89).

CONCLUSIONS

International comparisons of the relationship between pay determination and unemployment would seem to offer some considerable support for the conclusion that those economies with more centralized or coordinated pay bargaining structures have been better able to avoid the crippling rises in unemployment experienced by many of the larger OECD economies since the 1970s. However, there are a number of reasons for expressing some caution over drawing this general conclusion too firmly on the basis of the empirical literature reviewed in this chapter.

Manning (1993) has raised a fundamental problem concerning the empirical implementation of structural models of the aggregate labour market, models on whose results the alleged benefits of corporatism have be examined. This problem concerns the lack of econometric identification of the wage equation. In any example under consideration the real wage and unemployment data in question will reflect simultaneous movements in both bargained real wage and feasible real wage curves. The problem for the econometrician is to separately identify shifts in each curve in order to calculate the position of the other. Theory tells us that the bargained real wage will depend on union preferences, reflected by levels of unemployment benefit etc. and on technological conditions underlying the production function. One cannot rule out that in principle all of these may influence the feasible real wage – for example firms' price mark-ups may depend on taxation policies which in turn may depend on governments' decisions

about the generosity of unemployment benefits. In practice applied
work is conducted by appealing to a number of (in Manning's view)
arbitrary exclusion restrictions – the ruling out *a priori* of the
possibility that variable x can affect the feasible or bargained real
wage. Thus, in practice the estimated sensitivity of the real wage to a
change in unemployment for a particular country may be sensitive to
just what exclusion restrictions have been made. We simply do not
know to what extent the higher real wage flexibility enjoyed by both
corporatist and decentralized economies is over- or understated, if at
all.

International comparisons of the determinants of unemployment rest
on a model of the labour market maintained across widely different
economies. For the decentralized economies it may be entirely
inappropriate to thrust upon actual data relating to a long time period
a uniform model structure based on a stylized single collective bargain
between a 'union' as one group and an 'employer' as another. Thus it
is perhaps no coincidence that union–firm bargaining models appear
from the literature to be of greater interest to Scandinavian authors
than to North American ones. A more appropriate model of a
decentralized economy might be one of competitive wage
determination (i.e. no collective bargaining at all). Newell and Symons
(1987) attempt to identify differences between periods under which
particular countries might be considered as pursuing corporatist policies
and periods when they might not. However, any attempt to divide a
time-series of data into corporatist and non-corporatist sub-periods is
likely to be substantially *ad hoc*, though possibly just as arbitrary as
identifying countries as either corporatist or non-corporatist. For
example, the Calmfors–Driffill hump would appear to offer some sort
of policy choice for those countries dogged by poor unemployment
levels and intermediate levels of bargaining centralization. This is
misleading for the simple reason that the industrialized world is
unlikely to conform to a single model of pay determination in which
the degree of centralization enters as an explanatory variable. To
change the degree of centralization may require a change to a wholly
different system of pay determination. So the decentralization
alternative may in fact require the total abolition of collective
bargaining, a policy change with rather wider ramifications than first
seems to be the case. Empirical analysis of wage determination which
makes use of disaggregated data, for example the work of Holmlund

and Zetterberg (1991), suggests a further reason why the decentralization policy option is misleading. This is because more decentralization of bargaining may result in the greater influence of 'insider' power in wage determination and thus less responsiveness of wage-setting to prevailing economic conditions.

A more obvious point is that correlation need not imply causation. For example, one could associate lower levels of unemployment in the Nordic countries in the early 1980s with their systems of unemployment insurance which, while relatively generous initially, provide support for only a short period of time and may be conditional on the individual being prepared to participate in training programmes (Calmfors 1990). Unemployment may be lower because the rate of outflow from unemployment does not fall to the same extent as in other countries during recessions. High rates of unemployment outflow are bolstered by large-scale active labour market intervention, especially in Sweden.

This leads to the point that by defining corporatism in terms of the structural characteristics of national labour markets one is ignoring the question of how that centralization is made workable. In practice this is likely to be the outcome of a wider political process which may entail consideration of other aspects such as the nature of the welfare state and the level of government policy intervention. However, for writers such as Calmfors and Driffill it is apparent that such a wider conception, incorporating consideration of the political consensus-forming process leads to a too nebulous definition of corporatism. Our own view is that this need not be the case and many insights can be gained from a broader perspective. In conclusion we have to state, as Bean (1992) does, that the economic literature on the role of labour market institutions leaves many questions still unanswered. Specifically, in the narrow confines of the analysis of labour markets, we may not be able to quantify the role of such institutions in any simple way such that useful policy conclusions can be reached. So in the next chapter we cast the net more widely into the political economy literature.

APPENDIX

Derivation of bargained real wage curve

The model here is as described by Carlin and Soskice (1990, pp. 389–91).

Assume that the union in industry i wishes to maximize the average utility of it membership U_i, both employed and unemployed. Those employed receive a real consumption wage w_i, and those unemployed receive a reservation income. Each worker has a probability E_i/L_i of being employed, where E is employment and L total union membership. One minus this probability is therefore the probability of being unemployed. So union utility is

$$U_i = (E_i / L_i) \, v \, (w_i) + (1 - (E_i / L_i) \, v \, (z_i) \tag{A3.1}$$

Those union members who do not get a job in the industry will either obtain an alternative real wage w^* or unemployment benefit b. The probabilities for each are given by one minus the unemployment rate and the unemployment rate itself respectively. Thus we can write z as

$$z = (1 - U) \, w^* + U \, b \tag{A3.2}$$

Labour demand (employment) in industry i is assumed to be decreasing in the real consumption wage and increasing in the level of aggregate demand y^D (see Carlin and Soskice for a fuller derivation of this in the context of constant mark-up pricing and the constant labour productivity)

$$E_i = E \, (w_i, \, y^D) \tag{A3.3}$$

So the union's constrained maximization problem is to maximize utility subject to the labour demand curve

$$\max \, (E_i / L_i) \, v \, (w_i) + (1 - (E_i / L_i)) \, v \, (z) \tag{A3.4}$$

subject to $E_i = E \, (w_i, \, y^D)$.

Aggregate demand is assumed held constant. Assuming risk neutrality on the part of the union and treating L_i as a numeraire, then, by substituting $E(w_i)$ for E_i, we can write

$$\max E\ (w_i)\ w_i\ +\ (1\ -\ E\ (w_i))\ z \tag{A3.5}$$

with respect to choice of w_i. The solution can be found by differentiating equation A3.5 with respect to w_i and setting equal to zero to obtain

$$w_i\ +\ dE\ /\ dw_i\ +\ E\ -\ (dE\ /\ dw_i)\ z\ =\ 0 \tag{A3.6}$$

Substituting for z in (2) and assuming that the wage setting is the same in all industries, such that $w^B = w_i = w^*$ we obtain

$$w^B\ +\ dE\ /\ dw^B\ +\ E\ -$$

$$(dE\ /\ dw^B)((1\ -\ U)w^B\ +\ Ub)\ =\ 0 \tag{A3.7}$$

Rearrangement of equation A3.7 gives

$$w^B\ =\ b\ (1\ -\ 1\ /\ (\eta U))^{-1} \tag{A3.8}$$

where $\eta = |\ (dE/dw^B)\ (w^B/E)\ |$

NOTES

1. The most commonly discussed difficulty with this model is that it generates a wage-employment outcome that is Pareto sub-optimal. It is well known in the literature (Oswald 1985) that by bargaining over both wages and employment Pareto gains to both union and firm are possible, the so-called 'efficient bargaining' outcome. However, the right-to-manage model is usually justified by appealing to the empirical fact that very little collective bargaining is conducted over both wage and employment jointly (Oswald and Turnbull 1985). If workers care only about wages then such bargaining is 'efficient' (Oswald 1987).
2. This can be justified by appealing to the 'normal-cost hypothesis' (Coutts, Godley and Nordhaus 1978) which suggests that firms price according to a mark-up on normal costs, i.e. average costs over the cycle.
3. The model can be extended to an open economy by incorporating import prices and thus international competitiveness (Carlin and Soskice 1990).
4. Holmlund (1986) argues that wage drift may arise because of uncertainty at the time of the central negotiation about aggregate labour demand. Once that uncertainty is

eliminated wage drift operates to clear those labour markets which turn out to be in excess demand.

5. For a discussion of these issues, see Chapter 7.
6. Jackman (1990) also provides similar statistics in tabulated form.
7. In empirical work the appropriate price deflator for the nominal wage must also take account of direct taxes so that $w-p$ measures the log of the real consumption wage.

4. The Political Economy of Durable Compromise

The focus of much of the previous chapter was concerned with the question of whether corporatism as an institutional arrangement can facilitate macroeconomic adjustment especially in the presence of adverse economic shocks. Real wages which are inflexible to unemployment are seen to be the problem to which corporatist institutions can provide a solution by helping to improve the inflation–unemployment trade-off. In short, centralized wage-bargaining may not entail formal incomes policies, which are treated with suspicion in most of the economics literature. But it can lead at least to a situation where the 'going-rate' of wage inflation is sensitive to external macroeconomic conditions and where perversely coordinated 'leap-frogging' wage settlements across separate bargaining groups are avoided.

In this chapter we argue that this emphasis on labour market characteristics is only part of the story, and leads to at best an incomplete understanding of the role of wage-restraining policies in corporatist societies. Rather than focusing predominantly on problems of short-term macroeconomic management, we argue that corporatist institutions provide the foundation for relationships between organized interests (especially those of capital and labour) and the state. These relationships are both longer-term and broader in scope than is allowed for in the literature on international comparisons of wage-setting behaviour. It is these relationships which are important to the understanding of economic performance in corporatist economies.

To shed some light on these issues we turn to the political economy literature on corporatism. This draws together work developed by writers from a number of academic disciplines, in particular political science and sociology. We begin with the theory of political exchange which analyses the process by which organized interest groups, especially those of labour, may exercise restraint in the labour market in exchange for other 'goods' in the political market. The idea of political exchange can be seen as a macroeconomic equivalent of the contracting concept discussed in Chapter 2. We highlight the difficulties inherent in this political exchange process. These are the need for national-level or 'peak-level' interest groups (trade union confederations and employers' associations) to aggregate effectively the preferences of their constituents and the 'interpretation gap' which may undermine the credibility of the parties to this exchange process. We then, in a second section, examine the emphasis placed by many writers within the political economy approach on the importance of the state in its capacity to harmonize public and private interests in successful corporatist countries. In a third section we shift attention from the state to the objectives of the organizations, such as trade unions, which operate within the framework of corporatist institutions. We examine the ways in which different objectives can lead to different forms of corporatism. In the final two sections we discuss further the different forms of corporatism that exist and review cross-country empirical evidence that they lead to differing economic performance.

CORPORATISM AND POLITICAL EXCHANGE

A seminal contribution to the theory of political exchange has been made by Pizzorno (1978). Pizzorno begins his analysis by trying to understand how it is that political factors, such as legislation, union strategies with respect to the political process, and government intervention affect bargaining. For Pizzorno political exchange is where workers offer restraint in the labour market in exchange for greater influence in the political sphere, which may in turn be directed to the achievement of their social and economic objectives. Reflecting the concern of writers on corporatism with the question of order in capitalist societies (see Chapter 2), Pizzorno argues that workers, or their unions, obtain increased political power in exchange for social consensus, or a reduced threat of labour militancy. Consequently their market power depends not on the demand for labour but on the need for consensus. The underexploitation of the short-run labour market bargaining power of workers may occur either to further the interests of the union as an organization or to further the future interests of the workers. An important point, therefore, is that unions have 'a capacity for strategy'. Under certain circumstances where they feel that they can exercise a degree of control over future events this may induce moderation in wage demands and in strike militancy. In effect workers face a long-run utility maximization problem in which they seek to trade-off higher short-run current incomes with the long-run benefits they might derive from current wage restraint. The latter might include future provision of desirable 'goods' such as improved future employment opportunities, social benefits etc. Whether such control of future events is indeed possible is a critical element in any political exchange and we return to this later.

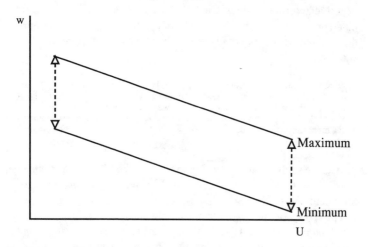

Figure 4.1 Bargaining discretion and the level of unemployment

In terms of the model presented in the previous chapter, Carlin and Soskice (1990) suggest that the bargained real wage curve might be replaced by a zone of bargaining discretion bounded from below by the minimum acceptable real wage across the range of levels of unemployment and from above by the maximum bargained real wage (see Figure 4.1). In this context a policy of income restraint can be seen as a attempt to induce unions into accepting a wage–unemployment outcome towards the lower bound of the zone of discretion. As Carlin and Soskice point out, successful restraint may be based not simply on the *quid pro quo* of economic goods, such as increased government spending in exchange for bargaining restraint, but also as payoffs of a more political nature. For example, the unions may secure an enhanced role in economic policy making or changes in industrial relations legislation. (op. cit., p. 178)

However, unions are unlikely to be merely interested in the unemployment–inflation trade-off, in so far as it allows a simple exchange of moderation in wage-bargaining for greater employment. This brings us to another limitation of the analysis in Chapter 3 where an implicit assumption was made that formal incomes policies or greater centralization in wage-bargaining could be a rather limited and depoliticized affair. Shonfield (1965) was an early critic of the idea that some form of an incomes policy, together with appropriate demand management, could easily solve the problem of inflation once and for all:

> What the fashionable exponents of incomes policies seemed constantly to ignore was that they were asking wage-earners to accept [that] the existing division of wealth and the income derived from it was basically fair ... Labour is really being asked to give its consent to a particular *status quo* ... the practical approach to a more rational wage policy must be deliberately and extensively political. (op. cit., pp. 217–18)

And as we shall see when turning to the practice of political exchange, it is not even the case that political exchange can be limited, as Shonfield assumed, to such issues as price controls, dividend restraint and policies sustaining growth and employment. The exchange process is a dynamic one and through it labour experiences a 'learning curve' which tends to expand workers' demands or aspirations (Goldthorpe 1987). To give one example, if income restraint encourages investment, eventually workers are likely to seek some control over the ensuing process of capital accumulation, and on the level and type of investment undertaken. As we shall see later, this is what happened in Sweden.

Political exchange may be conditional on the level of success which trade unions, and employers' organizations, can achieve in the aggregation of members' interests. The theory of social choice shows us that from a theoretical point of view aggregation of preferences in democratic societies is fraught with problems (Craven 1992). The 'preference-aggregation' problem faced by peak-level organizations entails attempting to harmonize interests within the organization in order to reconcile the different demands of different sections or groups. It requires the leaders of trade unions and of employers' confederations to focus their attention on those aims to which most of their members feel some attachment (Goldthorpe 1984). The degree of centralization is, therefore, important for the enforceability of political exchange and without it many trade-offs and deals would be difficult to envisage (Pekkarinen *et al.*, 1992).[1]

An equally serious problem for labour in any strategy of political exchange is what Pizzorno has called the 'interpretation gap'. That is, if workers are to offer restraint they must have some confidence that the benefits promised will be forthcoming. This problem is rooted in the inevitable uncertainty entailed in a strategy which tries to balance the short-run and long-run interests of workers – sacrifices in the present for benefits in the future. In other words, a political exchange process may come unstuck if it becomes clear that future gains for one reason or another will fail to materialize. The process may not even get off the ground if there is widespread cynicism about the state's capacity or willingness to deliver its side of the bargain (Regini 1984). A similar problem may arise on the employers' side if current investment plans are dependent on future wage moderation which employers are uncertain that unions will deliver. As we shall explore later, the viability and nature of corporatist institutions rests to some extent on how the problems of aggregation and the interpretation gap are dealt with.

For Pizzorno the interpretation gap is significant mostly in the importance it attaches to the role of the union organization over and above the role of individual workers. Regini (1984), however, is more interested in focusing on the objectives of those involved in the political exchange process. He argues that the main benefit for labour lies in the ability of the process to modify market outcomes to labour's advantage. He suggests a number of reasons why unions may want to indulge in political exchange. Firstly, they may have more power in the political arena than in the labour market (due to a pro-labour party in government, for instance). Secondly, the state may offer greater social benefits than their employers (social policies, industrial policies which favour employment creation). Thirdly, there may be risks within the context of a weak, possibly open economy in utilizing full bargaining power. This may undermine the economy further through loss of competitiveness and result in lower incomes for union members in the future (Regini 1984).

In this explanation of political exchange, we have left rather vague a distinction which is of importance when looking at the economic performance of corporatist economies – is economic performance the result of the underlying institutional structure, such as the extent of centralization in wage bargaining, or is it the product of the objectives of the organized interests and state policy-makers?[2] By focusing almost entirely on structure this distinction was obscured in much of the analysis of Chapter 3. Bruno and Sachs (1985) discuss this issue and point out that economic performance may diverge between countries because of both 'technology' (economic structure) and 'tastes' (policy objectives). However, in their empirical work they ignore the latter because of the difficulties entailed in specifying and econometrically estimating a policy preference function alongside a structural model of the economy. The issue is also ignored in the analysis of Calmfors and Driffill (1988). In his discussion of Calmfors and Driffill, Honkapohja (1988) points out that they assume that:

> the objectives and means of influence of the unions are kept unchanged when the economy becomes more centralized. While the assumption may be a natural starting point, it must be recognized that, in reality, more encompassing unions typically have different goals and means of influence when compared with small unions. (op. cit., p. 48)

Honkapohja goes on to state that these objectives may include political influence over such issues as working time or profit-sharing. These are issues very much consistent with the view that unions seek to engage in a political exchange. For the moment, however, it needs to be underlined that the specification of these objectives is bound to be important to the nature and performance of corporatist institutions. We return to this issue later in this chapter.

THE ROLE OF THE STATE IN THE CONCERTATION PROCESS

A large part of the literature on corporatism in the political economy tradition looks at political exchange from the perspective of the state. Writers have shown a good deal of interest in the decline of the post-war 'golden age' and the loss of state control over social order in the late 1960s. In the most general terms the state, or governments, required workers' and employers' organizations to share the responsibility for economic and social order. This was necessary in order to legitimize the conduct of economic policy in democratic societies in the face of stagnationary conditions. As Crouch (1991) indicates:

> almost everywhere in western Europe there was a thickening of the texture of relationships between employers and unions during the course of the 1970s; and in particular in the acceptance of these organizations that they had some responsibility for *national* success and stability. (op. cit., p. 50)

In some countries, Crouch argues, this entailed a deepening of corporatist institutions that already existed (Austria, Sweden, Norway and Denmark), while in others it constituted a new departure (Finland, Britain, Ireland and Italy). The state was involved in creating or developing institutions to harmonize public and private interests. In different countries rather different degrees of success were achieved.

Writers on corporatism have been particularly interested in developing the theory of the state and its relationship to organized interests. A discussion of this goes beyond our present scope in so far as we are concerned with economic outcomes. However, an important distinction has been drawn by Gamble (1993) which has a bearing on the state's capacity to harmonize public and private interests. Gamble contrasts the 'despotic power' of the state, that is the power to issue orders and to command obedience, with 'infrastructural power'. The latter entails 'the power of the state to penetrate and coordinate the activities of civil society through its own agencies' (op. cit., p. 50). British political scientists, such as Gamble, and Marquand (1988) have argued that corporatist institutions in Britain have never become particularly developed or stable because of the very underdeveloped level of 'infrastructural power'. To this end they argue that the Westminster approach of parliamentary sovereignty has proved to be a severe handicap and 'has hindered rather than aided the development of a capacity to carry through complex long-term policies by organizing the necessary policy networks and forms of interest representation' (Gamble 1993, p. 46).

This infrastructural power is also an important element in Lehmbruch's conception of corporatism as a 'concertation' process. The concertation process is defined as one through which the conflicting actions of different interest groups in the economy together with those of the government are managed in order to achieve various commonly agreed national economic objectives. Illustrations of this include the Monnet plan for an *économie concertée* in France and the *Konzertierte Aktion* programme of the West German Grand Coalition government in the late 1960s.[3] Not all writers on corporatism have been happy to see 'concertation' as the essence of corporatism. Schmitter (1982), in particular, has tried to force a distinction between the idea of 'interest intermediation' and 'concertation', in order to explore the interrelationship between the two. Interest intermediation he sees 'as a distinctive mode for organizing the conflicting functional interests – whether these are based on social class, economic sector or professional status' (op. cit., pp. 262–3). Here the emphasis is on structure – for instance, whether an organization is hierarchical or whether it is the sole representative of a group or class. 'Concertation', on the other hand, describes the conduct of policy-making. Schmitter sees it as 'a distinctive mode for making and implementing public policy ... as distinguished from its polar opposite mode of policy-making which [he terms] "pressure"' (op. cit., p. 263).[4] Policy-making in response to 'pressure' characterizes, for example, the UK and the USA. Here politicians are subject to enormous influence from lobbyists and single-issue pressure groups.

It may in practice be very difficult to force this distinction between the structure and the conduct of policy-making under corporatism. Even Schmitter's 'interest intermediation' allows scope for a large state role in ensuring interest organizations share some responsibility for public policy-making.[5] Thus for both 'interest intermediation' and 'concertation' the role of the state is of importance since the state may grant rights of recognition and rights to operate as single representative to organizations (Regini 1984). It may delegate public functions to certain organizations, for example mandating employers' organizations or trade unions to manage the provision of training.

Lehmbruch (1984) identifies various levels or degrees of concertation. The level of concertation is related to the level of development of longer-term political exchange relationships. The first level Lehmbruch associates with a type of indicative planning, or exchange of information, on interrelated macroeconomic indicators such as wages, profits, investment and employment. Concertation in this sense does not entail an explicit *quid pro quo* but rather the creation of consensus on the needs of the economy and the appropriate policy responses to achieve those needs. Lehmbruch's model for this kind of exercise is the West German *Konzertierte Aktion* experiment over incomes policy. The weakness of this approach is one of an 'interpretation gap', as discussed earlier. In the German case unions quickly began to treat the stated expectations of the concertation process with suspicion.

The second level of concertation introduces a more formal *quid pro quo* between the parties in the form of an explicit barter transaction. A greater degree of formality in the conduct of bargaining attempts to reduce suspicion and uncertainty. Lehmbruch identifies the 'social contracts' of the 1970s as examples. Once again the interpretation gap proved to be a serious problem with such 'barter transactions'. The British experience with the Labour government's Social Contract in the 1970s is indicative of this – the uncertainty of the macroeconomic environment and other pressures operating on government policy-makers, such as IMF intervention, eventually made the assumptions and expectations underlying the original contract hopelessly irrelevant.

The third level of concertation Lehmbruch calls 'generalized exchange'. He argues that this exhibits greater stability, by entailing the promotion of longer-term relations between the state and the social partners. His discussion here has certain similarities with our account of networks in Chapter 2. There we saw that networks could build long-run trust relationships where there was no insistence on the immediate equivalence of benefits in any exchange or at least that the 'books could be left open' so that benefits could reach a rough parity over the long run. Thus, in the Austrian case of 'generalized exchange' where unions have been willing to underutilize their labour-market power over long periods there has been no explicit *quid pro quo*. Rather, as Lehmbruch argues, there have been 'the expectations that, thanks to the strong influence of the "social partners" on practically all aspects of economic and social policy, the national economy would be managed with the long-term interests of union members appropriately in view' (op. cit., p. 67).

Lehmbruch's other example of 'generalized exchange' is the Swedish case and in particular its experience with what has come to be known as the Rehn–Meidner model. The first element in this model was the Swedish labour movement's strategy of a 'solidaristic wages policy'. This sought explicitly to close differentials among workers

(Martin 1979, Pontusson 1992a). Such a policy creates problems for unions representing workers with significant market power. The exchange for their sacrifice is likely to benefit all workers, as well as other groups such as part-time workers and the unemployed. The second element of the Rehn–Meidner model follows on from the squeezing of the profitability of relatively unproductive firms (workers in low-paid areas would be paid more than would result from the market outcome). The approach of the Rehn–Meidner plan was to turn this 'problem' into the centrepiece of the strategy. For low-profitability firms would either have to innovate through product development or technological innovation – the path of reducing wages being firmly closed by centralized wage-setting – or go out of business. In order to ensure a continual transfer of resources to higher-profitability areas, the Rehn–Meidner plan entailed active labour market policies to retrain those workers released from unprofitable firms. Of course, Swedish practice was more complex than this highly stylized description and we will return to it later in this, and other, chapters. For the moment we need to point out that, as in the Austrian case, the 'generalized exchange' operated over the long run and its stability meant that there was less need for the benefits to workers and employers to accrue simultaneously.

What is important in concertation can be brought into even sharper focus by comparing the Austrian and Swedish examples with the British case. Britain has, in comparison, had a very limited experience with corporatist arrangements – in Lehmbruch's typology Britain is a 'weakly corporatist' economy.[6] They have often been introduced in an *ad hoc* and temporary manner (Gamble 1993, Marquand 1988). Critics of corporatism in Britain are thus highly dismissive of any suggested benefits to be gained from concertation attempts. They are critical of the crisis-management nature of much of the tripartite discussions that took place during the Labour Governments of the 1960s and 1970s, discussions that an unfriendly press characterized as 'beer and sandwiches at 10 Downing Street'.[7] Unsuccessful British attempts at concertation during this period culminated in the experience of the Social Contract, which ended in the industrial unrest of the so-called 'winter of discontent'.

A rather weak corporatist institutional structure was created in Britain in the early 1960s in the form of the National Economic Development Council (NEDC) but this lay dormant during the 1980s, almost entirely ignored by the Thatcher Conservative government until it was finally abolished in the early 1990s. The weakness of the NEDC is indicative of the, already noted, weak 'infrastructural power' of the British state.[8] As Marquand (1988) points out, the British state has rarely attempted to use 'public law to define the powers and responsibilities' (p. 161) of organized interests. Intervention in industrial relations has usually been limited to either reducing trade union legal immunities (usually Conservative governments) in order to remove restrictions to the market or to restore these immunities (Labour governments).

Both Marquand (1988) and Therborn (1992) point to the importance of common law in the British case. This contrasts with the Roman law tradition elsewhere which is much more positive in its articulation of the public functions, rights and duties of trade unions and employers' organizations. Furthermore, Marquand argues that corporatism in Britain has usually been covert and unexplicit, operating through unwritten and changing conventions and understandings. Procedures were not clearly-defined, and so British attempts at corporatism have been fluctuating and unstable. They can perhaps be summarized as 'crisis-corporatism'. Marquand contrasts this with institutions such as the self-governing chambers of Commerce, Labour, and Agriculture in Austria, or the Swedish Labour Market Board which are long-standing bodies, with public status or high public profile, and which 'have had sufficient time (and been sufficiently successful) to acquire moral authority as well as coercive power, where they have it' (ibid.).

Lehmbruch (1984) describes those countries which have been able to achieve a durable concertation process as 'strong corporatism'. They are characterized by the participation of workers' and employers' organizations in both formulation and implementation of policy. He contrasts this with 'weak corporatism' where participation is only limited to certain sectors or stages of policy formulation, and 'medium corporatism' where the scope of collective bargaining is wider but concerted attempts at incomes policy have met with only temporary success. Table 4.1 summarizes his categorization of various OECD countries on this basis. The absence of any form of concertation is described as 'pluralism'. France and Japan are placed in a separate category termed 'concertation without labour' to indicate the absence of trade union involvement despite a durable concertation between employers and government in each case. This categorization is

conditioned by the time period under consideration (in this case up to
the early 1980s), and countries may well move between groups over
time. On the basis of the experience of the whole of the 1980s we
might want to indulge in some reclassification – notably the UK is

Table 4.1 Degrees of 'concertation' in OECD countries

Pluralism:	US, Canada, Australia, New Zealand
Weak corporatism:	UK, Italy
Medium corporatism:	Ireland, Belgium, Germany, Denmark, Finland, Switzerland (borderline)
Strong corporatism:	Austria, Sweden, Norway, Netherlands
Concertation without labour:	Japan, France

Source: Lehmbruch (1984), Table 3.1

now more pluralist than weakly corporatist. We might also want to add
a 'concertation without capital' category to describe recent Australian
experience.

Three features are associated with the durable concertation which
exists in Lehmbruch's 'strong corporatism' category. The first is that
the concertation process involves a much wider policy agenda than that
entailed in traditional incomes policies. This broader scope is implicit
in the dynamics of political exchange and important for its stability
over the long run.

The second is the need for the achievement of consensus about
macroeconomic objectives. Later in this chapter, in discussing various
types of corporatism, we will draw on a distinction between corporatist
arrangements which attempt to provide a framework for explicitly
recognized conflict and those which are based on the idea of an
underlying harmony or consensus in social relations. Here we mean
consensus broadly defined in the sense of at least a *modus vivendi*
between the parties. Successful corporatist arrangements usually imply

that the state and the social partners have both shared objectives and a common understanding of how the economy works (Scharpf 1984). This point has also been made by Giavazzi (1988) in his discussion of Calmfors and Driffill (1988). He points out that centralized wage-bargaining may be a necessary prerequisite for national-level bargaining but that it is not a sufficient condition for the success of such arrangements. Giavazzi notes that other studies such as that of Newell and Symons (1987) suggest that the performance of the same labour market institutions may be different when there is consensus from where there is not.[9] This reinforces the point made in the previous chapter that the use of a single model to describe the labour markets of very different countries may present serious problems.

The third feature associated with concertation is the establishment of 'long-term' relationships, or 'relational contracting'. Just as contract law establishes institutional constraints governing the conduct of atomistic market transactions so corporatism attempts to establish institutional guidelines for 'relational contracting'. Lehmbruch (1984) argues that 'generalized exchange' cannot be based on 'unstable and shifting' coalitions. It is therefore the opposite of a pluralist mode of regulation where such unstable and shifting coalitions of interest groups are seen to be the source of the strength of the system.

Many of the OECD economies – the principal exceptions being Canada and the United States – have experimented with national economic consensus agreements which attempt to establish a set of agreed economic goals and policy objectives. Such attempts are listed by country in Table 4.2. In most cases these have been transitory, as for example in Germany and in the UK. In the late 1980s a number of the less rich members of the European Community, such as Ireland, Spain and Portugal, attempted to conclude such agreements. The difficulties experienced in reaching agreement in these cases do not bode well for continued durability.

OBJECTIVES, ORGANIZATIONS AND SOCIAL DEMOCRACY

The three features we have isolated as important for more durable corporatist compromises should not be allowed to obscure the fact that

100 *Corporatism and Economic Performance*

Table 4.2 Economic consensus-forming arrangements in OECD economies

EC:	
Belgium	'Social Compact', under strain since 1975
Denmark	SDP attempted national consensus, 1979–82
France	indicative planning system: 'concertation without labour'
Germany	Concerted Action program 1967–77
Greece	state-dominated arbitration
Ireland	developing in the 1980s
Italy	attempted but not successful, focused on controversial national wage indexation procedures
Netherlands	not very successful since 1970
Portugal	emerging in mid-1980s
Spain	developing in 1980s
UK	some institutions existed 1963–1991 but were moribund since 1979
Non-EC :	
Austria	highly developed
Finland	more recent than other Nordic cases but now well established
Norway	well developed
Sweden	traditionally very important, though under pressure in 1980s
Switzerland	strong established links between government and employers
Non-Europe:	
Canada	none
USA	none
Japan	strong linkages between finance capital, industrial conglomerates and government
Australia	Labour-government 'Accord' since 1984
N. Zealand	none

there is more than one path to establishing longer-term, broad and consensual relationships. This means that different corporatist economies can have very different institutions and ways of approaching the process of concertation. Before examining such differences in more detail in the following section, we look here at the way some of these differences are related in part to how the problems of political exchange – namely the preference-aggregation problem and the interpretation gap – are resolved. How these twin problems are confronted will determine not only whether long-run corporatist arrangements are possible but also will greatly affect the type of corporatism that is established and thus have important implications for economic performance.

The previous section discussed corporatism from the perspective and needs of the state. As we have seen, this approach has met with considerable criticism from those who stress that such an approach leads to too functionalist a description of corporatism and diverts attention from the important issue of investigating the objectives of the organizations involved in corporatist arrangements (Regini 1984, Therborn 1992). The work of Lange and Garrett (1985) has been very influential not least because it tries to redress this overemphasis on the state. They address the question of whether what is important is the capacity of labour organizations to be encompassing enough to be able to aggregate their members' interests in order to enforce collective discipline. Have they thus been able to exchange quiescence for greater investment and more stable growth rates, thereby improving the prospect for union members over the medium to long run? Lange and Garrett offer a sustained critique of this idea. They argue that the approach is theoretically underdeveloped in that it ignores the fact that investment in capitalist economies depends largely on the decisions of capitalists. So workers face considerable uncertainty over whether their restraint will result in more investment and greater growth.[10] There is in other words an acute interpretation gap:

> in the presence of encompassing unions, the expected behaviour of the state ... can become an essential element in reducing unions' uncertainty, and thus increasing the probability that they will regulate their militancy. (Lange and Garrett 1985, p. 797)

This explains why policies of wage restraint have of necessity to be expanded in corporatist economies to incorporate the wider questions of investment, productivity and international competitiveness. Lange and Garrett postulate, in this context, that better economic performance, in terms of growth, would result from encompassing unions and the presence of a sympathetic government of a social democratic persuasion.

The objectives of interest organizations are also of importance with respect to the problem of aggregation. We have already noted that preference-aggregation requires more than centralization, especially since the trade-off in any political exchange may benefit other groups beyond those making the sacrifices. Some have therefore argued that a prerequisite for exercising the necessary group solidarity may be that workers act as a class in order to internalize this potential 'free rider' problem. This may be linked to a particular labour heritage:

> under the influences of Marxism in its social-democratic variant, these movements saw themselves as acting in the interest of an encompassing working class, and the development of corporatism of the present day cannot in fact be adequately understood without reference to this emphasis on class as distinct from narrower sectional interests. (Lehmbruch 1984, p. 77)

Lehmbruch contrasts this social democratic heritage with that of revolutionary syndicalism (traditionally strong in France, for example) with its distrust of tying too closely the functions of trade union organizations and political party. He also contrasts it with British experience where the nature of trade unionism, and its roots in nineteenth-century liberalism, prevented the establishment of a strong class ideology. Maier (1984) argues in this respect that the ideal, from the perspective of establishing corporatist arrangements, may be a labour movement whose political and industrial wings have grown together with neither wing being powerful enough to dominate the other.[11] The need for solidarity is vital because the lure of dualistic solutions is never far away. As Goldthorpe (1987) points out, strong trade unions, even when they have a strong social democratic class heritage, always face the temptation of 'dispersing' the costs to weaker groups of workers rather than 'internalizing' them.

The references above to Goldthorpe, Maier and Lehmbruch provide evidence that these writers, who are associated with the tradition of looking at corporatism from the perspective of the state, have not neglected the importance of organizations and their objectives. In this respect the criticisms of certain observers such as Therborn (1992), who have stressed the importance of a 'socially minded' labour movement and the balance of power between capital and labour, are rather misplaced. But it is fair to say that others have concentrated much more on objectives. Thus, some Marxist writers – often referred to as 'power resource theorists' in the political science literature – consider the corporatist literature as either unhelpful or misleading in understanding economies such as Sweden, and have instead emphasized the objectives of the labour movement and the politics of social democracy. To simplify greatly, their idea is that the underutilization of labour market power exercised by the labour movement should be seen as part of a broader political and economic strategy to establish an alternative to capitalism. If such a strategy of moderation can lead to increased investment and employment, it avoids the weakening of the labour movement that accompanies slow growth and rising unemployment.

Such 'societal' bargaining – a concept which is not too far removed from our discussion of corporatist networks – may be equated with the incorporation of workers within the capitalist state, by allowing them a degree of control over policy. The incorporation thesis is associated with Marxist critics of corporatism, such as Panitch (1980), who argue that corporatism cannot provide a route to the eventual aim of the replacement of capitalism with a socialist alternative.[12] But as Crouch has argued, the incorporation thesis assumes that:

a corporatist strategy employed by dominant elites is actually successful. There is one major condition for this success: the organizations which simultaneously represent and discipline the working class have to operate primarily downwards, ordering their members. If instead they ... convey demands, to the state and organized capital, not only do they impart a strong element of pluralism, but it is pluralism which is less constrained by the market and by the institutional segregation of policy and economy characteristic of liberal capitalism. (Crouch 1979, p. 22)

Thus 'societal' or 'political' bargaining can create a 'balance of class forces' or a 'class compromise' which can work to labour's advantage and can expand the possibility for future advances (Higgins and Apple 1983, Pontusson 1984).[13] For authors such as Korpi and Shalev (1980) such a 'class compromise' can extend labour's power away from the industrial arena to the political one, and at the same time weaken the position of employers.[14] This, of course, is a direct link back to those such as Lange and Garrett (1985), discussed earlier, who stress the importance of the control of government by social democratic governments. Other writers see this strategy of temporary compromise as a feasible social-democratic reformist path to the market socialist alternative to capitalism.[15] And even those who express scepticism about this latter claim do accept that corporatist institutions can be seen as providing a 'distinctive context' for the expression of class conflicts within capitalist economies, one where labour may be able to enhance its political role (Goldthorpe 1984). Thus, many comparative economics textbooks, for instance Zimbalist *et al.* (1989), have entitled their discussion of economies such as Sweden as 'the Middle Way'.

The stress on interest group objectives in what we will loosely term the social democratic tradition has a number of further implications. The first is that there may be different types of corporatism which result from differences of objectives. We take up this issue in the following section.

A further important implication concerns the stability of corporatist arrangements. If objectives are important then corporatist arrangements may come under pressure if these are not met. This is important in the analysis of Regini (1984), who discusses the unsuccessful corporatist episodes in Britain and Italy in the 1970s. In the Italian case many of the benefits for labour did not materialize either because of opposition from government bureaucracy or because the government itself was not willing to pursue the logic of its corporatist policy. Thus, the unions' eventual disillusionment with this embryonic attempt at corporatism had little to do with their ability to aggregate their members' interests, or to integrate those interests with the interests of other groups. It was more to do with their perception of the declining benefits actually received from a strategy of moderation. The trade-off was increasingly unacceptable. We have already discussed the British case where towards the end of the 1974–79 Labour government trade unions became less and less willing to accept wage restraint. Matters came to a head in the industrial conflict of late 1978 and early 1979.

The emphasis on the objectives of labour movements also raises the question of the objectives of employers. If, as Rowthorn (1992a) argues, what he calls the 'inclusive' corporatism of the Swedish model – a description which we discuss further in the next section – can be seen in terms of labour's struggle for 'democracy and equality' why should employers be interested? In fact, in much of the corporatist literature the role of employers has been given considerably less attention than has that of labour.[16] This is a deficiency which needs to be rectified since the objectives of employers and the logic of their collective action must be an important component in understanding corporatism.

Martin's (1979) typology of three stages of Keynesian political economy demonstrates the importance of both workers' and employers' objectives (see also Higgins and Apple 1983, and Gamble 1993). His typology fits in well with the concerns of the corporatism-as-social-democracy literature discussed here and is also based specifically on the experience of an actual corporatist economy – namely Sweden. The first stage Martin associates with traditional Keynesianism and entails no more than a loose political commitment to full employment. In the Swedish case this was in practice underpinned by a political alliance between the social democratic and the agrarian parties. The second stage is close to the type of 'generalized exchange' discussed earlier in this chapter and entails the incorporation of labour into the public policy arena. But as we have seen, the 'generalized exchange' entails more than just a fiscal guarantee of full employment combined with an incomes policy to regulate any resultant inflationary pressure. It extends to both welfare provision and active labour market policies.

The third stage was planned but never materialized in Sweden. It follows from the logic of political exchange and in particular the need to ensure sufficient investment and growth to underpin the commitment to welfare provision and active labour market intervention. In Sweden social democratic proposals ranged from active industrial policies to the radical idea for wage-earner funds, a system of collective worker share ownership financed from a profits tax on employers (Pontusson 1992a). The Meidner committee, which led to the creation of the Rehn–Meidner Plan, saw wage-earner funds as complementing the solidaristic wages policy of the unions. A system of collective profit-sharing could, it was thought, convince higher-wage earners not to push for higher wages (in the face of excessive profits). By allocating a certain percentage of profits in the form of newly issued shares to wage-earner funds administered by the unions themselves, the radical implications of this *quid pro quo* for income restraint emerged. In due course a form of market socialism would emerge as the wage-earner funds became majority stock-holders in the economy's private enterprise. In fact, due to the opposition of the private sector and the lack of the social democratic party support, this strategy was never implemented.[17] As Martin (1979) points out, there is no guarantee that a corporatist-leaning country will move rapidly from stages one through to three. On the contrary, he argues that most economies hardly made it to stage two before the onset of the stagnationary crisis of the 1970s (see also Gamble 1993).

For our purposes the changing objectives of different groups may be important for the durability and development of corporatist arrangements through these stages. Thus, for instance, if labour expands its objectives too far towards a form of social ownership, employers may feel that any corporatist trade-off is no longer worth it. They may then look to dualist solutions, where workers and employers formulate and select strategies in isolation and where actual outcomes depend on relative bargaining power (Goldthorpe 1984). Not only may the objectives of the parties change but the capacity of their organizations to follow particular strategies may be altered by internal economic developments (for instance the form that economic restructuring takes in the aftermath of a macroeconomic shock) or by other exogenous events stemming from the world economy (Pontusson 1992b). We return to such issues later in the book when we examine the stability of corporatism and its future prospects.

FORMS OF CORPORATISM

In the previous section an important distinction has been implicit: that different types of corporatism may occur where the inherent conflict between different groups is explicitly recognized from where such recognition is absent. A number of authors have attempted to distinguish between the corporatism of Scandinavia and that as practised in the Germanic countries. Katzenstein, for example, in his influential book *Small States in World Markets* (1985), makes a distinction between liberal corporatism and social corporatism. In the former group he includes Switzerland, Netherlands and Belgium, and argues that their distinguishing features are politically strong, centralized employers' groups but rather weak and decentralized union organizations. For him the latter group contains Austria, Norway and Denmark, with Sweden combining aspects of both types. Here trade union movements are much stronger and more centralized, and employers' organizations weaker. Katzenstein argues that the effects of these differences are to be seen in terms of differing approaches to industrial policy, broadly defined. We shall turn to this in greater detail in the next chapter but he summarizes the ways in which the two types respond to economic change as follows:

> Liberal corporatism accepts market-driven change but makes the political gestures necessary to keep disadvantaged industry segments, firms, or regions integrated in an overarching consensus. Social corporatism seeks to cushion change within the limits that markets permit. (op. cit., p. 134)

In his social corporatist examples he argues that state institutions are much more pre-emininent in coordinating active policy responses to economic shocks.

A vital institution in this respect may be the welfare state. Cornwall (1989) notes the correlation between the level of social welfare provision and corporatism. If corporatism entails a political exchange process then social protection is likely to be identified as an 'economic good' that might be provided in return for wage restraint. However, the political exchange process may not in itself be sufficient to bring forth a commitment on the part of the state to generous levels of social expenditure. In so far as corporatism is a mechanism for articulating the interests of producers and suppliers of labour (Williamson 1989), the ability of corporatist arrangements *per se* to reflect the interests of other groups such as the non-economically active and the unemployed may be limited. In Scandinavia corporatism is associated with a generous and universalist welfare state. Elsewhere corporatism is not so closely allied with generous social welfare provision because the welfare state has arisen from Catholic democratic and Bismarckian social insurance traditions. Esping-Andersen (1990) and Baldwin (1990) make this distinction between the nature of the welfare state in those countries which fall into the liberal corporatist and social corporatist categories.

Thus, Pekkarinen *et al.* (1992) describe the social corporatism of Scandinavia as having a non-exclusive nature. The meaning of social corporatism here is therefore somewhat different from that of Katzenstein. This inclusiveness means that a greater commitment will exist to ensuring that the burden of adjustment to shocks to the economy are shared by all groups and do not fall disproportionately on the least advantaged. So a strong sense of social solidarity will be a feature of such inclusive corporatism. In less-inclusive forms of corporatism the burden of adjustment may be less equally spread.

Therborn (1992) argues that successful strife-free adjustment to economic shocks can be achieved in two ways. In the liberal corporatist cases (his examples are Austria, Netherlands and Switzerland) the social partnership or consensus between labour and capital is institutionalized through formalized decision-making bodies and legal institutions. The use of words such as 'partnership' and 'consensus' here highlights the criticisms of some Marxists of the concept of corporatism. The historical origins of the liberal form of corporatism can be identified as rather different to social democratic origins of social corporatism. A key basis for the former is to be found in Roman Catholic social teaching of the late nineteenth and early twentieth centuries, and in particular in the two papal encyclicals *Rerum Novarum* of Leo XIII (1891) and *Quadragesimo Anno* of Pius XI (1931).[18] Neither document explicitly mentions 'corporatism', however *Rerum Novarum* broke new ground in terms of Catholic teaching by acknowledging the legitimacy of trade unions but propounding the opinion that workers and employers should work together to solve social problems in a context of an accepted harmony of interests. *Quadragesimo Anno* is acknowledged by many authors (Pryor 1988, 1993, Williamson 1989) to have provided unwittingly a spur to the creation of the authoritarian anti-democratic corporatism of the fascist regimes in Catholic countries such as Italy and Spain.[19] The association between a form of corporatism and fascism has contributed to the highly sceptical position adopted by many of the left. Writers such as Panitch (1980) and Offe (1985) hence view corporatism as entailing a more or less tacit acceptance on the part of workers of the *status quo* of the capitalist economy.

However, the existence of consensus-forming arrangements need not imply the existence of a harmonization of the interests of workers and employers – on the contrary they may facilitate the achievement of compromise. Thus, the Lehmbruch (1984) explanation of corporatism as 'concertation' need not contradict the distinction here between liberal and social forms of corporatism. In social corporatism conflict between labour and capital is accepted as given and institutionalized, or even as Therborn says 'ritualized'. The important distinction between liberal and social corporatism is that in the former the state seeks to harmonize common interests and objectives. In the latter case the two sides of the labour market, and the state, explicitly recognize that they have different interests and objectives. Sweden and Finland are identified by Therborn as the principle examples of where the latter occurs. Therborn regards the post-war German experience as lying between the two types. The origins of social corporatism can be seen in the realignment of Scandinavian Social Democratic parties in the 1930s in the light of the emerging character of the Soviet Union and of the rise of fascism.[20] The appeal of a form of 'middle way' led to electoral success for Social Democrats across Scandinavia in the 1930s. However, if the motivating ideology and the understanding of conflict entailed in this form of corporatism entails questioning the very legitimacy of capitalism, then corporatism may be viewed as merely a staging post to some form of socialist system. The earlier discussion of the fate of the Swedish wage-earner funds serves to illustrate this point. This raises further grounds for questioning the long-run stability of corporatist arrangements since the progressive development of both inclusive and exclusive forms of corporatism may eventually be questioned by employers and workers respectively.

The earlier sections of this chapter have focused on the importance of durability in the relationships between interest groups if corporatism is to be successful, and on the importance of the scope of the exchange process involved. The nature of the compromise or consensus, in particular the extent to which it is premised on a creative tension between groups or on the assumption of an underlying harmony, adds a third dimension. This is summarized in Table 4.3. The extent to which each of the features listed in the table are necessary conditions for the successful operation of corporatism is open to question – for example, Sweden is characterized by a relative absence of formal consensus-forming arrangements and has relied more heavily on the high durability and scope of collective bargaining agreements whereas in the Germanic countries (Germany, Austria, Switzerland) more emphasis has been placed on the establishment of formal 'concertation' arrangements. None of the conditions is sufficient on its own. It is this multidimensional nature of corporatism that leads some authors such as Therborn (1992) to argue that as a concept it is not particularly useful. We would argue, in contrast, that it necessitates sophisticated but careful consideration of different countries on a case-by-case basis, as conducted, for example, by Therborn's co-contributors in Pekkarinen *et al.* (1992). Those OECD countries which have exhibited corporatist features, to different degrees, in the late twentieth century

Table 4.3 Elements of corporatist arrangements

	Pluralism	Moderate forms of corporatism	Strong forms of corporatism
Scope of bargaining arrangements:			
a) centralization	low	medium or high	high
b) coordination	low	high	high
Scope of 'agenda':	pay and working conditions	pay, income restraint, employment levels, economic policy	pay, pay inequality, income restraint, employment, social and economic policy
Inclusiveness:			
a) workers	nil	low (Japan) to high (Austria)	high
b) employers	nil	high (e.g. Japan, Switzerland.)	high
c) others	nil	low (e.g. Austria)	high
Durability of relationships:	short and transitory	medium to long	long
Examples:	Anglo-Saxon economies	continental European economies, Japan	Scandinavian economies, Austria is borderline

do differ considerably, as we have seen, in the scope of bargaining arrangements, in the durability of corporatist compromises, and in the degree of inclusiveness of the corporatist exchange process. Thus, actual examples cannot be classified as 'corporatist' or 'non-corporatist' but rather should be investigated on the basis of the extent to which they display particular identifiable features of corporatist arrangements.

CORPORATISM, POLITICAL POWER AND ECONOMIC PERFORMANCE

In the previous chapter we saw that economists have tended to concentrate on the structural characteristics of labour markets in attempting to define the degree of corporatism of different countries, and in particular on the degree of centralization of collective bargaining. Not surprisingly, political scientists have, in contrast, focused on the correlation between economic performance and the socio-political characteristics of corporatism.

The empirical literature in political science on corporatism takes its lead from earlier work on political alignment and the inflation–unemployment trade-off (Hibbs 1977, 1979, Payne 1979). This investigated the possibility that, given the existence of a Phillips curve trade-off between inflation and unemployment in the 1960s, countries with governments of more left-wing orientation preferred to position themselves at the lower-unemployment, higher-inflation side of the trade-off. In other words, it was suggested that a Phillips curve could be identified cross-sectionally across countries and the position of countries along that trade-off was determined by political considerations. However, while this simple correlation can be observed using data relating to the 1960s it is apparent from subsequent experience that certain countries were able to enjoy lower unemployment at no greater cost in terms of higher inflation. This is the same observation as noted in the previous chapter – that more corporatist countries appeared to inhabit a lower Phillips curve.

Cameron (1984) demonstrates the existence of a positive relationship across OECD countries between low unemployment rates and low wage and price inflation over the period 1965–1982. This could indicate that in low unemployment countries employers are better able to resist wage pressure or that in such countries there is an absence of militancy on the part of workers. The absence of militancy might simply indicate the existence of very weak labour movements, however this does not appear to be borne out by the fact that those countries with the lowest level of strike activity in the late 1960s and 1970s include Austria, Netherlands, Germany and Norway (Cameron 1984, Table 7.3). Cameron describes such countries as having labour movements which are 'quiescent', in the sense that the use of the strike weapon for short-term wage gain is strategically forgone in order to promote the maintenance of a high level of employment.

Political scientists have, not surprisingly, been concerned to explain this phemonenon in terms of political factors. A number of authors including Cameron (1984) demonstrate a positive correlation between the absence of strike activity and the presence of governments of a social democratic persuasion (Hibbs 1978, Shalev 1978, Korpi and Shalev 1979, 1980). However, left-wing government need not imply industrial calm – the British experience of 1978–79 is a notable example. We have already discussed theoretical reasons for supposing that social democratic government might form an important precondition for the successful operation of corporatist arrangements. Cameron demonstrates positive bivariate correlations between left-wing dominance in government and certain alleged structural characteristics of corporatism, including the organizational structure of labour movements, the power of union confederations over constituent unions, the degree of bargaining centralization and the existence of worker participation and co-determination arrangements. More recently Lijphart and Crepaz (1991) have presented similar evidence. In their case the corporatism measure used is the average standardized ranking of each country from twelve previous studies of corporatism. One immediate problem with this approach is that these twelve different authors use very different criteria for ranking countries – for example, the list includes Bruno and Sachs who rank on the basis of bargaining centralization and Lehmbruch who classifies on the basis of 'concertation' arrangements. Furthermore, different authors have looked at different time periods. The resulting average is therefore heavily influenced by the preferences of these twelve studies rather than determined by the criteria Lipjhart and Crepaz themselves deem to be important. Nevertheless the exercise is instructive in the sense that, unlike any earlier work, the authors demonstrate the degree of expert (dis)agreement about different countries (see their Figure 1). In view of our earlier discussion it is unsurprising to discover that least agreement is reached on how corporatist Japan and Switerland are.

The relationship between corporatism and unemployment has been extensively discussed. Political scientists are generally dissatisfied with the varying response to supply shock explanations and the real wage inflexibility explanations of cross-country variations in unemployment, as proposed by economists (Korpi 1991). However, it has to be said that, in contrast to the economic literature on unemployment, the statistical analyses of political explanations for international variations in unemployment contained in this literature are generally conducted at a rather crude level. Korpi (1991) for one expresses doubts about the usefulness of attempts to quantify political factors and correlate them with indicators of economic performance. We have some sympathy with this position.

Schmidt (1982) classifies countries into strong, medium and weak corporatism. Strong corporatism is where there exists an ideology of social partnership, where the labour movement cooperates in policy formulation, where strike activity is low, and incomes policies, when used, are agreed upon rather than imposed in an authoritarian fashion. Weak corporatism is where there is an absence of these features altogether and medium corporatism is a central residual category. Schmidt finds a weak rank correlation between this typology and average unemployment for the period 1974 to 1978. Cameron (1984) obtains a negative correlation between each of his structural attributes of corporatism, listed earlier, and the average level of unemployment between 1965 and 1982. Castles (1987) uses the binary classification of Crouch (1985) into countries with a corporatist 'industrial relations system' and those without and obtains a significant negative correlation with average unemployment in each of the three periods 1960 to 1973, 1974 to 1979, and 1980 to 1984.

A small number of further studies attempt a multiple regression analysis. Crepaz (1992) pools average unemployment data for eighteen countries for the three periods 1961 to 1973, 1974 to 1982, and 1982 to 1988, and regresses this data on the averaged ranking calculated by Lijphart and himself (1991), discussed above. He interacts the corporatism measure with dummy variables for the second and third of these periods in order to investigate whether the effectiveness of corporatism has weakened in the 1980s. His results suggest that corporatism was most strongly associated with lower unemployment in the 1974 to 1982 period, but was still significantly associated with lower unemployment in the later 1982 to 1988 period. However, one serious difficulty with Crepaz's results is that the corporatism variable as defined does not change over time. The variable is based on studies which consider the period up to but not beyond the early 1980s. His estimated effect of corporatism on unemployment in the 1980s will be biased by the unknown extent of this measurement error.

Boreham and Compston (1992) seek to test for differences in the effect on unemployment between countries where corporatism is predominantly incomes-policy-based and those where it is more participative and broader in scope. They suggest that the former type can be captured through the effect of an index of union political power in collective bargaining in an unemployment regression and the latter through the effect of an index of the extent to which national labour movements are involved in economic policy formulation. A series of other control variables are also added, including a measure of left-wing political dominance in government, and several economic cyclical variables. The data used are for eleven countries and are pooled annually for the years 1974 to 1986. The explanatory variables do vary over time and are, in essence, constructed on the basis of subjective judgement. Their main conclusion is that union participation in policy-making appears to be the most important of the political/institutional factors in explaining variations in unemployment over time and across countries.

A serious limitation of the focus on unemployment is that the analysis is still concerned with short- or medium- term adjustment in the face of adverse economic shocks. The earlier discussion in this chapter has been concerned with the possibility that the greater benefits of corporatist political arrangements will only be observed over the longer run. If this is the case then our concern might be with examining the growth performance of corporatist countries. The evidence so far on this is rather inconclusive. Two studies already discussed, Castles (1987) and Crepaz (1992), present correlations between economic growth and extent-of-corporatism indicators. Neither find a statistically significant correlation between the two. Furthermore, Crepaz reports a significantly negative association between GDP growth and the presence of social democratic government.

The question of whether political factors can explain differences in growth rates across the developed economies is also addressed by Lange and Garrett (1985), in a multivariate framework. Their important contribution is to argue that beneficial effects on growth are more likely to occur where a country enjoys the joint presence of a strong, centralized labour movement organization and a left-wing government. The justification for this is that an encompassing labour organization will feel more secure in pursuing 'collective gain' strategies if it operates in the climate of a sympathetic government. In other words, the authors seek to test directly the point made earlier that social democratic government may act to bridge the 'interpretation gap'. They demonstrate that on their own the effects of strong union organization and left-wing government on GDP growth over the period 1974 to 1980 are negative, but when the two are jointly present (captured econometrically by an interaction variable) the effect is a positive one.

Lange and Garrett's work has generated a substantial and, at times, quite heated debate (Jackman 1987, Lange and Garrett 1987, Hicks 1988, Jackman 1989, Hicks and Patterson 1989, Garrett and Lange 1989). In particular, Jackman is concerned that Lange and Garrett's central result is driven by the presence of Norway, whose superior growth is, he argues, entirely the result of the discovery of North Sea oil. It is hardly worth rehearsing here the statistical nit-picking that has taken place in this debate – certainly further investigation of the robustness of the conclusion begs the use of larger datasets. Nevertheless, the Lange and Garrett conclusion does importantly point to the fact that the socio-political factors at work in corporatist countries operate in a complex and interactive way, for precisely the theoretical reasons developed in this chapter.

In conclusion, the transition from political theory to empirical specification has resulted in a good deal of subjectivity in the definition and measurement of explanatory variables. Paucity of very aggregated time series data has meant that degrees of freedom in much of the ensuing empirical work have tended to be rather low and the statistical procedures used relatively unsophisticated. Thus the results obtained point to possible associations that might exist between economic and political factors, and certainly do not offer anything like conclusive evidence of causation. Thus, what is perhaps needed is a synthesis of the vast work on the economic modelling of unemployment and of growth and the important insights of political scientists into the structural preconditions for the successful operation of corporatism.

NOTES

1. Pekkarinen *et al.* (1992) also suggest that the importance of centralization may be most important at times of crisis 'where there is little use for learning from experience'. We provide some evidence for this view in the following chapter where we discuss how corporatist and liberal economies coped with two major episodes of profit squeeze since the 1970s.
2. This distinction is also made by Pekkarinen *et al.* (1992).
3. See Scharpf (1991) for a detailed discussion.
4. In other words the counterfactual is the usual image of pluralist politics, where organized interests – including shifting coalitions – pressurize the government but remain outside the policy-making process.
5. Therborn (1992) also argues that both Lehmbruch's and Schmitter's conceptions share a similar focus on the 'steering of society' to promote social order.
6. This was of course in 1984, and by the early 1990s little existed of even this version.
7. Pimlott (1992) recounts the possibly apocryphal story that when Harold Wilson's Labour government left office in 1970 the only items found in the Downing Street larder were several bottles of beer and some sandwiches.
8. State structure may not, of course, be the only reason explaining the unhappy British experiment with indicative planning and a form of corporatism. Rowthorn (1983), for instance, argues that British employers may have been wary of entering into any corporatist arrangements because of the strength of British trade unions and the fear that indicative planning may have legitimized socialist values. In France, where such indicative planning was more of a success, the unions were in a far weaker position. This type of argument focuses our attention on the importance of the objectives of trade unions and employers' organizations, an issue to which we return later in this chapter and in the conclusions of the book.
9. An example of this is the West German experience when consensus was forthcoming under SPD governments. This is also added support for the view of Lange and Garrett discussed below.
10. See also Przeworski and Wallerstein (1982). There is also a literature in economic theory concerned with the long-run objectives of trade unions where wage bargaining behaviour may influence investment decisions (Lancaster 1973, Grout 1984, van der Ploeg 1987, Manning 1987). We shall discuss this point in greater detail in Chapter 5.
11. On the nature of British trade unionism and its unsuitability for developing corporatist institutions, see also Therborn (1992) and Marquand (1988). Therborn's three forms of labour organization – Anglo-American, Latin and Germanic – are similar to the distinctions made by Lehmbruch.
12. For Panitch and other radical critics corporatism is less an institutional framework or a relationship between interest groups and the state and more an outcome (i.e. wage restraint).
13. Again the distinction with mainstream corporatist writers should not be drawn too sharply. Thus Schmitter argues that one reason why the state may look favourably on corporatist situations is the existence of a rough parity in the power of capital and labour, see Pryor (1988).

14. See Cameron (1984), especially p. 144.
15. See Esping-Andersen (1985) and Stephens (1979).
16. Soskice (1990) is a notable exception to this generalization and he argues that the position taken by employers is crucial to successful coordinated bargaining in many corporatist economies. Katzenstein (1985) also highlights the importance of employers' organizations in distinguishing between types of corporatism. See also Swenson (1988).
17. Instead a watered-down version was introduced, which was essentially a share investment scheme – taxes on profits above a certain level were used to buy shares (Pontusson 1992a).
18. Both are reprinted in English translation in O'Brien and Shannon (1992).
19. See Pryor (1988) for further discussion.
20. See Katzenstein (1985, Chapter 4), for an extensive discussion.

5. Growth, Competitiveness and Income Distribution

In the previous chapter we attempted to demonstrate that, although there are many variants of corporatism, most corporatist arrangements are motivated by concerns beyond short-term macroeconomic management. The chapter examined how institutions which underpin relationships between organized interests and the state can ensure that those relationships are both long-term and broad in scope. We develop this theme here by taking a closer look at the three important longer-term economic issues of growth, competitiveness and income distribution.

In the first section we discuss further specific economic mechanisms through which corporatism as a form of institutional and political configuration is linked to growth performance. The relationship between economic growth and corporatism may not necessarily be that corporatism seeks to influence the *level* of economic growth, as assumed in the empirical political science literature. In practice corporatist economies tend to enjoy levels of GDP *per capita* which are well to the top of the ranking of industrialized countries. The recent literature on economic catch-up and growth rate convergence suggests that in the developed world there is a tendency for the less rich to 'catch-up' those with the highest *per capita* GDP.[1] Therefore it may be inappropriate to hold too high expectations concerning the ability of corporatist economies to achieve absolutely higher rates of growth. Instead it is more pertinent to consider whether corporatist economies seek to achieve greater long-run stability in economic growth. Stable growth is particularly important in corporatist economies because it provides a climate for fulfilling the commitment to full employment. Once more Kalecki's (1943) desire for institutional arrangements that would overcome political pressures to abandon full employment policies is of relevance. To shed light on this issue of stability we examine the relationship between corporatism and corporate profitability, and in particular whether corporatist economies are better able to avoid destabilizing episodes of profit squeeze. We also discuss whether corporatism succeeds in providing conditions for more stable rates of investment.

The second section asks whether corporatist arrangements are better equipped to adopt policies, aimed at the supply-side of the economy, to preserve, or enhance, long-run international competitiveness. If corporatist economies cannot maintain such competitiveness then sooner or later the long-run viability of corporatist arrangements will be brought into question. It is therefore appropriate to consider if corporatist 'concertation' may facilitate the development of industrial policies to manage the process of economic change. Such policies aim, on the one hand, to manage the economic decline of some sectors of the economy in a strategic manner and, on the other hand, to accelerate growth in nascent sectors of the economy through, for example, the promotion of technological change. In short, these constitute policies to optimize the productivity of the capital stock and the adaptive efficiency of the economy. This interesting aspect of corporatism has been the concern of a small number of influential writers. We also examine active labour market policies (ALMPs). These are typically viewed as policies to alleviate unemployment. In the context of corporatist economies we consider that they also comprise a form of 'indirect' industrial policy. Thus corporatist arrangements may lead to a more successful management of the productive potential of both physical and human capital stock. The rejection of decentralized wage-setting and the commitment to full employment in corporatist economies means that in the 1970s and early 1980s the strategy adopted by more liberal economies of allowing rising unemployment to introduce real wage discipline could not be pursued. To maintain international competitiveness in key exporting sectors corporatist economies have therefore found it necessary to place a greater emphasis on forward-looking policies such as product development and the introduction of new technologies.

The final issue concerns an aspect of economic performance that was rather neglected in the 1980s, but which fortunately has been receiving much greater attention more recently, namely income distribution. It is important to explore the way in which the proceeds of economic growth are shared out, in terms of the distribution of income and also in terms of the distribution of access to income and consumption opportunities. The ability to promote stable growth and international competitiveness over the longer term will depend critically on the extent to which different groups perceive that they are benefiting from the proceeds of that stability. In corporatist countries the durability of the corporatist compromise will quickly be called into question if it is felt that certain groups are benefiting disproportionately. The observed association between corporatism and social democracy, at least in the strongly corporatist economies, has imparted a strong egalitarian commitment. The end of the long post-war boom has in many parts of the industrialized world heralded an end to the progressive narrowing of the income distribution. This reversal of trend has largely been avoided by the most corporatist countries and so in the final section of this chapter we examine the relationship between corporatism and trends in income inequality.

While the issues above may appear quite distinct, they are in fact interrelated. To take just one example, a commitment to the maintenance of full employment and the use of ALMPs may lead to a more equal society, but that in turn may be associated with a preference for more forward-looking economic strategies since reactive strategies (such as the use of unemployment to discipline real wage determination, or extensive use of defensive industrial policy) are ruled out. We shall attempt to highlight these interrelationships in greater detail.

INVESTMENT AND PROFIT SQUEEZE

The importance of stable growth follows, as we have already indicated, from the commitment to full employment. Typically in capitalist economies cycles in the level of investment are of much greater amplitude than cycles in the level of economic activity. Investment growth outstrips output growth during booms and falls more sharply during recessions. Thus in this section we consider whether corporatism can promote more stable rates of investment.

The importance of investment as part of the corporatist *quid pro quo* should be clear from the previous chapters. If increased investment enhances the level of future incomes, then workers and capitalists will have a shared interest in seeking to optimize the level of that investment. Thus improved investment may be a vital joint instrument in the compromise at work in corporatist economies. As we have discussed in the previous chapter, the problem for workers is the possibility that employers will renege on a future commitment to invest in return for present wage restraint. Employers face a similar uncertainty in that workers may also renege by abandoning quiescence once investment has been undertaken in order to appropriate a larger share of the returns, so undermining earlier estimates of the profitability of that investment.[2] As seen in Chapter 2, such a situation can be characterized as a prisoners' dilemma game. Lange (1984) demonstrates just such an eventuality, and therefore the motivation for sustained and repeated cooperation over wage restraint and investment in corporatist economies. Initially a strategy on the part of workers of forgoing current consumption in order to increase future consumption levels will be rational.[3] However, in a stagnating economy, such as followed the end of the 'golden age', the theoretical analyses of Przeworski and Wallerstein (1982) and Schott (1984) suggest that compromise, in the sense of workers forgoing the use of immediate maximum wage-bargaining strength, may become more and more difficult to sustain. This is because under conditions of stagnation the returns to workers from further investment are eroded away. In game-theoretic terms, unions and capitalists are engaged in a dynamic, repeated game where capitalists choose a particular level of investment and workers a wage. Over time the dynamic externality faced by workers, in that the future benefits of wage moderation may be very uncertain, leads to a breakdown in this form of cooperation and to a level of capital stock which is suboptimal.[4] All this points to the importance of maintaining buoyant levels of investment, even if immediate macroeconomic conditions suggest unfavourable rates of return, to maintain the durability of the corporatist compromise.[5]

Investment depends on the diversion of income from consumption to saving. Savings may be generated in various different sectors of the economy. However, in the context of less than perfect capital markets the present ability of employers to generate profits will be of critical importance, both as an indicator of credit-worthiness and general business confidence and, where credit is rationed, as a source of funds. Worker militancy, in so far as it is indicative of conflict over the distribution of income between wages and profits, will undermine the accumulation process. Thus, where workers are strong capitalists have an interest in maintaining worker quiescence through the promotion of consensus or compromise. In terms of the prisoners' dilemma they may choose to play the cooperative strategy. If investment performance is the means to the success of corporatist arrangements, then corporatist economies need to enjoy conditions where each cyclical downturn does not lead to a rapid abandonment of trade union quiescence and thus profit-squeezing real wage increases. As an alternative, or in addition to this, it is desirable that investment activity is relatively insensitive to movements in profitability (Marglin and Bhaduri 1990). In other words, investment activity will be preserved in the face of an economic shock if investors' confidence can be maintained. This confidence can be established if a shared commitment to the maintenance of full employment exists. In the absence of either or both of these, an economic shock will lead to a decline in investment and an intensification of conflict over the distribution of income, as workers and employers switch to non-cooperative strategies.

Schwerin (1984) summarizes OECD data which shows that the Scandinavian economies were no less immune than other developed economies from the secular decline in aggregate rates of profit over the post-war period.[6] In fact, the measured share of operating surplus in GDP has declined in the corporatist economies, amongst other reasons, because of the growing size of the government sector, a point which Schwerin recognizes. As we discuss later in this chapter, this growth can be associated with a quite deliberate strategy of employment 'restructuring' through the growth of public employment schemes (Glyn and Rowthorn 1988). However, Schwerin argues that the growth of the government sector and the associated increase over time in government borrowing, particularly in Sweden and Denmark, has led to a 'crowding out' process which has made it increasingly difficult for the private sector to obtain funds for investment purposes and has raised the cost of capital. While this process may benefit the financial sector it places even greater importance on the 'distributional compromise' since an increased cost of capital risks damaging competitiveness in exporting sectors and thus leads to greater urgency in wage restraint.

In earlier work, the present authors (Henley and Tsakalotos 1991) estimate an econometric model of profit share for nineteen of the OECD economies. The results of this exercise are rather less pessimistic than Schwerin's conclusions. Controlling for the effect of government 'restructuring' and other trend effects on the functional distribution of income such as technology and long-run changes in the relative bargaining power of labour, the data indicate that the more corporatist economies experienced a somewhat slower rate of decline in their profit share over the period 1956 to 1986. A further interesting conclusion from the exercise is that a given rise in worker militancy, measured as working days lost through strike activity per employee, had a larger detrimental impact on profit share in the liberal economies than in the corporatist ones, suggesting that the former are more susceptible to overt distributional conflict. We conclude overall that:

> *ceteris paribus*, the more corporatist economies appear to be much better placed to avoid a long-run squeeze on private sector profitability. (Henley and Tsakalotos 1991, p. 439)

A consideration of the two sharpest episodes of profit squeeze across the OECD, namely 1973 to 1975 and 1978 to 1982, highlights the past ability of corporatist economies to moderate distributional conflict in the interests of a shared interest in maintaining the level of economic activity. Tables 5.1 and 5.2, taken from Henley and Tsakalotos (1991) provide rates of growth of key variables for each period. (The classification of countries follows Lehmbruch, 1984, see Table 4.1.) The tables provide details of average annual percentage growth of income, investment, profit share and real wages for the two periods of profit squeeze (measured across the OECD as a whole, see Henley and Tsakalotos, 1991, Figure 1). Table 5.1 shows that the more corporatist economies, particularly Norway, Sweden and Finland, were able to continue to grow through the 1973 to 1975 period, and furthermore were able to secure sustained growth in investment. The only countries able to achieve positive real investment growth outside the Nordic group during this period were Canada and Spain. However, the table also shows that the profit squeeze during this period affected all countries. But Sweden, Norway and Austria did manage to achieve rates of profit squeeze slightly below average. The least affected economies were in North America. This is probably explained by the high degree of nominal rigidity in wage setting in North America. This would have particularly worked to the advantage of the United States and Canada because the period was a time of very rapid price inflation.

To investigate further the issue of profit squeeze we calculate what we term the 'warranted rate of real wage growth' and this is included in the two tables. This is the rate of growth of the real wage which

Table 5.1 The 1973–1975 OECD profit squeeze

% per annum	Real income growth[1]	Real invest- ment growth	Profit share growth	Real wage growth	Warr- anted real wage growth[2]
Pluralism:					
Australia	1.90	−3.05	−4.16	4.76	2.52
Canada	4.59	3.94	−1.14	3.31	2.86
N. Zealand	2.67	−3.99	−10.30	1.27	−4.74
USA	−1.91	−12.35	−2.02	−2.16	−2.82
Average	1.81	−3.86	−4.41	1.80	−0.55
Weak corporatism:					
Italy	−0.12	−9.11	−5.47	3.03	−1.23
Spain	3.89	2.62	−2.26	6.18	4.79
UK	−0.27	−11.12	−13.11	4.03	0.47
Average	1.17	−5.87	−6.95	4.41	1.34
Medium corporatism:					
Belgium	1.39	−2.29	−6.91	4.39	1.15
Denmark	−0.93	−14.15	−7.29	3.86	0.68
Finland	2.72	8.31	−7.98	5.66	2.47
Germany	−1.00	−11.98	−4.20	2.78	1.15
Ireland	6.15	−8.13	−5.59	4.26	1.60
	−2.25	−15.20	−4.86	1.15	−0.83
Switzerlan d	1.01	−7.24	−6.14	3.68	1.04
Average					
Strong corporatism:					
Austria	2.96	−5.97	−4.16	4.76	2.52
Netherlands	1.74	−7.11	−6.43	4.41	1.81
Norway	5.04	9.58	−5.14	4.63	3.08
Sweden	3.75	7.53	−4.01	4.61	3.36
Average	3.37	1.01	−4.94	4.60	2.69

Table 5.1 (continued)

'Concertation without labour'

France	1.27	−5.26	−8.69	4.98	0.84
Japan	1.69	−7.21	−8.37	3.40	−1.30
Average	1.48	−6.24	−8.53	4.19	−0.23

Notes:
1. Income refers to total factor income and is defined as GDP minus indirect taxes plus depreciation plus subsidies.
2. The warranted real wage growth is that rate of real wage growth which is consistent with zero profit share growth assuming actually observed productivity and price changes. Applying the consumer price deflator to obtain real wages and the GDP deflator to obtain real output, it is calculated as: warranted real wage growth = growth in real productivity − growth in (consumer price deflator/GDP deflator).

Source: Henley and Tsakalotos (1991)

would be consistent with a constant profit share, given observed movements in real labour productivity and the prices of consumer goods and producer output. In other words, if labour had settled for this annual rate of growth of real wages there would have been no profit squeeze. Thus, in most cases the warranted real wage growth is considerably lower than actual real wage growth. In Table 5.1 we see that the smaller profit squeeze in Norway, Sweden and Finland is indicated in the narrower divergence between actual and warranted rates of real wage growth. The average warranted real wage growth rate for the strongly corporatist group is 2.7 per cent *per annum*. This contrasts with the 'pluralist' or most liberal economies where warranted real wage growth was in fact negative. The corporatist economies, by managing to maintain rates of investment, enjoyed a position of being able to continue to provide considerable real wage growth without risking conflict over the distribution of income.[7] Profit squeeze was greatest in those economies with fairly strong trade unions and collective bargaining systems, where labour was not prepared to accept the rather low warranted rates of real wage growth.

Similar conclusions emerge for the 1978 to 1982 period in Table 5.2. During this episode the superior performance, from the point of view of distributional conflict, of the strongly corporatist economies is more pronounced. In all of the strongly corporatist group, and also in

Table 5.2 The 1978–1982 OECD profit squeeze

% per annum	Real income growth	Real invest-ment growth	Profit share growth	Real wage growth	Warr-anted real wage growth
Pluralism:					
Australia	0.92	−1.77	−3.22	1.49	−0.22
Canada	1.14	−0.45	−1.43	−0.43	−0.97
N. Zealand	1.34	5.77	0.46	−0.16	0.07
USA	0.10	−5.46	−4.06	−1.54	−2.56
Average	0.88	−0.48	−2.06	−0.16	−0.92
Weak corporatism:					
Italy	2.46	2.08	0.41	1.64	1.93
Spain	−0.45	−1.85	1.84	1.84	0.62
UK	−1.38	−3.83	−2.58	0.81	0.06
Average	0.21	−1.20	−0.11	1.43	0.87
Medium corporatism:					
Belgium	1.54	−4.52	−0.09	0.47	0.44
Denmark	1.17	−6.24	−0.86	0.04	−0.28
Finland	4.64	7.85	0.69	1.93	2.18
Germany	0.75	−1.63	−1.65	0.47	−0.15
Ireland	1.33	3.23	−6.21	1.63	−1.24
Switzerland	2.00	4.21	−1.56	1.35	0.79
Average	1.91	0.48	−1.61	0.98	0.29
Strong corporatism:					
Austria	1.88	−1.09	1.44	1.28	1.78
Netherlands	0.18	−5.61	1.81	−2.37	−1.62
Norway	2.78	4.14	10.40	−1.14	0.59
Sweden	1.27	1.46	6.41	−1.59	−0.20
Average	1.53	−0.28	4.95	−0.96	0.14

Table 5.2 (continued)

'Concertation without labour'

France	1.51	0.85	−3.65	1.82	0.52
Japan	3.43	2.37	−2.06	1.62	0.63
Average	2.47	1.61	−2.89	1.72	0.58

Notes: See Table 5.1
Source: Henley and Tsakalotos (1991)

the case of Finland (which is probably by this time better classified as strongly corporatist too) there is no profit squeeze at all. Profit shares in fact rise. With the exception of The Netherlands investment growth rates remain positive. The growing profit share implies that actual real wage growth is below the warranted rate of growth. In fact, in the strongly corporatist group, real wages fell during the period by almost one percent *per annum*. The preservation of constant income shares could have allowed a slight growth in real wages. In contrast warranted real wage growth in the pluralist group is almost minus one percent *per annum*. In practice they were only, on average, able to secure reductions of 0.16 percent *per annum*. The average income growth rate achieved by this group is only slightly more than half that achieved by the strongly corporatist group. The highest average income growth is achieved by the medium corporatist group, but this high average is entirely due to the exceptional performance of Finland (which as already indicated, may be better regarded as strongly corporatist).

So the ability to create a climate for sustained investment in the face of economic shocks, particularly among the Scandinavian corporatist economies, appears to have been greatly helped by a capacity to avoid distributional conflict. This is true in a relative sense *vis-à-vis* the more pluralist economies in the aftermath of the first OPEC oil price rise, and in an absolute sense in the aftermath of the second oil price rise.

The second relevant aspect of investment is its degree of sensitivity to movements in profitability. As we have seen, the corporatist economies may have suffered less from potentially damaging episodes of profit squeeze. Henley and Tsakalotos (1991) present further evidence from the econometric estimation of investment functions to suggest that the strongly corporatist group, as classified in Tables 5.1

and 5.2, jointly possess long-run elasticities of investment with respect to changes in profitability which is significantly lower than that of the other groups of countries. This enjoyment of investment levels which have been less sensitive to movements in profitability suggests that investment performance in corporatist economies would have been better, *ceteris paribus*, even if the extent of distributional conflict in these economies had been the same as elsewhere.

ADJUSTMENT TO ECONOMIC CHANGE AND INTERNATIONAL COMPETITIVENESS

It is not only the maintenance of buoyant and stable levels of investment which is of importance in the provision of stable and sustained economic growth. The quality of that investment needs to be such that it preserves, and at best enhances, the international competitiveness of an economy. The growing volume of world trade that has resulted from the progressive opening up of world markets in the post-war period has placed a growing pressure on the industrialized economies to maintain international competitiveness. If corporatist economies fail to compete, with consequent loss of export earnings, the durability of corporatist compromises will be increasingly questioned. Individual economies have to varying degrees employed specific policy instruments in the attempt to promote competitiveness. Corporatist economies are no exception. We examine the extent to which corporatism is compatible with industrial policies, or whether corporatist economies have been more successful in their use of what can be termed 'indirect' industrial policies. The main example of the latter is active labour market policy.

Industrial policy is a rather wide-ranging term which is used to cover various forms of government action aimed at changing the allocation of resources between firms or between sectors.[8] A wide range of specific instruments fall into this definition. They include subsidies, tax incentives, investment incentives and import restrictions. The connection between corporatism and industrial policy has been discussed quite extensively. Katzenstein (1985) argues that the establishment of corporatist institutions, in themselves, can be seen primarily as one form of policy response in the face of the economic change in the latter half of the twentieth century. They represent a response that has in particular been adopted by a number of European economies which are small and open. 'Smallness' and 'openness' have therefore brought to the forefront the need for corporatist compromise in a number of such European countries. The growing international-ization of the world economy has left these economies particularly vulnerable to fluctuations in international economic activity, in exchanges rates and in commodity prices. A strong commitment to free trade and a belief that the gains from a strategy of trade protection will be more than outweighed by the counter-effects of retaliation have led these economies, Katzenstein argues, to accept a liberal world economy as given and to place emphasis on a 'strategy of domestic compensation' to smooth out the effects of international fluctuations. Katzenstein interprets the definition of what constitutes an industrial policy in a wider sense to include incomes policies and strategies concerning the structure of collective bargaining. For Katzenstein the important elements of such policy, as practised in the small corporatist European countries, are that it is incrementalist and flexible and that corporatist arrangements allow economic flexibility and political stability to be 'mutually contingent'.

Several authors (Kenworthy 1990, Pontusson 1991, 1992a) suggest that corporatism and industrial policy, as conventionally understood, may be incompatible because the latter is selective in nature and will fail to command consensual support from all employers and all groups of workers. Landesmann (1992), in contrast, argues that the Scandinavian economies have each successfully adopted varying approaches to industrial policy. For example, Sweden successfully managed the total decline in its shipbuilding industry between the early 1970s and mid-1980s from a position of being the second largest in the world with virtually no increase in unemployment (Standing 1988). Landesmann also discusses at length the case of Austria, but argues that it has not succeeded to anything like the same extent in the effective design and implementation of industrial policy. On the other hand, in his comparison of Austria and Switzerland, Katzenstein (1985) argues that Austria has since the late 1960s adopted an interventionist approach to industry through the promotion of rationalization, the management of declining sectors and promotion of high technology.

Landesmann argues that, although specific industrial policies may be directly targeted to benefit particular groups, it is important not to miss the point that the overall goal of any industrial policy must be to increase national wealth. Thus, leaving aside issues of dynamic externalities and interpretation gaps, industrial policies ought to command widespread support. Presumably the extent to which 'losers' accept the acceleration of resource reallocation will depend on the overall environment of policy formulation. A state guarantee of full employment implemented through temporary public employment and retraining programmes, and more generally a commitment to an egalitarian society, may make such change more acceptable and less threatening for workers and their union representatives. Thus the efficacy of 'offensive' industrial policies is related to the discussion which follows on ALMPs and income distribution.

While the use of what Landesmann terms 'change-promoting' policies may be motivated by a desire to improve national wealth, this objective becomes less certain when considering the effects of 'structure-preserving' policies. The latter have tended in liberal and corporatist economies alike to be targeted at maintaining the financial viability of ailing firms and industries.

A widespread criticism of the latter kind of industrial policy is that it is almost inevitably adopted at the cost of investment in new or more dynamic sectors of the economy. This alerts us to the problem that within the long-term consensual relationships associated with corporatism it may be difficult to employ selective policy to promote economic change and increased efficiency. 'Regulatory capture', a situation where the administration of industrial policy, say, is 'captured' by organized groups to serve their own interests, is a distinct possibility. In Britain during the 1960s and 1970s industrial policy was managed through the weakly corporatist tripartite National Economic Development Committees ('little Neddies') and sectoral working parties. Experience suggests that the operation of these entailed a danger that tripartism had become the be-all and end-all of economic strategy. Under certain circumstances tripartism can operate to the detriment of the promotion of change and the improvement of competitiveness. Hall has noted that this British experience of tripartism helped to perpetuate rather than eliminate structural defects. These institutions left:

the initiative for rationalisation up to private sector actors themselves, and, faced with a relatively unchanged set of market incentives, they clung to traditional practices. (Hall 1986, p. 91)

Experience elsewhere, for instance in Sweden, Japan and South Korea, suggests that there is no inevitability about this and that industrial policy can be strategic and forward-looking. There are ways, as we shall see, in which stronger forms of corporatism can better facilitate change-promoting policies. Nevertherless, the tension between such policies and the preservation of an existing industrial structure is probably not easily eliminated.

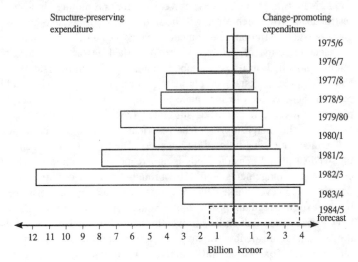

Figure 5.1   The structure of industrial support in Sweden
Source: Landesmann (1992, figure 8.6)

Even in the Swedish case, while change-promoting expenditure continued to increase in absolute terms in the 1960s and 1970s, the majority share of total expenditure on industrial policy was, by the late 1970s, being directed as state aid to ailing firms, see Figure 5.1. This was particularly directed to firms in shipbuilding industry. Nevertheless, aid to this industry was, by the 1980s, seen as assisting a managed closure operation rather than as a permanent subsidy. The shift of emphasis in Swedish industrial policy was largely the result of the increasing pace of global economic change and the increasing difficulties involved in maintaining a strategy of full employment in the face of a stagnating global economy.

Even if we accept that particular forms of direct industrial policy are associated with corporatism, as Landesmann does, there remains the question of whether such policy is actually formulated and implemented using corporatist institutional structures. Pontusson (1991) argues that less emphasis has been placed on direct industrial policy in Sweden than in countries such as Japan and France. This is not only because of the much greater importance attached in Sweden to the solidaristic wages policy as a vehicle for promoting industrial restructuring (of which more will be said presently), but also because corporatist concertation arrangements have proved much less amenable to selective forms of policy. Sweden launched an 'active industrial policy' modelled on its active labour market policy in the late 1960s and attempted to establish corporatist arrangements which would parallel those created to formulate and implement the labour market policy. However, it has been suggested (Zysman 1983, Pontusson 1991) that the increasingly defensive orientation of industrial policy was indicative of institutional deficiencies. The tripartite management of Swedish public pension funds is an exceptional example of where corporatist arrangements could be brought to bear on investment decisions. However, these decisions were often heavily circumscribed by the external regulation of capital markets by the central bank. We have already seen that further moves in the 1970s and 1980s towards the 'socialization' of investment were seen by business as a step too far. The role of the central union confederation, the LO, in the industrial policy process was, in Pontusson's view, a marginal one throughout the 1970s and 1980s. He attributes this to a lack of an overall trade union strategy for policy and a lack on the part of the LO of independent information and expertise.

Authors such as Pontusson (1991) and Kenworthy (1990) contrast the experience of the highly corporatist economies, and especially Sweden, with those countries such as France and Japan where industrial policy over the post-war period has been very prominent. Both France and Japan are characterized by Lehmbruch (1984) as 'concertation without labour' (see Table 4.1). It seems likely that the most developed forms of industrial policy have evolved in countries where corporatist arrangements, such as centralized wage-bargaining and consensual macroeconomic policy formulation, were not forthcoming, due to the absence of strong trade union movements. On the other hand, in Japan sectoral employer organization has been traditionally very strong and in France a strong commitment to a statist mode of policy intervention has characterized post-war economic development.

However, as we have noted already, corporatist economies have tended to rely to a greater extent on indirect forms of industrial policy. The commitment to full employment has required policy-makers to implement specific arrangements for handling the displacement of workers from declining sectors, in particular through the use of ALMPs. As Jackman *et al.* (1990) demonstrate from cross-country evidence, the use of active labour market policies is able to significantly and beneficially affect the reduction in unemployment arising from a given improvement in the number of job vacancies. In a more general sense the rejection of a strategy of allowing unemployment to regulate labour markets has required the development of ALMPs as an alternative. The point has been forcibly made by Pekkarinen *et al.* (1992) who draw on the distinction made in the previous chapter between inclusive and exclusive forms of corporatism:[9]

> The implicit premiss of a high employment rate with fairly equal pay characteristic of the inclusive type of corporatism may cause a pressure to strategic, forward-looking behaviour in industrial adjustment, whereas the groups privileged in the decision-making in a corporatist economy of the exclusive type may well tend to preserve their own status and shift the burden of adjustment to others. Apart from differences in the capacity to adjust to new circumstances, this difference in the fundamental constraints of industrial adjustment may be reflected, for example, in the greater emphasis on active manpower policies prevalent in the inclusive corporatism of the Swedish type. (Pekkarinen *et al.* 1992, p. 15)

This commitment to 'strategic, forward-looking behaviour in industrial adjustment' was, of course, explicit in the Swedish Rehn–Meidner model from its inception in the 1950s (see Chapter 4). The solidaristic wages policy of the Rehn–Meidner plan can be understood as an indirect form of industrial policy. It should be seen not just as a vehicle of short-term wage restraint but also as an attempt to accelerate long-term restructuring of the economy. The policy of forcing less-efficient firms to pay a centrally determined wage level would accelerate the movement of employment from declining sectors to high-profit, high-productivity sectors. To make this work the model also entailed a tight demand-management policy in order to prevent weaker firms from sheltering behind buoyant demand conditions.

The solidaristic wages policy is indirectly selective in that it implicitly rewards certain sectors and firms and penalizes others. The question then arises of whether such an approach would command the extensive support of employers. One might expect that the 'losers' would be strongly opposed to centralized wage setting. However, at the time of the inception of centralized bargaining, the Swedish employers' organization (SAF) agreed to the policy with little serious dissension. Kenworthy (1990) attributes this to the fact that the largest members of the SAF were also at that time the most profitable. The Rehn–Meidner plan found easy favour with the trade union confederation (LO) because it entailed the retraining and re-employment of displaced workers.

The Swedish system of active labour market policy is the most comprehensive in the world, and so it is particularly worthy of discussion. As Table 5.3 illustrates, Sweden spends the greatest proportion of GDP on ALMPs among the OECD economies. However, because of its success in maintaining very low rates of unemployment, total labour market expenditure including income maintenance (i.e. unemployment benefits) is lower as a proportion of GDP than in several other countries.[10] Sweden stands out particularly because of the very high spending of ALMPs proportional to income maintenance spending. The Swedish ALMP strategy involves a number of aspects.[11] Unemployed workers are guaranteed extensive facilities for job placement, assisted by a national vacancy computer system which matches unemployed workers with available vacancies, and would-be employers with suitable job candidates. The state will subsidize interview and mobility expenses and will also subsidize employers in certain cases to employ those who have been unemployed for more than six months. This subsidy can amount to fifty percent of wages in the first six months of employment. Failing successful job placement the unemployed are guaranteed very comprehensive job training,[12] or temporary employment on public employment programmes. Vital to the Swedish strategy is the conception of the right to work. Conversely, there is no right to unlimited unemployment insurance. Thus, while unemployment insurance is very generous (replacement ratios are typically eighty percent, OECD 1988), payment is strictly limited to a period of fourteen months.

A social-corporatist ethos underpins the operation of the ALMP and training systems. Both the National Labour Market Board (AMS) and the National Employment Training Board (AMU) are tripartite bodies managed jointly by government, employers and trade unions. The

Table 5.3 Public expenditure on labour market programmes

Average % of GDP 1985–88	1 Active Labour Market Programmes	2 Income maint-enance	3 Total expend-iture	4 Ratio 1 over 2
USA	0.26*	0.51*	0.77*	0.51
Canada	0.58	1.74	2.32	0.33
Australia	0.36	1.20	1.56	0.30
New Zealand	0.73	0.78#	1.48#	0.94
Japan	0.19+	0.40+	0.59+	0.48
Euro-core				
Belgium	1.27	3.21	4.48	0.40
Denmark	1.13*	4.07*	5.20*	0.28
France	0.74#	2.34#	3.08#	0.32
Germany	0.95	1.36	2.31	0.70
Italy	0.67	0.88	1.55	0.76
Netherlands	1.12	2.88	4.00	0.39
UK	0.80	1.89	2.69	0.42
Corporatist				
Austria	0.31	1.03	1.34	0.30
Finland	0.89	1.46	2.35	0.61
Norway	0.51	0.44	0.95	1.16
Sweden	1.96	0.80	2.76	2.45

Notes: * 1986–88, + 1987–88, # 1985–87
Source: OECD Employment Outlook, July 1989, Table A.1, pp. 206–7

lower-level county boards and local offices of both organizations have tripartite representation. While other corporatist countries do not spend anywhere near the same proportion of GDP on ALMPs (Table 5.3), they share with the Sweden the same high degree of administrative and policy coordination (OECD 1988).

Among the European Community members Germany is often cited as an example of where ALMPs have been used successfully, particularly in the area of employment training and specifically the training of young people (Layard and Philpott 1991, Disney *et al.* 1992). Again policy implementation is characterized by a high degree of national coordination through the *Bundesanstalt für Arbeit* (Federal Employment Institute). The key aspect of the German training system is its dual nature – involving placement in firms and vocational school attendance. While Germany's attempts at economic concertation at the national level were rather short-lived, it is well known that Germany possesses a long-established and well-developed system of worker codetermination. Similarly it has enjoyed considerable success in its operation of microeconomic supply-side labour market policies. This emphasis on microeconomic effectiveness has meant that Germany has not traditionally viewed active labour policy as an instrument of macroeconomic stabilization (Disney *et al.* 1992).

The link between corporatism and the supply side of the economy rests on more than just the use of ALMPs. In Chapter 3, it was argued that both centralized and decentralized labour markets may be superior in operation to those with intermediate levels of centralization. In addition to the point made in that chapter that decentralization may not be a feasible option, there are further reasons for believing that centralized bargaining may be preferable. Decentralized labour markets may be able to provide real wage flexibility but they have not been very successful in generating the sustained productivity growth that allows workers to enjoy sustained growth in the real 'social' wage. In this respect the US and the UK are seen by some to have suffered most from the liberal strategy of decentralization and flexibility which has focused too narrowly on the problems of wage determination.[13] Within the non-EC corporatist group of countries and within the EC itself policy-makers are reluctant to pursue this option too since it may provide an incentive structure which leads firms to avoid competition through innovation in production methods (Grahl and Teague 1990).[14]

A alternative strategy rejects international price competition as a sole response but rather emphasizes the ability to provide a higher-quality product, through the use of a whole range of non-price factors such as research initiative, product development and consumer after-sales service. One precondition of the ability to deliver these is a high-skilled, flexible and motivated workforce. As we saw in Chapter 2, Soskice (1991) introduces the term 'flexibly coordinated systems' to the institutional arrangements adopted in some economies. Micro-corporatist arrangments are an important aspect of these systems, and may comprise a vital element in the superior competitiveness of more corporatist economies.[15] As was mentioned in Chapter 2, such systems seem better able to avoid the problems of short-termism which bedevil more decentralized or market-liberal arrangements. They are characterized by strong employer organizations which provide infrastructural services (in areas such as research and development, marketing, and training). As a result they are able to exercise leverage over individual firms in the centralization and coordination of wage-setting. As with macro-corporatist arrangements the openness of these economies is an important spur.

Decentralized labour markets may not provide a favourable environment for such systems of production. Where there are considerable externalities associated with training it will be undersupplied by individual firms. Firms have an incentive to 'poach' rather than train, and in order to do so they may need to reduce the level of coordination in wage-setting. Beyond the provision of training, deregulated labour markets may be unable to provide the motivated and flexible workforce that is required. The uncertainties involved in decentralization may deter workers from thinking strategically and actively cooperating in the introduction of new technologies and production systems (Grahl and Teague 1990).

On the other hand, micro-corporatist features such as worker participation and codetermination provide considerable scope for the negotiated introduction of approaches to improving productivity. Furthermore, micro-corporatism may have positive feedbacks on macro-corporatism. The moderation of plant-level wage drift may depend on the scope for widening the bargaining agenda beyond wage determination to longer-term productivity issues. We have already seen that there are sound theoretical reasons for workers to underutilize present labour market power in return for investment. This investment may be as much in human capital as in physical capital, taking the form of training provision. Training reinforces internal labour markets and help to create a sense of long-term job security (Soskice 1990). However, there is a clear danger that such micro-corporatist features may tie workers increasingly to the concerns of their firm, or industry, and therefore disconnect them from the rest of the economy. This may imply that centralized wage-bargaining may become more difficult. We return to this issue and that of whether the drive for labour flexibility is undermining corporatist arrangements in the concluding chapter.

A final point that links with the issue of income inequality, to be taken up in the next section, is that a more participatory and cooperative relationship between workers and management has implications for the degree of egalitarianism. As Gordon has argued, micro-corporatism:

> probably requires considerable solidarity among workers in order most effectively to tap the potential for worker participation and involvement. And that, other things equal, probably requires relatively high levels of equality in the distribution of labour earnings. (Gordon 1991, p. 203)

To conclude this section, there are a number of approaches that have been adopted by corporatist economies with respect to enhancing international competitiveness. These include both direct and indirect forms of industrial policies. Kenworthy (1990) suggests that the contradictions between industrial policy, in its more conventional narrower definition, and corporatist wage determination and labour market policies lead to four possible policy configurations. Firstly, corporatism and industrial policy may, due to the inclusive nature of the former and selective nature of the latter, be incompatible and so highly corporatist economies will avoid the use of industrial policy. However, actual experience does not bear out this prediction.[16] Secondly, corporatism and industrial policy may coexist if they attend to different policy domains. This configuration seems most feasible if industrial policy is of a more defensive nature, as it has tended to be in both corporatist and non-corporatist economies alike since the late 1970s. Thirdly, corporatist arrangements may be used to implement a *de facto* industrial policy. The Rehn–Meidner plan typifies this. Finally, industrial policy may be formulated and implemented in a corporatist fashion through tripartite consultation but will be openly selective and discriminatory. Kenworthy argues that the second of these accords most with the actual experience of corporatist economies. While most of the highly corporatist economies have each attempted to bring a corporatist mode of policy formulation and implementation to bear on the use of industrial and labour market policies, experience has shown that the institutional infrastructures have been much less well developed for the former when compared to the latter. The use of policies to manage economic restructuring is far from anathema to corporatist economies, as it has been in liberal economies such as the UK and US in the 1980s, and it is in this sense that corporatism and industrial restructuring policies are strongly associated.

CORPORATISM, THE WELFARE STATE AND INEQUALITY

While the processes of industrial change and restructuring have been experienced by all the industrialized economies since the end of the post-war 'golden age', different countries have managed these processes very differently. Interventionism through labour market and industrial policies is one approach. The alternative approach that has found favour, particularly among English-speaking economies, is the *laissez-faire* response – supply-side policies aimed at a reduced level of government involvement in both labour and product markets. Evidence, which we shall review here, suggests that corporatist and liberal responses have had very different distributional implications. The strong egalitarian commitment of governing social democratic parties in many of the corporatist economies, particularly in Scandinavia, has precluded, at least until recently, the use of a liberal policy response. Corporatism may have explicitly been adopted in order to manage industrial restructuring with a more equal sacrifice in the burden of adjustment. Furthermore this, egalitarianism may, in turn, as we have seen, contribute to more forward-looking approaches to economic restructuring. So the third theme we take up in this chapter is to examine the corporatist economies' record on income inequality, pointing to the important interdependence between corporatist institutions and those of the welfare state.

Table 5.4 shows movements in Gini coefficients of personal and household incomes for a number of both corporatist and non-corporatist economies. Comparisons between countries using the table are not meaningful due the different definitions of income and different samples used, however the data do give an indication of trends within countries. In most countries a trend towards greater equality occurred between the end of the Second World War and the onset of stagnation in the 1970s. However, the table demonstrates that the more corporatist countries, particularly in Scandinavia, have avoided the dramatic reversal in the trend that has occurred elsewhere.[17] Figures 5.2 and 5.3

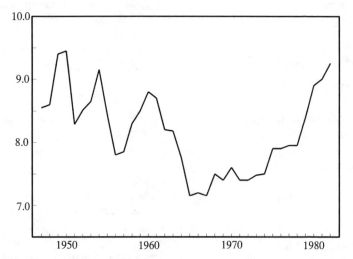

Figure 5.2 Income ratio of top to bottom quintiles of families, USA
Source: Beach (1989)

illustrate this contrast by comparing what Bluestone and Harrison (1988) term the 'Great U-Turn' of the United States with the much greater stability in income inequality after 1975 in Sweden. A more substantial review and discussion of other cross-country comparative evidence is provided by Green, Henley and Tsakalotos (1992).

The most obvious factor in the corporatist economies' experience which would lead to an expectation of less inegalitarianism is their avoidance of high rates of unemployment in the early 1980s. The commitment to full employment that provided the spur to the development of corporatist arrangements arose because of a view that

Table 5.4 Trends in Gini coefficients of income inequality in selected countries

USA		Canada		UK		Germany	
1949	0.378	1951	0.390	1965[a]	0.326		
1959	0.361	1961	0.368	1970	0.339	1969	0.313
1969	0.349	1971	0.400	1975	0.347	1973	0.294
1979	0.365	1981	0.377	1980	0.358	1978	0.307
1984	0.385			------	------	1983	0.317
				1979[b]	0.239		
				1988	0.310		

Austria		Norway		Sweden		Finland	
		1970[a]	0.305	1967[a]	0.295	1966	0.318
		1973	0.348	1975	0.214	1971	0.270
		1976	0.319	1980	0.202	1976	0.216
		1979	0.314	1985	0.207	1981	0.206
		------	------	------	------	1985	0.200
1981	0.238	1979[b]	0.346	1975[b]	0.233		
1983	0.227	1982	0.334	1980	0.206		
1985	0.235	1986	0.330	1985	0.221		
				1989	0.223		

Definitions and sources:
USA: family gross income, Levy (1987)
Canada: family gross income, Vaillancourt (1985)
UK: [a]household gross income, Moohkerjee and Shorrocks (1982), [b]equivalized household disposable income, Johnson and Webb (1993)
Austria: net individual income, Guger (1989)
Norway: equivalized household disposable income, Ringen (1991), [a] self-employment income component is net of depreciation, [b] self employment income component is gross of depreciation
Sweden: [a]equivalized household disposable income, Gustafsson and Uusitalo (1990), [b]equivalized household disposable income, Bjorklund (1992)
Finland: equivalized household disposable income, Gustafsson and Uusitalo (1990)

rising unemployment in the inter-war period indicated that some groups were bearing disproportionately the costs of economic decline. The obvious way to avoid this unequal burden was to avoid the cause of it. The observed egalitarianism of corporatist countries also comes about because centralized wage-bargaining is associated with a lower dispersion of wages across industries (Rowthorn 1992a, 1992b). Related to this is the feature that corporatist economies have higher levels of union density (see Table 3.2). Cross-country evidence suggests that unions are associated with reduced wage dispersion (Blanchflower and Freeman 1990).

Of course, not all corporatist economies have the same record on income inequality and, in this respect, the distinction made earlier between exclusive and inclusive forms of corporatism is relevant. Thus, Austrian corporatist institutions and the social compromise which underlies them have not encompassed activity by trade unions to promote wage equality (Guger 1992).[18] Furthermore, while Austria has maintained low rates of unemployment, its record on employment growth has not been impressive, since it has allowed the cost of reduced employment growth to be largely borne through the

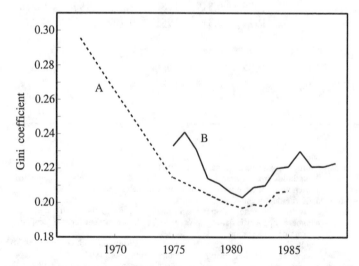

Figure 5.3 Household equivalent net income inequality in Sweden
Source: A: Gustafsson and Uusitalo (1990); B: Bjorklund (1992)

repatriation of overseas workers. It is in this sense that Austria constitutes an exclusive form of corporatism[19]. However, at least for Austrian workers this lack of wage solidarity is to some extent compensated by a generous welfare state. State expenditure was particularly strong in the 1970s, rising from 42.4 percent of GDP in 1970 to 49.7 percent in 1975 and then again to 56.3 percent in 1987 (Guger 1992).

The preference for the use of ALMPs may also play a complementary role. ALMPs can be seen as an 'employment strategy' as opposed to unemployment insurance arrangements which represent 'cash-assistance strategies'. Thus the state acts as guarantor of work rather than of income (Layard and Philpott 1991). The way that ALMPs are financed has an important influence on their ability to prevent rising inequality. In Sweden, where the use of ALMPs has been most comprehensive, financing has been directly from the state budget, rather than on an individually defined contributions and benefits basis. This contrasts, for example, with Germany. Direct state financing signals that ALMPs exist to pursue general employment policy objectives (Schmidt and Reissert 1988). As Jackman *et al.* (1990) note, there is a further feedback mechanism between greater egalitarianism and the effectiveness of ALMPs. Where the wage distribution is narrower wage offers to unemployed workers will be more uniform, meaning that the returns to job search will be lower. Thus unemployed workers in more egalitarian, corporatist economies may be less likely to decline job offers, when they appear, in the hope of improved future offers. Finally, in the previous section it was noted that micro-corporatist participatory institutions may also require a fair degree of egalitarianism to be effective.

The wider socio-political emphasis in corporatist countries on high levels of social welfare provision[20] and greater egalitarianism is developed by Glyn and Rowthorn (1988). They argue that 'post-tax wage restraint' has enabled corporatist economies to finance structural change. In this context Glyn (1992) develops the concepts of 'employment-spreading' and 'consumption-spreading'. Employment-spreading entails both the maintenance of employment in the private, market sector and the creation of employment opportunities in the state sector. This process, by widening access to consumption opportunities, leads to consumption-spreading. The extent of consumption-spreading will also depend on the generosity of the social insurance system.

However a key prerequisite for the greater egalitarianism implicit in this spreading of employment and consumption opportunity is 'a high degree of social solidarity on the part of those with secure jobs' (Glyn 1992, p.133). If wage-earners seek to offset the spreading effect through higher wage claims to restore their level of post-tax pay, this tends to reduce the impact of the increase in state employment by encouraging faster restructuring and employment loss in the private sector. In the short run the costs of this process may be met through a rising government deficit and reduced public expenditure. In due course, though, these costs will require financing through increasing tax rates and will result in a reduction in the growth rate of the standard of living for the employed. A lack of commitment on the part of those in jobs to accept this growing need for restraint in post-tax wage growth will mean that the burden of adjustment is increasingly borne by a rising number of unemployed.

Glyn argues that consumption- and employment-spreading played an important role in the ability of the corporatist economies to adjust to the economic shocks of the 1970s without incurring high unemployment. After 1979, he argues, the corporatist economies reached the limits of politically acceptable income redistribution through these methods. But a reversal in this trend, allowing the possibility that income inequality might begin to widen, did not emerge because, at least in the first half of the 1980s, these economies managed to maintain levels of social welfare provision and maintain very low levels of unemployment.[21] He interprets this as indicating that the social solidarity implied by consumption- and employment-spreading was not entirely reversed.

Given the importance of the above, it is important to consider the relationship between corporatist institutions and those of the welfare state. Esping-Andersen (1990) examines the differing character of the welfare state in economies with different institutional structures. Advanced industrial economies can, he argues, be distinguished according to three broad 'types', although in practice particular countries may display characteristics of more than one type. Firstly, he identifies the 'liberal' welfare capitalism of the Anglo-Saxon world (United States, Canada, Australia, New Zealand) as one type. Welfare systems in these countries generate a high level of social stratification through typically flat-rate means-tested social benefits. The flat-rate nature of benefits encourages the better-off to seek private forms of insurance leading to the development of a dual structure. A second cluster of countries is in continental Western Europe, where welfare states developed from within a strongly Christian Democratic tradition, and rely on a social insurance approach but lack any overt commitment to egalitarianism. This model is confusingly (in the present context) termed 'corporatist' by Esping-Andersen, because its origins are in the guild-corporatism of Germany and Austria in the early twentieth century. The final model, which is exemplified by the Nordic economies, exhibits a much stronger commitment to universalism and egalitarianism, and is seen as developing from a social-democratic tradition.

Esping-Andersen argues that on the basis of egalitarianism this third model provides the most successful social welfare framework for full employment, in the context of private enterprise and powerful trade unions. Esping-Andersen also identifies as a key aspect the ability of the corporatist economies (in our terminology) to provide a collective bargaining framework within which full employment inflationary wage pressures can be contained through the post-tax wage/social wage wedge. The ability of trade unions to accept such a strategy depends critically on the universal and non-stratifying nature of the welfare state. Under such conditions employers and state have emerged as co-providers of social protection. This has been achieved through the commitment to full employment and the avoidance of creating a secondary 'sometimes-working' class reliant on meagre state income support during periods of recession. Such a system is in stark contrast to the privatized insurance protection available to primary workers alone under the liberal model.[22]

In conclusion, the commitment to full employment, narrow wage dispersion and centralized bargaining, societal consensus concerning the ends and means of economic adjustment, are all associated to some degree with corporatist institutions. It is therefore not surprising that the evidence shows that corporatist economies have been more likely to avoid a significant trend towards inequality since the end of the post-war 'golden age'. By contrast, the liberal economies have experienced, to a greater or lesser extent, rising inequality in the 1970s and 1980s. The use of approaches to labour market flexibility which entail allowing rising unemployment to discipline wage determination along with other forms of 'numerical flexibility' have contributed to this. These, together with stratified welfare states which increasingly rely on means-testing of benefits (Esping-Andersen 1990, Baldwin 1990), have led observers to point to the growth of the phenomenon of the 'two-thirds' society in many economies (Therborn 1986). The one-third, comprising the unemployed, the low paid and part-time workers in low-paid jobs, are those who have in these economies disproportionately carried the costs of economic stagnation.

The preservation of an egalitarian income distribution is, arguably, in itself an impressive aspect of the economic performance of corporatist economies. However, in this chapter, we have also argued that this egalitarianism may have contributed to other aspects of economic performance in corporatist economies. It has, at least until the mid-1980s, provided a framework of social solidarity which has facilitated the adaption to economic change without either high unemployment or an unequal sharing of the burden of adjustment. Many argue that by the late 1980s the ability to avoid a reversal in the sustained trend towards a more equal income distribution had reached it limits. This may be indicated by the growing opposition in corporatist economies to welfare state dependency, high marginal tax rates, and narrow occupational wage differentials. We take up the question of current pressures on and future prospects for corporatism in the concluding chapter.

NOTES

1. See Dowrick and Nguyen (1989) for evidence on this and Crafts (1992) for further discussion.
2. This dilemma for both workers and capitalists forms the essence of the 'dynamic inefficiency of capitalism' in the theoretical presentation of Lancaster (1973).
3. Of course, the extent to which they will be prepared to intertemporally substitute consumption will depend on their rates of time preference.
4. A formal presentation of this is provided by the models of Lancaster (1973), Grout (1984), van der Ploeg (1987) and Manning (1987) and also discussed in Landesmann and Vartiainen (1992).
5. This need for resilience of investment in the face of declining profitability is made as a general observation concerning the growth of distributional conflict at the end of the 'golden age' by Marglin and Bhaduri (1990).
6. The sources of this decline have been extensively investigated. See Henley (1990) and Weisskopf (1987).
7. The smaller extent of profit squeeze in the corporatist countries in the 1970s is also noted by Glyn (1991).
8. Geroski (1989) provides an introduction on the rationale for industrial policies as well as a discussion of their relevance in a European context.
9. Pekkarinen *et al.* (1992) also argue that in this respect exclusive corporatist

economies, especially during structural crises, may resemble those pluralist economies which adopt dualistic solutions.

10. A further breakdown of active labour market expenditure into separate components is provided by OECD (1988), and is discussed by Jackman *et al.* (1990).

11. The Swedish ALMP system is discussed in greater detail in Robinson (1989) and Layard and Philpott (1991). In addition to these authors, the unemployment insurance system is covered in detail by Bjorklund *et al.* (1991).

12. Employment training in Sweden is reviewed by Standing (1988). He sounds a sceptical note about the efficiency of the system, arguing that training has tended to be viewed as an alternative to unemployment rather than as a mechanism for improving efficiency, and thus that the social rate of return may have been low.

13. The productivity 'slowdown' in the US has been extensively discussed, for example Bowles *et al.* (1983), Clark (1984). In the UK the evidence for a 1980s Thatcher productivity miracle is very mixed. The most sophisticated recent analyses (Crafts 1991, Stoneman and Francis 1992) are very sceptical that British productivity performance in the 1980s was exceptional.

14. The Social Chapter of the Maastricht Treaty is indicative of this. Britain's opt-out of this element of the European integration process highlights concern that its policy-makers remain wedded to the efficacy of the 'labour flexibility' strategy.

15. Soskice's main example, which acts as a model for 'flexibly coordinated systems' is Germany.

16. Detailed discussion of the development of industrial policies in corporatist economies is provided by Landesmann (1992). Detailed comparisons between corporatist and non-corporatist cases are provided by Pontusson (1991) for Sweden and France, and by Kenworthy (1990) for Sweden, Japan and Germany. A very sceptical empirical assessment of the effectiveness of Swedish industrial policies is provided by Carlsson (1983).

17. For an extensive discussion of this reversal in the United States context see Levy (1987) and Bluestone and Harrison (1988).

18. Rowthorn (1992b) finds that wage dispersion amongst manufacturing industries declined slightly between 1973 and 1985: albeit from a very high level. There is some evidence, however, that, from the point of view of earnings distribution, there was some increase in inequality over the period (Green, Henley and Tsakalotos 1992).

19. To explain the difference with Sweden, when so much of the institutional corporatist framework is similar, political scientists have pointed to the extent to which the social democratic parties have been hegemonic in their respective corporatist arrangements (Esping-Andersen 1985).

20. Green, Henley and Tsakalotos (1992) also provide a more extensive discussion of the relationship between corporatism and social welfare expenditure.

21. As already mentioned, in the case of Austria this was achieved through the export of unemployment through the reduced opportunities for foreign-worker employment (Guger 1992).

22. It is important to point out, though, that the social democratic model is not without its costs and difficulties; for example: the high level of female absenteeism despite very high participation in Sweden (Esping-Andersen 1985).

6. Corporatism and Macroeconomic Policy

In the previous two chapters we have suggested that durable corporatist arrangements extend beyond negotiations to improve the unemployment–real wage trade-off. Corporatism inherently leads to a broadening of the bargaining agenda to cover other areas of economic policy. This chapter develops this theme by examining the role of macroeconomic stabilization policy in corporatist economies and the question of why, in corporatist economies, we might observe greater interdependence of macroeconomic and other policies. It is this broadening and interdependence of policy concerns into areas beyond wage determination which dismays many critics of corporatism. So, in this chapter we assess the criticisms made of corporatist arrangements as they relate to macroeconomic policy formulation.

The first section reviews the literature on the policy credibility and time consistency (PCTC) of macroeconomic management. This literature argues that, rather than state policy-makers having discretion to negotiate and bargain with organized interests, the optimum stabilization strategy is to ensure that policy-makers enjoy little room for manoeuvre and that their actions should be limited through the consistent enforcement of policy rules. Behind this is a concern to uphold the market mechanism as the predominant means of coordinating economic activity at the macroeconomic level. By examining the coherence of these ideas we assess some of the criticisms of allowing organized interests to influence macroeconomic policy.

The next section examines the practice of macroeconomic policy in corporatist economies. Discretionary macroeconomic policy has provided a strong pillar of support for corporatist arrangements and has allowed improvements in economic performance. The final section casts a wider net by considering the underlying differences between a corporatist approach and one based on policy rules. These differences revolve around the extent to which democratic processes are allowed to impinge on economic policy. By looking at these differences we confront directly some of the arguments of those, in particular the 'public choice' school, who are critical of corporatist arrangements.

NEW CLASSICAL MACROECONOMICS AND POLICY RULES

The argument against discretionary macroeconomic policy and in favour of a minimalist role for state economic intervention is particularly associated with monetarism, and more recently with new classical macroeconomics. At the heart of new classical models is the idea, discussed in Chapter 2, that the market economy has strong equilibrating tendencies and will work well if 'rigidities' and 'imperfections' are removed. If this proposition is correct then state intervention, in the form of corporatist arrangements or in other forms, is nonsensical – there is literally no need for it. In the area of macroeconomic policy an implication of this is that policy-makers should target monetary variables rather than real variables. By controlling the money supply the authorities can control inflation and provide the best framework for market activity to generate economic growth. In the absence of 'imperfections' the real economy will function best if optimizing economic agents are left to their own devices.

In new classical models stabilization policy is typically ineffective and a credible disinflationary strategy can reduce inflation with no output cost (Sargent and Wallace 1975). Models which incorporate total policy ineffectiveness can been seen as more radical versions of the monetarist model behind Friedman's original critique of the Phillips curve (Friedman 1968). Friedman was prepared to countenance some policy effectiveness in the short run and so his model implied some initial output cost to any disinflationary strategy. However, for our purposes, the differences between the monetarist and new classical models need not be exaggerated.[1] Monetarists in general, and Friedman in particular, have argued since the 1950s that monetary policy is best undertaken using a simple policy rule.

However, this preference for rules over discretion has developed considerably in the 1980s in the literature on policy credibility and time consistency of policy.[2] The essence of this approach is illustrated by a simple non-economic analogy. Mankiw (1990) compares the public policy issues faced by monetary authorities with that of negotiators who have to deal with hostage-takers. It could be argued that hostage crises could be eliminated once and for all by always refusing to negotiate with the hostage-takers. The insight of the PCTC literature is that the mere announcement of such a strategy is unlikely to prove sufficient to ensure its success. Hostage-takers may believe, and they may be proved correct, that in an actual hostage crisis the authorities, irrespective of the previously announced policy, may be tempted to negotiate because of political pressure to resolve the crisis. Therefore, the remedy to hostage-taking lies in ensuring the authorities are allowed no discretion to negotiate.

The relevance of this to the control of inflation is that an announcement by the authorities of strict monetary targets may not be credible. One reason for this may be that, if the government sets monetary targets that are believed and acted upon by other agents in the economy, it has an incentive to allow the money supply to increase above those targets in the short run, thereby reducing unemployment below its natural level. The question arises of why within the new classical/monetarist framework, with a vertical long-run aggregate supply curve, anybody should seek to reduce unemployment below its natural rate. The answers have not been particularly convincing – see Goodhart (1989). But if this incentive to cheat is understood by rational agents, then the monetary targets will be disbelieved and the credibility of the strategy undermined. The approach has been developed to incorporate, for example, uncertainty about the nature of the government and the establishment of reputation by governments.[3] However, the basic conclusion of the literature remains that it is desirable to remove the discretionary power of governments by binding their actions to a fixed policy rule (Mankiw 1990).

The PCTC literature is concerned with understanding the political processes which allow the growth of the money supply, and thus also inflation, to get out of control. This interest in political processes may seem to contradict the opinion expressed in Chapter 2 that much of neoclassical economics exhibits rather autarkic tendencies. However, the PCTC approach is very specific in its interest in the political process. Tabellini (1987) points out that new classical economists are very precise about the questions asked of political scientists. They are solely concerned with the way in which decisions are reached by monetary authorities. The analysis used to reach an understanding of that decision process is one which emphasizes the incentives and constraints faced by individual decision-makers. The virtue of the PCTC literature, according to Tabellini, is that its game-theoretic approach focuses attention on the game between the monetary authorities and the private sector. An approach which explicitly considers conflict over income distribution, institutional aspects of labour markets etc. is rejected. Tabellini rejects the view that price stability is a public good, and that inflation results from the possibility of conflict over income distribution through price formation in product and labour markets. In his words this confuses

> absolute with relative prices: in the presence of a nominal anchor provided by the monetary authorities, the bargaining process of contracting parties determines only relative prices and not their absolute level. (Tabellini 1987, p. 459)

This is a restatement of the familiar Friedmanite position that inflation is always and everywhere a monetary phenomenon. If the monetary authorities stand their ground by not giving in to the demands of organized interest groups to print money, then there can be no inflationary problem – just as it is clear, in the earlier analogy, that hostage-taking will cease when the authorities spell it out that no negotiation will be undertaken.

It cannot be over-emphasized that the simple logic of the PCTC literature is derived from its monetarist view of the world. This view assumes perfect markets, which always clear to equate supply and demand. These in turn ensure that the reduction of inflation is painless, if policy is credible. As we argued in Chapter 2, it is all too easy to believe that when all markets clear the result will be accepted by market participants and therefore harmony will prevail. If capitalist economies are free from conflict over income distribution, and if market forces can be relied on to bring about full-employment equilibrium, then theories of inflation need only address a limited number of issues. They are confined to such problems as information and coordination failures, expectational inconsistencies and the problem of time inconsistency. If this is so then the regulation of organized interests through corporatist institutions is at best an irrelevance.

But the implications of economic and social institutions for the determination of price stability cannot be wished away by definition or by assumption. The new classical explanation of inflation assumes all that is of interest away and produces an analysis that is too simplistic. In particular, economic agents may not passively accept market outcomes but may rather attempt to organize, in Goldthorpe's phrase, 'against the market'.

It may be the case, as monetarists have argued, that distributional conflict need not result in inflation if the authorities refuse to accommodate it through expansionary monerary policy.[4] However, distributional conflict does pose considerable obstacles to the more sanguine expectations of monetarists. Monetary targets (or exchange rate targets if the exchange rate is the nominal anchor) are often seen as a threat to everybody in general but nobody in particular (Layard 1990). For example, the threat that a wage increase may lead to unemployment (when there is no monetary/exchange-rate accommodation) will not influence all workers with equal weight. Many workers may rationally consider that, even if unemployment goes up, this is unlikely to influence pay and employment determination in their industry or firm. Once again we return to the point that the alternative to centralized wage-bargaining is rarely the textbook neoclassical labour market. Rather, distributional conflict will become manifest in phenomena such as insider power in wage determination. So it can lead to high unemployment, contradicting monetarist expectations concerning the output costs of disinflation.

A more sophisticated interpretation of the preference for pre-announced monetary rules in the 1970s and 1980s suggests that the reality of distributional conflict was not ignored. Bleaney (1985) suggests that monetary policies during this period were a pre-announced signal that levels of employment would not be protected from excessively inflationary wage-bargaining. In other words, the use of rules constituted an informal incomes policy which would remain in place until wage-bargaining moderated, signalling that only once wage pressure had abated would macroeconomic policy return to is conventional objective of controlling the level of output. So, for example, it was frequently stated during the brief 1990–1992 period of British membership of the European Exchange Rate Mechanism that a fixed exchange rate would require severe wage discipline before the recessionary conditions of the time could be brought to an end. Thus, attempts to reduce inflation, in the absence of other mechanisms for controlling distributional conflict in liberal economies, have since the 1970s relied on restrictive aggregate demand policies. These in turn have led, as they did in the early 1920s, to high unemployment and low rates of capacity utilization, investment and productivity growth (Cornwall 1987).

The fact that output costs are much higher than monetarism predicts suggests there are two important implications of the use of monetary rules to control inflation. Firstly, the transmission mechanism between the money supply and prices is rather different from that envisaged in the monetarist literature. Secondly, the reduction in inflation may prove to be highly conditional and temporary. Goldthorpe (1987) states that, if a period of monetary contraction reduces wage claims, wage moderation may have occurred because of the shift in relative bargaining power between employers and workers in a depressed labour market. It does not indicate a downward shift in inflationary expectations because of workers' 'conversion' to the logic of monetarist macroeconomics. This means that the underlying causes of inflation have been suppressed rather than cured.

To illustrate the limitations of the PCTC literature consider an analogy not from politics but from psychology. Some of these criticisms of PCTC mirror the Freudian critique of behaviourist theories. In very simple terms, Freudians are critical of behaviourists for concentrating too much on symptoms, preferring to examine the underlying psychological structures in order to gain a better understanding of the symptoms. For example, a Freudian might be critical of a behaviourist technique to sort out someone's nervous tic fearing that the underlying neurosis may merely re-emerge in a different form.

The simplicity of the PCTC prescription, although theoretically ingenious, may be misleading. Returning to Mankiw's analogy, a response to the problem of hostage-taking relies on an understanding of the underlying cause of discontent, the internal interest of the parties involved, the international relations context and so on. It may not just rest with the appropriate design of incentive structures to ensure that governments do not negotiate. If it did, a strategy which ends hostage-taking may merely lead to increases in other forms of terrorist activity. The same point applies in the case of inflation. Without an accurate understanding of the process of inflation generation, and in particular the importance of distributional conflict over income distribution, then monetary rules will merely suppress inflation and will not provide the longer-term goal of sustained and stable growth.[5]

For this reason the case for discretionary macroeconomic policy, formulated in the context of a consensual, corporatist environment, is not undermined by the recent preoccupation of new classical macroeconomics with 'rules' and policy 'credibility'. Corporatism, if successful, has the ability to deal directly with distributional conflict. It therefore has the potential to deal directly with the macroeconomic problems that emerge from that conflict. Furthermore, we have seen that corporatist policy-making is more likely to be successful if the interdependence of macroeconomic, industrial and social policies is taken seriously. Distributional conflict is not easily resolved in a context of deflation, declining investment and poor growth. A coordinated response may be necessary to confront both inflation and poor growth. The best anti-inflationary strategy may be one based on achieving a working social consensus over appropriate ways to increase investment and therefore improve growth prospects.

There are other issues which arise from the differences between the rules-based policy approach and the consensual corporatist approach. These concern the appropriate role of the state and the relationship between political democracy and the formulation and conduct of economic policy. Before examining these we turn first to a brief review of the empirical evidence on the effectiveness of rules and policy credibility and to an examination of how macroeconomic policy has been carried out in corporatist economies.

DIFFERENCES IN MACROECONOMIC POLICY IN CORPORATIST AND LIBERAL ECONOMIES

We begin this section with some general evidence on rules and their success or otherwise in liberal economies in the 1980s and then look at corporatist economies to determine whether their preference for discretionary macroeconomic policy has been detrimental.

A casual investigation of the success of monetary targeting in halting moderate inflations does not provide much comfort for the supporters of PCTC approach. The monetarist experiments in the early 1980s in the UK, US and Denmark resulted in very high output and employment costs.[6] The literature on more sophisticated econometric testing of the credibility and time consistency hypothesis provides support that is very slight in comparison to the size of the theoretical work on the subject.[7] The implication of the PCTC literature is that over a period of time inflation will be lower when rules have been adopted in preference to discretion. There would seem to be little hard evidence for this proposition, irrespective of whether we look at the issue across time, say for OECD countries as a whole, or alternatively we compare the record of various OECD countries.

The obvious comparison is between the 1950s and 1960s, when discretionary monetary and fiscal policy was predominant, with the period after the first oil crisis, when monetary targeting began to be practised. The second period is associated with higher rates of inflation even though the switch to pre-announced monetary growth rates occurred. The question remains of why inflation was not more of a problem in the earlier discretion-dominated period.[8] The experience of the US from 1979 onwards may also provide a comparison. The Federal Reserve was at its most monetarist in the period 1979–82. After 1982 monetary targets declined in importance. Again the evidence for the PCTC approach here is hardly overwhelming. Krugman (1990) states that the US Federal Reserve's policy after 1982 was highly erratic. At times it allowed money supply growth to reach double-digit rates, at others it was negative, and in consequence monetarist observers, such as Friedman, forecasted accelerating inflation and severe recession. Yet for the US in the second half of the 1980s inflation and growth rates were more stable than during the earlier period.

The evidence from cross-country comparisons is no more convincing. A test that is often considered appropriate is to compare the record of countries which have tight incentive structures on the monetary authorities with those which do not. The obvious examples of the former are countries with an independent central bank. While there are economies, such as Germany, which have an independent central bank and low inflation, there are other low-inflation countries, such as Japan, where the central bank has virtually no independence from the government. As we have seen in earlier chapters, alternative institutions, such as centralized wage-bargaining or arrangements to promote social consensus, are just as able to achieve both lower inflation and more stable growth. If such features are empirically important then a focus on the nature of monetary institutions is too narrow.[9]

Of the OECD economies it is the corporatist ones where macroeconomic policy has generally been least bound by the adoption of rules. The evidence is that, as a result, there were periods when macroeconomic policy in these economies successfully complemented other economic policies and led to improved economic performance. The important difference in the approach of corporatist economies is that macroeconomic policy, albeit to differing degrees, has been included in discussions between the social partners. Consequently macroeconomic policy has not tended to act as a constraint set independently of the wage bargain, nor has it worked to undermine the corporatist agreement.

It is not possible within the space available to discuss the macroeconomic history of each corporatist economy. Instead, we highlight a number of salient features and examples of the way in which corporatist economies have organized macroeconomic policy. We first outline a stylized description of the role played by macroeconomic policy in the 'Scandinavian model'. This should not be taken as a complete description of all corporatist economies. Instead it is used merely to highlight some of the important issues involved in macroeconomic policy-making in a corporatist framework.

The 'Scandinavian model' of corporatism operates by defining a growth path for earnings. The upper limit of this path is determined by the minimum level of profits required to ensure that firms continue to undertake investment. If wages rise above the upper bound, then investment and productivity growth will fall against the interests of both workers and employers. If wage increases are less than the lower limit, then wage drift will tend to correct it (Faxen 1982). Macroeconomic policy will reflect the fact that most corporatist economies are small open economies which therefore face given international prices for their exports and imports. If the exchange rate is fixed it is possible to define a path for nominal wages which will maintain international competitiveness. The exchange rate can thus act as the nominal anchor in the system which keeps wages and hence prices under control.

However, this does not imply that there is no room for any accommodating exchange rate movement. Korkman (1992) provides two reasons why an accommodating devaluation might prove useful in such a model.[10] Firstly, it helps to reduce uncertainty about future profit levels and in this way encourages investment. The net returns on long-term investment projects could easily become negative where the exchange rate is fixed and an unanticipated wage increase or an unfavourable change in world economic conditions occurs. Thus, with a fixed exchange rate, profits can become uncertain. However, if employers know that the exchange rate can alter to accommodate such shocks, then uncertainty is reduced and hence investment is encouraged. The second advantage of the occasional use of an accommodating exchange rate devaluation is that it can help to reduce the effect of unsustainable nominal wage increases. Devaluation can reduce the real wage, particularly if reinforced by a tighter monetary and fiscal policy which limits the power of trade unions to restore pre-devaluation real wages.

This stylized account of the role of macroeconomic policy in corporatist economies is not a description of all countries at all times. Instead, it highlights the fact that bargaining between state, employers and unions in corporatist economies has an agenda expanded beyond wage determination to include exchange-rate policy, monetary and fiscal policy, investment, growth, productivity and so on. Macroeconomic policy can therefore be formulated to complement wage determination, rather than being taken as an independently set constraint on the bargaining process. A number of specific examples of the way in which macroeconomic policy operated in corporatist economies illustrate this.[11] We look firstly at some examples of the operation of monetary and fiscal policy in corporatist economies and secondly at exchange rate policy.

Scharpf (1984) examines the employment experience of Austria and contrasts it with that of Germany over the 1973–82 period. Table 6.1, using data reported in his article, shows that Austrian employment performance was considerably better than that of Germany. He argues that the poor German employment record can be explained by the fact that the Bundesbank operated independently of the wage-bargaining process. It set a tight monetary policy to control inflation in the aftermath of the first OPEC shock. Wage determination had then to be accommodated to that. However, Scharpf argues, if cost-push inflation arises (as it did in the 1970s due to the oil price increases) and monetary policy is kept very tight to try to control it, then aggregate demand will fall. The moderation of wage demands can do little to

Table 6.1 Employment, budget deficits and interest rates in Austria and Germany, 1973–1982

	Austria			West Germany		
	Employ -ment[1]	Deficit[2]	Real interest rate[3]	Employ -ment[1]	Deficit[2]	Real interest rate[3]
1973	100.0		1.1	100.0		2.3
1974	100.3	1.3	−1.0	98.7	−1.3	2.9
1975	98.5	−2.5	1.6	95.9	−5.7	2.6
1976	98.7	−3.8	2.1	95.1	−3.4	3.7
1977	100.0	−2.4	2.9	94.9	−2.4	2.7
1978	101.3	−2.8	3.6	95.5	−2.5	3.2
1979	102.6	−2.5	3.2	96.8	−2.7	3.3
1980	103.0	−2.0	2.7	97.7	−3.1	3.0
1981	104.4	−1.8	3.5	96.9	−4.0	4.3

Notes:
1. Index 1973=100
2. Total government deficit as percentage of GNP
3. Discount rate minus inflation
Source: Scharpf (1984, Tables 11.2, 11.5, 11.7)

help to maintain employment levels. One interpretation of this is the traditional Keynesian argument that, in cases where employment is constrained by aggregate demand, a cut in wages is not the appropriate response.

This was the scenario in Germany during the 1970s and it goes some way to explaining the rise in unemployment. In contrast, the policy pursued in Austria was one of wage restraint combined with demand reflation. Whereas fiscal policies in Germany and Austria was similar,[12] Table 6.1 shows that monetary policy was much looser in Austria, at least in the immediate aftermath of the oil shock.[13] This accommodating role played by monetary policy contrasts with the German experience and, Scharpf argues, accounts for Austria's better record on unemployment. In short, whereas in Germany the Bundesbank determines monetary policy and the rest of the economy has to accommodate to the tightness of that policy as best it can, in Austria monetary policy was determined as part of the economic concertation process.

Further evidence on the success of corporatist economies in including macroeconomic policy within the corporatist domain is given by Kurzer (1988). She examines the experiences of Austria and Sweden for the post-1974 period and compares them with those of Belgium and The Netherlands. She seeks to explain the better unemployment record of the former countries compared to the latter. Since all four countries are similar in that all have some form of centralized wage-bargaining, there is a need to look beyond wage-bargaining to explain their divergent employment performance. Monetary and fiscal policy in Belgium and The Netherlands was much more deflationary than in Sweden and Austria. This is because the Swedish and Austrian central banks are forced, by the nature of the corporatist arrangments, to cooperate with their governments. In contrast the Belgian and Dutch central banks have much greater independence to pursue their own aims.[14]

The final example which illustrates the view that corporatist economies have been much more successful at tailoring macroeconomic policy towards their needs is one relating to exchange rate policy. Korkman (1992) shows that the Nordic countries and Austria have successfully used exchange rate policy in the implementation of corporatist full-employment strategies. For example, in Sweden and Finland, devaluations were undertaken to help to restore competitiveness and industrial growth and, he argues, they generally succeeded in those aims. In Finland, in particular, investment levels remained high because exchange rate changes ensured an adequate and certain rate of return. Devaluations were usually successful in these two countries because trade unions did not press to restore real wage levels. On occasions when trade unions showed some hostility to devaluation, monetary and fiscal policies were tightened to prevent a wage–price inflation spiral. On other occasions, the unions accepted devaluation as a means of adjusting the level of real wages without affecting pay relativities. In Norway and Austria exchange rate policy has been less accommodating – both have followed a hard-currency policy. In the case of Austria this has been possible because wage restraint has operated so successfully that exchange rate changes were not considered necessary. In Norway it is a result of the fact that industrial development has been dominated by the growth of the off-shore oil and gas sector. Overall, Korkman concludes that there is a close association between exchange rate policies and corporatist policies in these countries. In Austria a fixed exchange rate policy has served as 'a cornerstone of the corporatist system of real wage regulation', and in Sweden and Finland, devaluation has been implemented following agreement between the government, trade unions and monetary authorities.[15]

Thus, in conclusion, these examples show how monetary, fiscal and exchange rate policies have all been brought within the corporatist arrangements of a number of countries. Policy in corporatist economies has not always been more expansionary or accommodating. Rather, macroeconomic policy has been determined within the corporatist domain. As such, it has been able to respond more flexibly to unanticipated changes in economic conditions. Such a flexibility or discretion runs counter to the recommendations of the new classical and PCTC literatures.

From the 1980s onwards, corporatist economies have been under increasing pressure resulting from the internationalization of capital movements and the deregulation of world financial markets. This has implications for the formulation of independent macroeconomic policy in the future. However, such changes do not necessarily negate the importance of discretion and flexibility within corporatist economies for two reasons. Firstly, financial liberalization was a policy choice which a number of corporatist economies opted for in the 1980s. Secondly, the prospects for macroeconomic independence are dependent on other decisions these countries might take, in particular regarding membership of the European Monetary System (EMS) and participation in the proposed Economic and Monetary Union (EMU) of the European Community. If the EFTA/corporatist countries opt to join the EC, and if the EC continues to move towards EMU, then the issue of what kind of macroeconomic policy is optimal will again become important. The EC, as a large monetary area, will have some monetary independence because it will be able to influence the world interest rate. The importance of these pressures and their likely influence on corporatist economies in the 1990s are taken up in the next chapter.

Other institutional arrangements in corporatist economies which have helped in the conduct of macroeconomic policy include the nonindependence of central banks and the relationship between finance and industry. Thus Epstein (1992) argues that monetary policy is determined not only by how the capital–labour relationship is mediated in an economy but also by the above two institutional arrangements and the interaction between them.[16] The examples above showed that a non-independent central bank allowed macroeconomic policy to be brought within the corporatist domain. Epstein concentrates on the relationship between the tightness of monetary policy and central bank independence. He suggests that a more independent central bank will favour a tighter monetary policy.[17] However, in corporatist countries the tightness of monetary policy is of less interest than whether or not monetary policy can be used in a discretionary way. Whether it is tight or loose will depend on the circumstances facing the economy in question. There is no presumption that monetary policy should always be expansionary in corporatist economies. Instead, the desirability of a non-independent central bank is that its policies – monetary, fiscal and exchange rate – are not set independently of the corporatist bargaining process.

The link between monetary policy and the relationship between industry and finance is of greater interest. An obvious distinction here is between the German/Japanese model with close ties between commercial banks and industry and the Anglo-Saxon model where the provision of corporate finance is dominated by the stock market. Epstein argues that, in the first of these, banks have a stronger interest in the performance of domestic industry, and monetary policy will hence be conducted in the interests of the capitalist class as a whole – it can be either tight or loose depending on the state of the economy and the power of labour. In the Anglo-Saxon model, where the links between industry and finance are weaker, the central bank is likely to favour more restrictive monetary policy because its interests are more closely allied to the financial sector than the industrial sector. Whether this applies in practice is a matter of debate – obvious counter-examples are Germany and, at certain times during the 1980s, the UK. In Britain and other countries there is a large and long-standing debate about appropriate finance–industry relations. This revolves around whether the two have different goals and thus policy preferences – with finance favouring a tighter monetary policy and a stronger exchange rate than industry.[18] A number of arguments are made. Firstly, finance may prefer lower inflation and hence a more restrictive monetary policy. Epstein and Schor (1990) cite evidence that suggests that inflation reduces the profits of financial firms, whereas it has less effect on industrial firms. Secondly, in the case where finance is only weakly linked to domestic industry, finance tends to prefer a strong and stable exchange rate. A strong and stable currency is an attractive asset to hold. Hence stability increases the pool of potential business which domestic banks can capture. Finally, where a central bank is keen to promote its country as an international financial centre, it will again tend to favour a restrictive monetary policy and a strong and stable exchange rate. Kurzer (1988) argues that a restrictive monetary and fiscal policy is beneficial to the balance of payments and hence makes it easier for the central bank to stabilize the exchange rate. This, in turn, tends to aid commercial banks and other financial institutions in attracting customers from international markets.

It is beyond our scope here to discuss these points in depth. However, the evidence does indicate that an independent central bank in conjunction with weak finance–industry relations may make it more difficult to incorporate macroeconomic policy into a corporatist dialogue and may lead to macroeconomic outcomes which make any corporatist agreement more difficult to achieve.

ECONOMIC DEMOCRACY AND THE POLITICS OF MACROECONOMIC POLICY

We have contrasted two views on inflation which lead to very different economic policy prescriptions. The first suggests that inflation is fundamentally a monetary phenomenon which can best be controlled through some form of fixed 'rule'. The second sees inflation as a manifestation of distributional conflict and in turn suggests that, if appropriate institutions exist for mediating that conflict, then macroeconomic policy can play a useful part in improving the performance of the real economy. These two views are associated, not only with different underlying theories about the nature of society, but also differences about the extent to which democracy, or democratic procedures, should inform the conduct of economic policy.

The first approach, by advocating policy rules, attempts to constrain the freedom of public authorities. This approach is part of a long-standing tradition and can be compared to the old 'Treasury View' (Clarke 1988). Since the nineteenth century, support for balanced budgets has been based on more than purely economic considerations. It was felt that a balanced budget would provide constitutional protection against state expenditures running out of control or, in more modern parlance, 'fiscal overload'. More recently, economists associated with market liberalism, have argued that the recurring US budget deficit problem can best be prevented through a constitutional amendment requiring balanced budgets.

These ideas are associated with a stance which has often been deeply suspicious about the nature of democratic politics, fearing that the conduct of modern politics leads to insatiable demands for new state spending programmes. These in turn could easily lead to financial instability. This somewhat cynical attitude to the nature of democracy is identified today with the Virginia School public choice literature, associated with James Buchanan and Gordon Tullock.[19]

Market liberals have been concerned about the 'economic consequences of democracy' (Brittan 1977).[20] The more the political sphere is seen as an alternative to market activity, especially in the provision of economic goods and benefits, the more dire are the consequences for economic efficiency. In the terminology of Olson (1982), 'distributional' coalitions, interested in increasing their share of the economic pie, can come to dominate 'productive' coalitions, whose aim is to increase the overall size of that pie. Those pressing for a higher share of the pie may not themselves have to bear the full costs of their actions. Thus, they have an incentive to press for larger and larger increases in government expenditure in their favour. The large literature on electoral business cycles emphasizes the electoral process, and on the assembling of 'arithmetic coalitions', all of whom have to be paid off after a successful election (Mullard 1992).[21]

It is, therefore, not surprising that market liberals are suspicious of attempts to incorporate organized interests into economic policy-making and are hostile to corporatist arrangements. As Mullard (1992) notes, their objection is that such supra-market arrangements distort the individual's right to choose, and place excessive expectations on government action. The result, they argue, is high taxation and high and growing levels of public expenditure. Mullard also points to the importance of the Conservative tradition, in which the possibility of distributional conflict is treated much more seriously. A recognition of this problem is usually associated with the other side of the political spectrum, but here it offers a rationale for opposition to corporatism. In the Conservative tradition the state performs the important role of preserving 'order'. To undertake this role, it must not risk compromising the authority and the legitimacy of the state by involvement with organized interests. British Conservative Party ideology in the 1980s incorporated both market liberal and Conservative themes in its opposition to what was seen as the corporatism of the 1960s and 1970s.

For some, then, 'rules' can play a useful function and set outside limits on the extent to which authorities may have discretion to react to organized interests and popular demands. In practice these limits can be prescribed in various forms: a fixed monetary rule, an independent central bank or, in extreme cases a return to the gold standard (supported by, amongst others, Robert Mundell). Each is derived from a common philosophical position.

Apart from an implicit distrust of democratic control over the policy-making process, there is a more obvious flaw in the approach. Whatever the precise form the policy 'rule' takes, it is unlikely to generate widespread acceptance or to be considered politically neutral. Goldthorpe (1987) argues that adherence to a strict monetary policy implies an underwriting by the government of the structural *status quo*, of current levels of market power and market advantage. However, if the latter are partly responsible for inflationary outcomes then monetary rules may achieve price stability but, as already discussed, at a price of suppressing rather than resolving distributional conflict. The government's monetary rule response will be seen, at least by those who bear the brunt of the costs of recession, as a partisan involvement in that conflict.

Monetarism is, thus, itself an exercise in political economy. It entails an individualistic philosophy, and a commitment to private ownership and minimal state interference. It contrasts with the corporatist strategy of inclusion, by seeking to weaken the capacity of certain groups to organize and act 'against the market' and thus leads to trade unions and business pursuing exclusionary, or dualistic, strategies. In supply-side policy form, the political economy of this exercise may be even more explicit. For example, it may entail, as in the British case, a legislative programme aimed at reducing trade union power. But efforts to detach the operation of the market place from politics tend to be spurious. In Maier and Lindberg's (1985) view they usually result in a buttressing of profits and managerial prerogatives. In Britain, in the 1980s, such a one-sided strategy included targeting the lowest rates of real income growth on groups who were in a poor position to organize their own defence, such as the unemployed, part-time workers and employees in small firms (Rubery and Wilkinson 1986).

Any particular 'rule' will not only be challenged by relatively disadvantaged social groups. There may also be a regional dimension to the unacceptability of its outcome. An example of this is to be found in the concern expressed about the workings of the proposed European Central Bank to be set up as part of the EMU process. There has been much debate recently concerning whether membership of the ERM entails acceptance of the monetary policy of the German Bundesbank. This makes it unlikely that the outcome of any monetary independence of the new European bank could easily appeal to both Germany and other states such as France and Britain, let alone the poorer economies of the European south. An earlier example is to be found in the nineteenth-century monetary integration of the States of the USA. Eichengreen (1990) writes about the early history of the US Federal Reserve and the bitter disputes between 'Easterners', associated with New York and other financial interests (committed to high interest rates), and the 'Westerners' (concerned with the perceived deflationary bias of the Federal Reserve). A similar phenomenon can be detected in British economic history and the dominance of the City (Leys 1985). The resolution of the conflict of interests between finance and industry may lead to the predominance of stock market institutions or to closer involvement of banks in industry. As we have already discussed, the nature of these institutions will affect the potential for successful corporatist arrangements.

CONCLUSION

The search for some credible policy rule, to be adopted with consistency, suggests that a narrow 'technical fix' can resolve macroeconomic problems. But this is a chimera. This technocratic approach is unlikely to acquire general support and any 'solution' that it provides is likely to prove temporary. From a viewpoint which envisages a role for corporatist institutions:

the retreat to a world of private choice implies a Utopia which is wholly unrealistic about the viability of dissolving group interests and the role of public institutions. The real world is constituted of strategic groups able to pursue very narrow and particularized interests which can destabilize the state and harm the general interest. They cannot be wished away nor made to disappear through the legislative process. (Mullard 1992, p.161)

This leads to an alternative view which emphasizes the need for institutions to promote economic consensus about the nature of the economy, the distribution of economic gains and the scope of economic policy. This too can never provide an easy solution. As the literature on corporatism makes clear, the process of consensus-building is not an easy one and is often subject to free-rider problems and breakdown in cooperative agreements. Furthermore, corporatism faces a number of the problems which are brought into focus by the public choice literature. Firstly, the combination of discretionary macroeconomic policy and consensual bargaining through organized interests can exclude various groups in society, such as the elderly, the self-employed or small businesses. This problem was highlighted in the distinction, made earlier, between exclusive and inclusive forms of corporatism. The success of inclusive corporatism in, for example, the Nordic countries demonstrates that this problem is not inevitable.

Secondly, the incorporation of organized interests into economic policy-making may lead to 'distributional' coalitions or, to use Olson's terminology, 'sclerosis' in economic affairs. This will have harmful consequences for technological dynamism, long-run competitiveness and economic growth. The corporatist response to this problem is two-fold. On the one hand, it is far from proven that the exclusion of organized interests will provide improved economic performance. On the other hand, as already made clear, it is possible for consensual bargaining to be based on a desire to maximize long-run joint gains through increased investment. If organized interests can cooperate with the state to promote long-term growth then this will have the additional advantage of alleviating distributional conflict. Without such conflict inflationary pressures will be less severe and so economic policy-makers can avoid the adoption of anti-inflationary strategies which are so often inimical to investment and growth (Maier and Lindberg 1985).

Discretionary macroeconomic policy can be a useful adjunct to corporatist arrangements without necessarily leading to problems of fiscal overload, inflation and electoral business cycles. This does not mean that corporatist economies enjoy fewer constraints on economic policy-making. Financial disequilibrium would be a clear sign that important priorities were not being met.[22] What is not present in successful corporatism is any inherent contradiction between the simultaneous existence of macroeconomic discretion and control over the processes which generate inflation.

There is one final attractive feature of corporatism as it might affect macroeconomic policy. It has a less cynical attitude towards democratic politics. Within corporatist economies economic policy results from democratic compromise, with participation at all levels of the state and society. In contrast, the public choice school, with its preference for economic liberalism, takes 'the preferences of individuals about politics and policies as fixed and unchanging' (Dearlove 1989, p. 226). This is not surprising since public choice theory is an application of the neoclassical economic world to political analysis. As such, it shares with neoclassical economics the difficulties of understanding and modelling institutions which were discussed in Chapter 2.

This limitation is particularly serious with respect to how democratic political institutions are dealt with in the public choice literature. Dearlove (1989) argues that it treats politics as a simple matter of individual preference aggregation,[23] with no weight given to '[d]iscussion; bargaining and reconciliation; the alteration of preferences in the face of divergences and interaction; the communal context; and individuals' views on the common interest' (op. cit., pp. 226–7).

There will necessarily be constraints on macroeconomic policy in corporatist economies, just as there are in more decentralized, liberal economies. But the expansion of the democratic process with the aim of generating economic consensus means that these constraints will not be seen as arbitrary or exogenous, set by some 'rule'. Rather, they will be seen as democratically self-imposed – people are more likely to accept the limitations of economic policy if they feel that they have had some say in determining those limitations through the process of economic concertation. This is true whether participatory decision-making is at the workplace level, or at the level of a national forum to establish consensus over macroeconomic problems and solutions.

NOTES

1. There are, of course, some important methodological differences between the monetarist and new classical schools. Hoover (1988) provides an excellent introduction to new classical theory and its differences from monetarism.
2. Amongst the most important articles in the PCTC literature are Kydland and Prescott (1977), Barro and Gordon (1983), Backus and Driffill (1985) and Rogoff (1985).
3. A thorough survey of theoretical and empirical developments in the PCTC approach is provided by Blackburn and Christensen (1989).
4. Strictly speaking it is possible for the banking system to initiate an increase in the money supply through credit expansion, but the monetary authorities need not react to such a phenomenon in a passive manner. If determined the authorities could bring monetary targeting to bear on the banking system.
5. For a theoretical analysis of inflation as the outcome of distributional conflict, in the context of imperfectly competitive market structures, see Rowthorn (1977) and Sawyer (1989, Chapter 11).
6. It is always possible to claim that any lack of success in practice was due to the policy's lack of credibility. In this sense it is very difficult to disprove the PCTC approach.
7. This is discussed in Blackburn and Christensen (1989).
8. For further discussion of this see MacDonald and Milbourne (1990).
9. As Peter Hall concludes, even in Germany low inflation may be more due to coordinated wage bargaining than the existence of an independent central bank: 'setting up an independent central bank that tries to impose its views on a reluctant government and a recalcitrant workforce is no more than a second best solution to problems that need to be tackled in wider terms' (*The Independent*, 21 January 1993).
10. This stylized account illustrates how the Scandinavian model operated in certain corporatist economies for most of the post-war period. Recent developments, particularly with respect to the liberalization of capital flows in some corporatist economies, have made a policy of occasionally changing the exchange rate much harder to implement. We discuss the implications of some of these recent developments later.
11. Macroeconomic policy in corporatist economies has not always been perfectly tailored to fit in with the other aims of agents in the economy. However, these historical episodes illustrate how the process of bringing macroeconomic policy into the discussions between social partners can help in certain instances to produce better economic performance.
12. Whereas the Federal government deficit as a percentage of GNP in Austria was consistently higher than in Germany from 1974–82, the Länder's (regional government) budget deficits were consistently higher in Germany (Scharpf 1984). Thus, Scharpf argues that the total government deficits of both countries were much the same (see Table 6.1). However, this evidence is not entirely conclusive. If the German economy was operating at less than full employment whereas the Austrian economy was at full employment, then comparing unadjusted total government deficits will not give us an accurate indication of the relative fiscal stance. It is more appropriate to compare, say, a full-employment budget deficit for both countries. In other words, the German fiscal deficit might be the result of the economy being at less than full employment and not because of a more expansionary fiscal policy.
13. Austrian exchange rate policy has consisted of pegging its exchange rate to the Deutschmark (because of the importance of Germany as a trading partner). However, the strength of the peg has varied over time. For example, after 1977 it became more formal, with the result that the room for independence in monetary policy narrowed. In addition there was a sharp separation between market interest rates linked to the

exchange rate policy and interest rates faced by firms. The latter were kept much lower through subsidized credit facilities (Kurzer 1988).

14. A possible criticism of such a view is that The Netherlands and Belgium were constrained by membership of the EMS. However, Kurzer (1988) is quite careful to take this into account. She divides the countries into two groups according to exchange rate policy. She, thus, compares Belgium (which devalued within the EMS) with Sweden (which followed a fixed exchange rate policy with occasional devaluations); and Austria with The Netherlands since these latter two both followed a policy of pegging to the DM. In both cases, monetary and fiscal policy was tighter in the less corporatist economies relative to the more corporatist economies.

15. However, in the concluding chapter we discuss the view that the Swedish devaluation in the 1980s was successful in the short run but was against the logic of the Rehn–Meidner model in the long run.

16. See also Epstein and Schor (1990). Kurzer (1988) also makes the point that the question of central bank independence and the relationship between industry and finance is important to determining the tightness of monetary policy.

17. Epstein's (1992) empirical evidence on the relationship between an independent central bank and monetary stance draws on a small number of observations from a limited sample of countries and should probably be taken merely as an indication of important underlying relationships that need further case study attention.

18. See Ingham (1984). There may be a conflict within industry – between domestically-oriented producers and transnational corporations. Kurzer (1988) argues that the latter will have similar objectives as finance – namely a stable exchange rate and low inflation.

19. The evils of Keynesian discretionary policy in this respect are articulated in Buchanan and Wagner (1977). For a critical review of the public choice literature, see Dearlove (1989).

20. For a good introductory review, see Mullard (1992, especially Chapters 1 and 4).

21. See Nordhaus (1975), Frey and Schneider (1975), Wagner (1977) and Macrae (1977). A review of these models is provided by Locksley (1980). The major difficulty, in the present context, with these models is the assumption a homogeneous electorate where each individual voter is able to exert the same degree of influence over the government.

22. On the link between macroeconomic control and consensual politics, see Tsakalotos (1991).

23. As texts on social choice such as Sugden (1981) and Craven (1992) show, this is a far from simple problem.

7. Conclusions: Problems and Prospects

Developments, both economic and political, in the traditionally highly corporatist economies suggest that the corporatist 'model' is under considerable strain. Some commentators have even announced the end of the line for a uniquely social corporatist mode of economic policy formulation. The purpose of this final concluding chapter is to address the reasons for an alleged decline in the viability of corporatism and to speculate about the extent and form of its survival in the future.

Corporatism is under pressure from forces both external and internal to the economies concerned. From outside the corporatist economies have found themselves under increasing pressure from the growing integration of the world and particularly the European economy. This has placed increasing constraints on the ability of corporatist economies to pursue macroeconomic policies which conflict with the more deflationary bias to macroeconomic policy in the rest of Europe. The background to this is that there is strong internal pressure in a number of the corporatist economies to accede to European Community membership and participate in the European economic integration process. In addition the internationalization of production and growth in transnational corporations, both domestic-based and foreign-based, has opened the alternative strategy of 'exit' rather than 'voice' to employers. If transnational employers within corporatist economies perceive that centralization is no longer in their own immediate interest then they can shift production and employment elsewhere. A further external pressure on corporatist economies arising from the nature of production may have come about because of the shift away from traditional mass-production technologies to forms of 'flexible specialization'. This has increased the tension between the need for centralization in pursuit of macroeconomic goals and the need for decentralization in order to implement the degree of labour flexibility required by new production methods. Flexible specialization may, as some argue, provide a fertile ground in which to cultivate

170

more micro-corporatist forms of worker participation, but it is open to question whether corporatism can continue to succeed at the macroeconomic level if it is to be based on a bottom-up form of worker involvement.

Internal pressure for decentralization has arisen because one or more of the parties to the corporatist compromise have in the 1980s become less convinced that the future long-run benefits will materialize from a continued commitment to corporatist strategies. In the case of organized labour, workers, or more precisely different sub-groups of workers have come to view a policy of accepting post-tax income restraint as no longer one which will maximize their long-run individual well-being, broadly defined. In the case of employers, as corporatism has evolved they have become concerned that the objectives of the social democratic/trade union movement will be extended, among other things, in the direction of social control over investment. The most explicit manifestation of this phenomenon was in the overt hostility of Swedish employers to the LO's proposal for wage-earner investment funds.

While this may present a rather pessimistic view of the prospects for a distinctively corporatist form of macroeconomic policy formulation it is important to emphasize once again the past achievements of the highly corporatist economies as presented at the very beginning of this book. They have been able to maintain high levels of employment and low levels of inequality. They have achieved this in the face of a world economy which in the last two decades has been unable to secure a return to the stable non-inflationary growth of the quarter century which followed the end of the Second World War. These past successes of corporatism illustrate very persuasively that an answer to the question of why economic performance differs across countries must take into account the factor of appropriate institutional design. While any institutional structure may have its failings, corporatism in the 1970s and 1980s succeeded where more liberal forms of economic organization so manifestly failed. This brings us to a final issue which must inevitably be addressed in any discussion of the comparative merits of different forms of economic organization – namely, whether corporatism is universalizable. If the European Community, or the individual members of it, were to adopt better-developed corporatist institutions would a solution (at least in part) be found to stubbornly high rates of unemployment?

MACROECONOMIC INTERDEPENDENCE

Compared with the 1960s, the world economy in the 1990s is much more highly integrated. This is true despite the fact that until the collapse of the Bretton Woods system in the early 1970s the international exchange rates of the developed world were quite rigidly fixed. In the 1990s trade flows are much larger and, whereas at the height of the post-war 'golden age' the majority of international capital movements were trade-related, they are now absolutely and proportionately much larger and dominated by speculative currency flows. As the 1992 British exit from the European exchange rate mechanism illustrates, international capital movements now have a much enhanced ability to undermine the macroeconomic autonomy of national governments. In addition within Europe the total removal of trade restrictions associated with the completion of the Single European Market has the aim of increasing further the volume of intra-EC trade. If the Europe Community succeeds in its aim, as stated in the 1991 Maastricht agreement, of the establishment of a European monetary union and a single financial area (and at the time of writing it is far from clear that it will), then the scope for monetary and possibly fiscal autonomy will be eliminated.[1] Even prior to the achievement of these aims ERM membership has for many European states severely constrained macroeconomic autonomy. The need for a tight monetary stance in one country may limit the scope of another to overcome an external deflationary bias which imposes suboptimal domestic economic performance. The ability to 'go it alone' for growth is limited and will in any case require sustained currency depreciation with concomitant consequences for the preservation of domestic price stability. Although the highly corporatist economies of EFTA at present remain outside the EC they have not been immune from the same problems.

There are specifically three potential sources of increased international interdependence between the corporatist group and other developed economies, particularly in Europe. The growing importance of all of these makes it increasingly difficult for corporatist economies to adopt independent macroeconomic strategies to maintain low unemployment in the face of a deflationary bias elsewhere. They are the growing volume of trade, the increased size of international capital movements and the importance of the exchange rate regime. All three

Table 7.1 Growth and structure of trade in corporatist economies

	Austria	Norway	Sweden	Finland
Imports as % of GDP				
1960	25.0	43.1	23.4	23.2
1970	30.2	43.1	24.5	26.9
1980	38.8	41.1	31.5	33.8
1989	39.5	37.6	32.0	25.3
Exports as % of GDP				
1960	24.3	41.3	22.8	22.5
1970	31.1	41.8	24.0	25.7
1980	36.8	47.3	29.6	33.0
1989	40.0	41.8	32.6	23.6
Source of imports as % of total, 1989				
EC	69.2	42.6	55.6	44.2
Other OECD	16.9	34.4	17.2	33.8
Rest of world	13.9	23.0	27.2	22.0
Destination of exports as % of total, 1989				
EC	66.7	63.9	53.7	42.8
Other OECD	18.0	26.6	19.4	31.3
Rest of world	15.3	9.5	26.9	25.9

Source: OECD National Accounts and Economic Surveys

have already been touched on.

The highly corporatist economies all have an historically long-established high degree of openness. Their small size has necessitated a reliance on imports in areas where they possessed comparative advantage and a high degree of industrial specialization. A dependence on the ability to trade in turn entails a large degree of economic dependence on the level of aggregate demand in importing economies. Table 7.1 shows the growth in the share of imports and exports in GDP for the four most highly corporatist economies between 1960 and

1989. The growth in the importance of trade is most pronounced for Austria and Sweden. Norway was already by 1960 a very open economy. Finland records a strong growth in the importance of trade until the 1980s. By 1989 it was beginning to suffer from the effects of the stagnant Soviet economy. Finland has a heavy reliance on its large neighbour for trade, and is therefore particularly vulnerable to economic collapse in Russia. The table also shows the breakdown of imports and exports by source and destination in 1989. In all cases the economies are particularly reliant on the rest of Europe as an export market. Finland is relatively less reliant than the other three, but this reduced share is made up by a much larger share of its exports going to former Eastern Bloc economies, particularly Russia.

Growth in trade between countries leads to increased spillover effects and therefore to a greater degree of interdependence. One implication of such interdependence is that there may be a bias towards fiscal conservatism in a more integrated European Community (Goodhart 1990). This is because any attempt by one country at uncoordinated expansion of government spending generates benefits for a trading partner and therefore domestic income does not increase as much and is therefore unlikely to generate significant additional tax revenues. Macroeconomic policy formulation within Europe will suffer from a prisoners' dilemma problem, in that countries will wish to avoid uncoordinated expansion. Applying this to the relationship between the corporatist economies and the EC suggests that it will be very difficult for corporatist economies to successfully pursue a more expansionary fiscal policy to maintain low rates of unemployment and counter this fiscal conservatism.

Free capital movement will undermine the full employment strategies of the corporatist economies for a number of reasons. Firstly, an economy which wishes a looser monetary stance than elsewhere in order to encourage investment will find that policy unsustainable since capital will flow out. Interest rates will need to be high and will therefore cease to operate as an effective policy instrument for stimulating investment. Secondly, capital flows may undermine the egalitarianism of corporatist economies. A commitment to egalitarianism may be a precondition for workers acceptance of a corporatist compromise. However, the high marginal tax rates and compressed wage differentials that this may entail may be perceived as detrimental to wealth-holders who in turn may move capital offshore. The high marginal rates of tax in Sweden (up to 72 percent in 1989) was one factor in the victory of the centre-right in the 1991 election. Thirdly, capital flows, as already mentioned, may very quickly undermine any exchange rate target policy. Finally, an increased ability by companies to access international capital markets may undermine their commitment to more long-term and intimate national-based systems of credit allocation, reducing the ability of the corporatist concertation process to influence the direction and scope of investment (Teague and Grahl 1992).

One solution to the adverse problems for domestic macroeconomic policy generated by increased economic interdependence may be found in the use of capital controls. Capital controls may help prevent destabilizing capital flight that may result from unilaterally adopting a monetary policy that becomes relatively looser than elsewhere. Most economies, including the corporatist ones, have therefore maintained capital controls until the 1980s. But stage 1 of the EC plan for economic and monetary union envisages total removal of capital controls throughout the EC. The prospective EC membership of the corporatist economies will require acceptance of this.[2]

The third channel of interdependence is the exchange rate regime. Orthodox economic theory suggests that flexible exchange rates allow for more independent economic policy. As discussed in Chapter 6, all the corporatist economies have attempted to pursue fixed exchange rate policies. Indeed, a fixed exchange rate was seen as a cornerstone to the corporatist model since it was required in order to rule out the route of currency depreciation to accommodate inflationary wage pressure. A hard-currency policy has been most consistently pursued in Austria, due to it physical proximity to Germany. The Scandinavian economies have also attempted to fixed currencies although they have been prepared to countenance periodic devaluations. Pontusson (1992b) argues that the 1982 Swedish devaluation, which marked the restoration of a Social Democratic government, was effective in restoring competitiveness and balance of payments equilibrium. Devaluation entailed a restoration of profits in exporting industries. However, this redistribution away from wages fuelled inflationary wage demands from workers in those sectors, undermining the ability of national union leaders to continue to press for a commitment to the solidaristic wages policy. In a number of ways the 1982 devaluation was against the logic of the Rehn–Meidner model, not only because it allowed wage drift but also because it removed the pressure on firms to seek productivity increases as a way of ensuring future profits.[3]

Since the mid-1980s Norway, Sweden and Finland have all pursued policies of trying to maintain a fixed parity against the ECU. Sweden and Finland in particular had to abandon this policy in the face of huge adverse speculative pressure and currency market turmoil in the autumn of 1992. The deflationary bias in economic policy during the late 1980s and 1990s presents serious problems for the stated social corporatist aim of the maintenance of full-employment. Any desire to maintain rates of unemployment far below those of the rest of Europe, as was achieved in the 1970s and early 1980s, requires a monetary and fiscal stance which is more accommodating than in the countries to which the corporatist currencies are pegged. This suggests a growing inconsistency between the full employment goal and exchange rate policy, which brings home very clearly the difficulties of a 'go-it-alone' strategy. It is widely thought that flexible exchange rates may offer some degree of economic insulation. However, abandonment of the currency peg may in turn require a tightening in domestic policy in order to contain the inflationary pressure of devaluation, particularly if, as we shall see shortly, the centralized system of wage restraint is also under strong internal pressures. The choice of appropriate exchange rate policy is therefore a difficult one – it is certainly not clear that opting for more flexible exchange rates would help the continued achievement of corporatist compromise. Furthermore, accession to the EC and participation in the EMU process will in due course require a return to fixed exchange rates.

It is therefore not surprising that writers such as Cornwall (1987) highlight the importance of an unfavourable world macroeconomic environment on corporatist economies. Corporatism is under pressure from the adoption of liberal/pluralist policies elsewhere in the world – policies which the corporatist economies themselves explicitly rejected in the 1970s and early 1980s.

CHANGES IN THE STRUCTURE OF PRODUCTION

The growing internationalization of capital has been suggested by a number of authors as a detrimental influence on the scope of corporatist arrangements. Transnational companies are less reliant on the well-being of a particular domestic economy and may therefore be less willing to participate in any form of corporatist compromise. As we have argued earlier, the organization of employers is an important aspect of the structural preconditions for successful corporatist compromise. Any division between the interests of national and transnational companies will weaken a centralized employers' organization. Increasing transnationalization of capital will undermine any form of corporatist employment restructuring. Furthermore if, as argued in Chapter 2, corporatism entails establishing long-term trust relationships then these are weakened by the internationalization of capital. These relationships rely on shared national and cultural values and it is not easy to see how these can be replicated at the international level (Teague and Grahl 1992).

In Sweden the Rehn–Meidner plan assumed that excess profits generated by centralized wage restraint in some sectors would accelerate restructuring of employment from declining to high productivity sectors. If those profits are simply repatriated abroad by transnational companies then this aspect of corporatism will fail. Pontusson (1992b) points to evidence that suggests that this may well have occurred in Sweden in the 1980s. While annual foreign net investment in Sweden has shown no upward trend between 1970 and 1990 averaging around 3 billion krona per annum in 1985 prices, Swedish net investment abroad has increased ninefold from 5 billion to 45 billion krona. Consistent with this is a rapid growth in employment in the foreign subsidiaries of Swedish-based companies. The growth of larger, increasingly transnationally based Swedish companies may have been unwittingly encouraged by the state through high company tax rates coupled with very generous investment allowances (*Economist* 1990). Smaller companies did not in the 1980s make enough profit to benefit from these subsidies. Privately owned companies, in particular, have responded to high effective personal and corporate tax rates by moving headquarters abroad. If corporatist countries pursue policies that squeeze post-tax rates of corporate return relative to that obtainable elsewhere then footloose transnational capital may be expected to move.

Further pressure on corporatism has arisen through longer-term changes in the nature of the production process. A number of authors (Pontusson 1992b, Teague and Grahl 1992, Streeck and Schmitter 1991) argue that corporatism is under threat from the retreat from

Fordist mass-production technologies towards forms of 'flexible specialization'. This change has come about because of increased competition between high-wage-cost OECD producers. In order to compete in terms of unit labour cost, in the face of little scope for driving wage costs down to the levels of the newly industrialized economies of the Far East and elsewhere, producers have been forced to develop strategies to improve product quality and customize production to individual customer requirements. This has necessitated developments in the organization of production. Earlier in Chapter 5 we argued that in fact corporatist economies may be better placed to respond to these international pressures because corporatist compromises explicitly rule out the regulation of labour markets through low wages and high unemployment. In consequence corporatist economies might be better placed to support this trend through the development of more participative, micro-corporatist forms of workplace organization. However, if this process in turn generates a dynamic of decentralization, which could undermine the centralized nature of wage restraint and macroeconomic consensus in corporatist economies, then the impact of 'flexible specialization' for these countries might be highly contradictory.

Pontusson (1992b) argues that mass producers in corporatist economies, such as Volvo, have been pushed into introducing decentralized forms of non-pay remuneration, through a process which he calls 'the functional equivalent of wage drift'. These moves have been complemented by pressure for an end to the solidaristic wages policy. In the 1970s and 1980s producers experienced very high rates of labour turnover and absenteeism, and have responded through 'work humanization' efforts, such as workplace arrangements to raise product quality consciousness and worker commitment (team production, 'quality circles', etc.). These are in addition to more direct pay decentralization moves such as bonus systems and profit sharing.

So there is a dilemma faced by corporatist economies, in the face of the declining importance of Fordist mass-production techniques, between maintaining wage solidarity and introducing flexibility in a 'labour-friendly' fashion.[4] It seems inevitable that the pursuit of production flexibility will increase a form of decentralized competition in the external labour market which can only be detrimental to economy-wide levels of employment (Grahl and Teague 1990). Microcorporatist arrangements through which workers participate in discussing non-pay conditions which affect the workplace may well, as Soskice (1991) contends, offer a useful bolster to corporatism at the macro level. However, if centralized bargaining collapses it seems much more unlikely that some effective form of corporatism can be resurrected from the 'bottom up'. Streeck and Schmitter (1991) discuss the possibility of greater geographical decentralization in corporatism, but conclude for several reasons that it would significantly undermine corporatism at the national level.[5]

EMPLOYER INTEREST IN CORPORATISM

The drive for production flexibility is one source of employer pressure on the centralized nature of corporatist arrangements, originating from increased competition in the global markets. However, there are other factors, internal to corporatist economies, tending towards a waning of employer interest in corporatist compromises, and the strongest demands for greater bargaining decentralization have, in the 1980s, originated from employers' organizations.

In the 1960s tight labour markets presented employers, particularly the larger ones, with problems of wage restraint. Their interest in bargaining centralization was therefore motivated by the view that it could best deliver wage restraint. In the 1980s the concern of employers has been for wage flexibility, for reasons already discussed concerning the changing nature of the production process. In Sweden from 1982 the SAF employers' association secured increasing provision for local flexibility within the centralized wage bargain. Pressure has arisen particularly from the metalworking sector (Lash 1985). Centralized bargaining for white-collar workers failed in 1983, because employers refused to mandate the SAF to bargain for these workers. The centralized bargain failed in 1988 and by 1990 the SAF was refusing to enter into further centralized negotiations (Edin and Holmlund 1992). In the 1980s centralized negotiations failed in Finland to produce a central wage agreement on three occasions (1980, 1983 and 1988). In 1988 the failure was because of union rejection. In Norway centralized bargaining, if faltering, did not fail completely in the 1980s. On occasions, such as after the 1986 devaluation, government intervention has legislated wage control. However, commentators (Pekkarinen 1992, Rødseth and Holden 1990) point to the importance of secondary local wage bargains for workers in many sectors, although as noted in Chapter 3 the bargainers seem in the past to have effectively anticipated any local wage drift. Of the corporatist economies, Austria seems to have experienced least employer pressure for decentralization.

Schmitter (1991) argues that the concertation process in corporatist countries has an intrinsic propensity to enlarge the social agenda. As pressure mounts for more and more generous social welfare provision employers will become alarmed by the extent to which corporate taxes will be expected to provide a rising contribution to financing this state expenditure. Kalecki (1943), in his discussion of the politics of full employment, noted that, under more prolonged conditions of full employment and tight labour markets, capitalists would become alarmed by the growing ability of labour to successfully demand higher levels of government spending. Trade union bargainers seek to extend the corporatist agenda as they learn more and more about how much state and employers are prepared to concede.

As we saw in Chapter 5, in Sweden attempts in the late 1970s and early 1980s by the LO to develop corporatism into a system which would generate a gradual socialization of investment were met with hostility. The vehicle for this was to have the system of wage-earner funds. For trade unions the corporatist agenda was being extended beyond full employment and reduced income inequality into a programme for social control of production 'through the back door'. The advantage of the wage-earner system to employers was that capital would be made available at a lower risk premium than could be obtained on international financial markets. However, a coalition of the SAF and white-collar workers were unconvinced and the scheme was eventually only introduced in a much-diluted form.

All this suggests that there may be limits to what corporatist institutions can achieve, and to that extent even corporatism may fail to overcome the problems which Kalecki identifies. In particular, if the employer side perceives that the balance of power is shifting too far away from them then it is likely that they will withdraw their support. This in part may explain some of the problems of corporatism in the 1980s, especially since the changes in production and the internationalization of capital have opened up alternative courses of action for employers. On the other hand, if corporatism is to evolve in even more favourable directions for labour then this cannot be done 'through the back door'. Such a strategy must rely on an explicit understanding that the balance of power has indeed shifted in favour of labour (Goldthorpe 1987). But this in turn entails both a strong and united trade union movement in alliance with confident social democratic parties. The prospects of both of these have receded, undermining even existing corporatist institutions, as we go on to examine.

LABOUR FRAGMENTATION

In addition to employer pressure, centralized bargaining in Sweden has been undermined because of a growing divergence of perceived interests among different groups within the labour movement. The decline of a predominantly manual and male working class is a phenomenon that has been experienced in all industrialized economies. In some this has occurred alongside the growth in part-time, often female, service sector employment. In corporatist economies, as we have seen, it has been countered through more explicit forms of employment restructuring involving the growth in public sector jobs. In Sweden a split both between blue-collar and white-collar workers and more latterly between public sector and private sector workers has resulted in pressure to decentralize and strike separate bargains (Ahlen 1989). The white-collar–blue-collar differences also run along private–public lines because of the growth in white-collar public sector employment. The divergence of interest arises for several reasons (Lash 1985).

Firstly, white-collar, public sector workers have in the 1980s grown discontented with their pay being governed through the centralized bargain by economic conditions affecting private sector workers, particularly in the key exporting metal-working and engineering sector. Traditionally the metalworkers union covering this sector has set the bargaining agenda for the whole of the LO union confederation. For the public sector as a whole, because their pay bill depends on government spending and taxation policies, they are more insulated from external economic conditions and so have been less ready to agree to wage restraint. Also there is, in part, a male–female conflict which again runs along private–public sector lines (Pekkarinen *et al.* 1992).

Secondly, within the public sector, because the total pay bill is often cash-limited, the more professional unions see themselves as involved in a zero-sum bargaining game with other administrative workers and municipal worker unions. Decentralization and an end to solidarity bargaining might improve the pay of the former at the expense of the latter.

Thirdly, white-collar professional workers have become less content with the progressive squeezing of wage differentials required by the solidaristic wages policy and have seen decentralization as the route through which wider differentials might be re-established. They are likely to be least content with very high rates of marginal personal taxation. They are also much less sympathetic to the aims of the LO/Social Democratic political position; for example, they were opposed to wage-earner funds.

This fragmentation in the political solidarity of the unions means that it is increasingly difficult for them to identify a common 'universal project for social transformation' (Teague and Grahl 1992, p. 22). The commitment from the union movement as a whole to corporatism as the route to a more socially acceptable form of market economy may be waning. The consequence of this is that sections of the movement in corporatist economies may be moving slowly towards a more North American industrial unionism model, as they have been in other European economies.

The fragmentation of labour and the decline of its capacity for political and social vision is related to the more general decline of social democracy (Scharpf 1991). This is important, since in Chapter 4 we argued that successful corporatist arrangements are usually associated with strong social democratic traditions. In conclusion it seems unlikely that any renaissance of corporatism will occur without a similar renaissance in the prospects of social democratic parties.

FUTURE PROSPECTS FOR CORPORATIST INSTITUTIONS

The issue that generally surfaces in most discussions of corporatism, and of the Nordic 'middle way', is that of the universalizability of the model. As we have stated earlier, there are a number of features of corporatist economies that are probably bound up with their past decisions to opt for a corporatist mode of policy formulation and wage restraint. The most obvious of these are the two highlighted by Katzenstein (1985). The first is that corporatist economies tend to be very open, being reliant on external trade and therefore very vulnerable to changes in economic conditions in the rest of the world. The second is that they are quite small in size, a factor which places greater emphasis on the need for industrial specialization and reliance on trade with other countries. Related to their small size they also tend to be societies with a high degree of social cohesion. This means that the problems of conflict accommodation between different competing groups is likely to be smaller because the number of those groups is limited.

It is this fact that corporatist economies tend to be small and cohesive which means that corporatism, in its most developed forms, is unlikely to be transferable to other much larger European economies. One can point to case-specific reasons why attempts at corporatism have failed in some of the larger European economies in the past, revolving around flawed institutional design or inadequate commitment from one or more of the parties concerned. However, the fact that French, Italian and British attempts at corporatist compromise in the 1960s and 1970s were short-lived and unsuccessful would suggest that size is important. Explicit attempts in the 1980s and 1990s to remodel industrial relations systems along Scandinavian or Austrian lines are rather few and far between. Australia is perhaps one notable exception, where the influence of the Nordic experience has been important in formulating policies to deal with inflexible wage determination (Archer 1992). Archer argues that a particular brand of social cohesion is to be found in Australia in the form of what he rather colourfully yet vaguely terms 'mateship'. The Australian experience so far has consisted largely of a wage restraint pact between unions and Labour governments – to extend Lehmbruch's (1984) taxonomy, a form of 'concertation without capital'. It has not developed the much wider agenda of more-developed Nordic corporatism.

Deliberate moves towards greater economic openness and trade through economic integration may motivate an interest in corporatism. Pekkarinen *et al.* (1992) suggest the democratic idealism of the new democracies in Central and Eastern Europe may provide one source of interest in corporatism. However, the problem in these countries is that any new institutional structure which entails some element of centralization is treated with suspicion because of the connection between the centrally planned economy and the former, now-discredited communist regimes. This is unfortunate since some Eastern European form of Rehn–Meidner plan for centralized and solidaristic wage determination might provide a form of accelerated industrial restructuring that would hasten the development of newly emerging profitable activities. This would allow an acceleration in the inevitable decline of others.

Another example of deliberate moves towards greater European trade is to be found in the Single European Market and EMU projects of the EC. Here the possible effectiveness of corporatist-type institutions is uncertain because the institutions would of necessity need to be supra-national. Among the majority of member states, the UK being the principal exception, the dominant view of European policy formulation is a neo-corporatist one (Henley and Tsakalotos 1992). However, at the EC-wide level the agenda is very limited. For example, the contentious Social Chapter of the Maastricht agreement avoids any attempt whatsoever to introduce Community-wide parameters for wage determination. European attempts at multinational collective bargaining are at present very limited (Northrup *et al.* 1988). European trade unions possess the inclination to coordinate wage-bargaining across countries but enjoy very little capacity to enforce its implementation. On the other hand, employers' organizations in the EC are less convinced of the need for any multinational coordination of wage bargaining.[6] Streeck and Schmitter (1992) also cast considerable doubt on the commitment of European business to any form of European corporatism. While the proposed European Works Council directive may necessitate greater international coordination, it is vehemently opposed by European employers' organizations (Hall 1992). The strongest support for a greater degree of corporatist-type arrangements in the EC comes from the European Commission itself (Henley and Tsakalotos 1992). As with trade unions, the Commission may possess a corporatist inclination but in practice possesses little ability to implement this in the face of strong national-level centrifugal forces. Teague and Grahl (1992) are more optimistic, arguing that we should not underestimate the potential for the Social Chapter, European Works Councils, and other embryonic institutions for the promotion of European-level dialogue between employers and workers to create conventions and forms of pattern bargaining which will have an influence beyond their immediate domain. This corresponds to the role for institutions which we developed in Chapter 2. Whereas these embryonic European-wide institutions may comprise an important first step, they will need to extend much further in the direction of incorporating European-wide coordination of wage determination (which at the moment is explicitly excluded) before even a weak form of coordinated European corporatism can come into existence.

The greater integration of Austria and the Nordic economies, through the creation of the European Economic Area and through possible future EC membership, may be important here. While the corporatist model may be under severe pressure in these countries there is beneath the surface a 'negotiation culture' which remains strong (de Geer 1993). One aspect of the 'corporatist model' which continues to command widespread support in the 1990s is the relevance of effective active labour market policies (*Economist* 1990, Layard and Philpott 1991). It seems quite practical that the EC should be capable of initiating a participative and internationally coordinated form of labour market intervention.

Corporatism in particular countries has been seen as a national-level response to the breakdown in international economic coordination in the late 1960s and early 1970s (Streeck and Schmitter 1992). Indeed, its ideological origins are in the nationalist movements in the inter-war period, although post-war social democratic corporatism did in fact evolve into a very different creature. Given the substantial preconditions for a successful national-level corporatism, outlined in Chapter 4, any international form of corporatist agreement will face enormous problems in its achievement. It is the failure of uncoordinated national policy responses to the slow growth of the 1970s and 1980s that has motivated moves towards greater EC integration. The question is whether such integration can promote an internationally coordinated corporatist solution as opposed to a liberal alternative which entails greater integration of trade through less regulation of economic activity. Streeck and Schmitter (1992) view the outlook as bleak, since European integration has so far relied on principles, such as 'mutual recognition' and other essentially deregulatory strategies, which have tended to strengthen the economic power of capital at the expense of labour. On the other hand, future international coordination of macroeconomic policy as envisaged through EMU would certainly form an important precondition for successfully internationally coordinated corporatism. If that coordination was premised by a commitment to overcome the current deflationary bias in Western Europe it would rule out for individual countries the use of policies designed to increase national competitiveness through pre-tax real wage flexibility. By default countries would be forced to turn to more corporatist forms of wage agreement. Corporatism and international economic cooperation may therefore not be substitutes for each other, as Streeck and Schmitter seem to suggest.

One final problem for a future international form of corporatist agreement concerns the very different nature of economic circumstances in the early 1990s compared to the immediate post-war period. At that time corporatist agreements emerged within individual economies as attempts to maintain non-inflationary full employment in the face of growing 'stagflationary' pressures in the global economy. In the highly corporatist economies the evidence shows that they succeeded for some considerable time. In the early 1990s most of the global economy is in a position of having experienced secularly rising rates of unemployment for over two decades. Many economies are now far from full employment and thus any future corporatist compromise will need to be designed towards restoring rather than maintaining full employment. The costs of such agreements will be much higher and the deferred benefits from wage restraint, for workers, and from the commitment to increase investment, for capital, will be much further in the future. The interpretation gap is therefore much wider.

CONCLUSION

The future for corporatist institutions may from the previous discussion appear very uncertain. However, the arrangements which have developed in the corporatist economies have done so over a considerable period of time. The nature and agenda of the corporatist compromise has also evolved over time. There may now be in operation strong pressures towards greater decentralization of wage bargaining in these countries but, while the structure of collective bargaining may continue to evolve, these changes will not in a few months or years destroy a now well-established corporatist culture.

This is a culture which recognizes the importance of negotiation. It also recognizes that industrial action, in the form of strikes and lock-outs, is not merely destructive but represents a failure in the operation of those conflict-resolving institutions.

The 'proof of the pudding' for corporatist institutions is, for us, in their past achievements, in terms of maintaining rates of unemployment far below those of most of the rest of the world for a considerable period after the end of the post-war 'golden age', and in terms of avoiding the socially corrosive growth in inequality that has accompanied the growth in mass unemployment in other liberal economies. This cannot be merely put down to conjunctural, fortuitous circumstances.

The past operation of corporatist institutions should be seen as a successful response to certain problems endemic in capitalist economies. We have isolated in particular the problems of uncertainty and the potential for conflict. Different types of market economy approach these in different ways, and those approaches vary over time. Thus corporatism is a multidimensional concept that has evolved through time and in different ways in different countries. This is because countries have had varying national needs and the parties involved have had different goals. For instance, in an economy such as Austria, the ability in the past to rely on foreign workers during periods of labour shortage has seen the development of a less-inclusive form of corporatism. In the Nordic countries, which have historically possessed a stronger tradition of social democratic welfarism, the nature of corporatism has developed around the idea that full employment is not only desirable in itself, but also because it is a route to achieving a greater degree of egalitarianism.

There are considerable present pressures on corporatism as an alternative to economic liberalism, which we have sketched out in this concluding chapter. Does this mean that the use of corporatist institutions as a useful adjunct to economic and social policy has passed its 'sell-by date'? The answer to this is no. The problems of uncertainty and conflict are no less prevalent in market economies in the 1990s than they were in any of the three previous decades. The implication of this is that the free market, liberal ideal of a perfect market economy where economic agents passively accept market outcomes, and where interest organizations can pose no threat, is a chimera. Thus the alternative to a corporatist form of economy is not one of perfect, decentralized markets, but rather one of unresolved conflict, dynamic instability and poor economic performance. Unemployment, the separation of powerful insider workers from weak outsiders, and the growth of inequality and poverty will be the mechanisms through which conflict is suppressed. Will the possible demise of corporatist arrangements in Europe lead to better economic performance? Again the answer must be no. We should not be surprised that if the demise of corporatism leads to an extended supremacy of market liberal analyses and policies then equilibrium rates of unemployment will rise or, where they are already high, remain stubbornly so.

However, what was appropriate in institutional terms for a Sweden or an Austria of the 1970s may not be so for a more integrated Europe of the 1990s. Institutions to deal with the deep-seated problems of market economies will remain necessary, but they may not take the same form as they have in the past. What precise form they might take is a difficult question to answer, and one which will inevitably involve a form of 'crystal ball gazing' in which we are reluctant to indulge. It remains sufficient to point out that institutional arrangements such as those in the corporatist economies are as relevant today as they have ever been.

NOTES

1. On the issue of whether EC member countries will lose fiscal autonomy, see Gibson and Tsakalotos (1991).
2. While the restoration of capital controls is unlikely, there has been some renewed interest in the Tobin tax which seeks to tax short-run speculative capital flows. For this to be a success it would rely on a great degree of coordination amongst OECD economies.
3. Some have argued as a result that the problems of Swedish corporatism in the late 1980s were the result of macroeconomic policy mistakes and the abandonment of the Rehn–Meidner model. But this does not explain why policy makers and others were so willing to accept the devaluation and for this reason an explanation for the problems of corporatism should be sought in the structural considerations which we discuss later (Pontusson 1992b).
4. There is some scepticism as to whether flexibility is always 'labour-friendly' and not merely an attempt to weaken trade unions or transfer the risk of economic activity to others, for instance sub-contractors. We do not consider this question in any depth because, whether flexibility is 'labour-friendly' or not, it still poses a problem for corporatist institutions, as we go on to discuss.
5. These problems include that central government sovereignty may be undermined; that regions may lack the capacity for the type of public support given to

corporatist institutions in the past by the nation state; that regional corporatism would by necessity be market driven, and that it would lead to further fragmentation of labour.

6.   Sisson (1991) points to several factors operating in favour of greater decentralization.

References

Aglietta, M. (1982), *Regulation and the Crisis of Capitalism*, Monthly Review Press, New York.

Ahlen, K. (1989), 'Swedish collective bargaining under pressure: inter-union rivalry and incomes policies', *British Journal of Industrial Relations*, vol. 27, no. 3, November.

Akerlof, G.A. (1970), 'The market for lemons: qualitative uncertainty and the market mechanism', *Quarterly Journal of Economics*, vol. 84, no. 3, August.

Akerlof, G.A. and Yellen, J. (eds.) (1987), *Efficiency Wage Models of the Labour Market*, Cambridge University Press, Cambridge.

Allsopp, C.J. and Helm, D. (1985), 'The political economy of economic policy', *Times Literary Supplement*, 6 December.

Alogoskoufis, G.S. and Manning, A. (1988), 'On the persistence of unemployment', *Economic Policy*, no. 7, October.

Archer, R. (1992), 'The unexpected emergence of Australian corporatism', in Pekkarinen *et al.* (1992).

Armstrong, P., Glyn, A. and Harrison, J. (1991), *Capitalism since 1945*, Basil Blackwell, Oxford.

Axelrod, R. (1984), *The Evolution of Cooperation*, Basic Books, New York.

Backus, D. and Driffill, J. (1985), 'Inflation and reputation', *American Economic Review*, vol. 75, no. 3, June.

Baldwin, P. (1990), *The Politics of Social Solidarity*, Cambridge University Press, Cambridge.

Barreto, J. (1992), 'Portugal: industrial relations under democracy', in Ferner, A. and Hyman, R. (eds) *Industrial Relations in the New Europe*, Basil Blackwell, Oxford.

Barro, R.J. and Gordon, D.B. (1983), 'Rules, discretion and reputation in a model of monetary policy', *Journal of Monetary Economics*, vol. 12, no. 1, July.

Batchelor, R., Major, R. and Morgan, A. (1980), *Industrialization and the Basis for Trade*, Cambridge University Press, Cambridge.

Beach, C.M. (1989), 'Dollars and dreams: a reduced middle class?',

Journal of Human Resources, vol. 14, no. 1, March.

Bean, C.R. (1992), 'European unemployment: a survey', *Discussion Paper*, no. 71, London School of Economics, Centre for Economic Performance.

Bean, C.R., Layard, P.R.G. and Nickell, S.J. (1986), 'The rise in unemployment: a multi-country study, *Economica*, vol. 53, no. 210, supplement.

Bils, M. (1987), 'The cyclical behaviour of marginal cost and price', *American Economic Review*, vol. 77, no. 5, December.

Bjorklund, A. (1992), 'The evolution of income inequalities in Sweden', paper presented to the Royal Economic Society, City University, London, March.

Bjorklund, A., Haveman, R., Hollister, R. and Holmlund, B. (1991), *Labour Market Policy and Unemployment Insurance*, Clarendon Press, Oxford.

Blackburn, K. and Christensen, M. (1989), 'Monetary policy and policy credibility: theories and evidence', *Journal of Economic Literature*, vol. 27, no. 1, March.

Blanchflower, D. and Freeman, R. (1990), 'Going different ways: unionism in the US and other advanced OECD countries', *Discussion Paper*, no. 5, Centre for Economic Performance, London School of Economics.

Bleaney, M. (1985), *The Rise and Fall of Keynesian Economics*, Macmillan, London.

Block, F. (1990), *Post-Industrial Possibilities: A Critique of Economic Discourse*, University of California Press, Berkeley.

Bluestone, B. and Harrison, B. (1988), *The Great U-Turn*, Basic Books, New York.

Boreham, P. and Compston, H. (1992), 'Labour movement organization and political intervention: the politics of unemployment in the OECD countries, 1974–1986', *European Journal of Political Research*, vol. 22, no. 2, August.

Boulding, K. (1968), *Beyond Economics: Essays on Society, Religion and Ethics*, University of Michigan Press, Ann Arbor.

Bowles, S. and Gintis, H. (1993), 'The revenge of homo economicus: contested exchange and the revival of political economy', *Journal of Economic Perspectives*, vol. 7, no. 1, Winter.

Bowles, S., Gordon, D.R. and Weisskopf, T.E. (1983), *Beyond the Wasteland: A Democratic Alternative to Economic Decline*, Anchor

Press/Doubleday, New York.

Boyer, R. (1987), 'Regulation', in Eatwell, J., Milgate, M. and Newman, P. (eds), *New Palgrave Dictionary of Economics*, Macmillan, London.

Boyer, R. (1992), 'Labour institutions and economic growth: a survey and a "regulationist" approach', *mimeo*, May.

Bradach, J.L. and Eccles, R.G. (1991), 'Price, authority and trust: from ideal types to plural forms', in Thompson *et al.* (1991).

Branson, W.H. and Rotemberg, J.J. (1980), 'International adjustment with wage rigidity', *European Economic Review*, vol. 13, no. 3, March.

Brittan, S. (1977), 'Can democracy manage an economy?' in Skidelsky, R. (ed.), *The End of the Keynesian Era: Essays on the Disintegration of the Keynesian Political Economy*, Macmillan, London.

Bruno, M. and Sachs, J. (1985), *The Economics of Worldwide Stagnation*, Harvard University Press, Cambridge MA.

Buchanan, J. M. and Wagner, R. E. (1977), *Democracy in Deficit: The Political Legacy of Lord Keynes*, Academic Press, New York.

Calmfors, L. (1987), 'Efficiency and equality in Swedish labour markets: comment to Flanagan', in Bosworth, B. and Rivlin, A. (eds), *The Swedish Economy*, Brookings Institution, Washington DC.

Calmfors, L. (ed.) (1990), *Wage Formation and Macroeconomic Policy in the Nordic Countries*, SNS Forlag, Stockholm, and Oxford University Press, Oxford.

Calmfors, L. and Driffill, J. (1988), 'Bargaining structure, corporatism and macroeconomic performance', *Economic Policy*, no. 6, April.

Calmfors, L. and Nymoen, R. (1990), 'Real wage adjustment and employment policies in the Nordic countries', *Economic Policy*, no. 11, October.

Cameron, D.R. (1984), 'Social democracy, corporatism, labour quiescence, and the representation of economic interest in advanced capitalist society', in Goldthorpe (1984).

Carlin, W. and Soskice, D. (1990), *Macroeconomics and the Wage Bargain*, Oxford University Press, Oxford.

Carlsson, B. (1983), 'Industrial subsidies in Sweden: macroeconomic effects and international comparison', *Journal of Industrial Economics*, vol. 32, no. 1, September.

Castles, F.G. (1987), 'Neocorporatism and the "happiness index", or what the trade unions get for their cooperation', *European Journal of Political Research*, vol. 15, no. 3, December.

Cheung, S.N.S. (1987), 'Economic organization and transactions costs', in Eatwell, J., Milgate, M. and Newman, P. (eds), *New Palgrave Dictionary of Economics*, Macmillan, London.

Clark, P.K. (1984), 'Productivity and profits in the 1980s: are they really improving?', *Brookings Papers on Economic Activity*, no. 1.

Clarke, P. (1988), *The Keynesian Revolution in the Making, 1924–36*, Oxford University Press, Oxford.

Clarke, R. and McGuiness, T. (1987), *The Economics of the Firm*, Basil Blackwell, Oxford.

Coase, R. H. (1937), 'The nature of the firm', *Economica*, vol. 4, no. 5, November.

Coase, R. H. (1960), 'The problem of social cost', *Journal of Law and Economics*, vol. 3, October.

Coe, D. and Gagliardi, F. (1985), 'Nominal wage determination in ten OECD countries', *Working Paper* no. 19, OECD Economics and Statistics Department.

Cornwall, J. (1987), 'Inflation and growth', in Eatwell, J., Milgate, M. and Newman, P. (eds), *New Palgrave Dictionary of Economics*, Macmillan, London.

Cornwall, J. (1989), 'The welfare state in a programme of economic recovery', in Davidson, P. and Kregel, J. (eds), *Macroeconomic Problems and Policies of Income Distribution*, Edward Elgar, Aldershot.

Coutts, K., Godley, W. and Nordhaus, W. (1978), *Industrial Pricing in the United Kingdom*, Cambridge University Press, Cambridge.

Cowling, K. (1983), 'Excess capacity and the degree of collusion: oligopoly behaviour in the slump', *The Manchester School*, vol. 51, no. 4, December.

Cowling, K. and Waterson, M. (1976), 'Price–cost margins and market structure', *Economica*, vol. 43, no. 171, August.

Crafts, N. (1991), 'Reversing relative economic decline? The 1980s in historical perspective' , *Oxford Review of Economic Policy*, vol. 7, no. 3, Autumn.

Crafts, N. (1992), 'Productivity growth reconsidered', *Economic Policy*, no. 15, October.

Craven, J. (1992), *Social Choice*, Cambridge University Press, Cambridge.

Crepaz, M.M.L. (1992), 'Corporatism in decline? An empirical analysis of the impact of corporatism on macroeconomic performance and industrial disputes in 18 industrialized democracies', *Comparative Political Studies*, vol. 25, no. 2, July.

Crouch, C. (ed.) (1979), *State and Economy in Contemporary Capitalism*, Croom Helm, London.

Crouch, C. (1985), 'Conditions for trade union wage restraint', in Lindberg, L.N. and Maier, C.S. (eds), *The Politics of Inflation and Economic Stagnation*, Brookings Institution, Washington DC.

Crouch, C. (1991), 'European trade unions: from conflict to concertation', in Espina, A. (ed.), *Social Concertation, Neocorporatism and Democracy*, Centro de Publicaciones, Ministerio de Tradajo y Seguridad Social, Madrid.

Davidson, P. (1991), *Controversies in Post Keynesian Economics*, Edward Elgar, Aldershot.

Dearlove, J. (1989), 'Neoclassical politics: public choice and political understanding', *Review of Political Economy*, vol. 1, no. 2, June.

Disney, R. and Gospel, H. (1989), 'The seniority model of trade union behaviour: a (partial) defence', *British Journal of Industrial Relations*, vol. 27, no. 2, July.

Disney, R., Bellman, L., Carruth, A., Franz, W., Jackman, R., Layard, R., Lehmann, H. and Philpott, J. (1992), *Helping the Unemployed*, Anglo-German Foundation, London.

Dore, R. (1983), 'Goodwill and the spirit of market capitalism', *British Journal of Sociology*, vol. 34, no. 4, December.

Dowrick, S. and Nguyen, D.-T. (1989), 'OECD comparative economic growth 1950–85: catch-up and convergence', *American Economic Review*, vol. 79, no. 5, December.

Dunford, M. (1990), 'Theories of regulation', *Society and Space*, vol. 8, no. 3, September.

Economist (1990), 'The Swedish economy', vol. 314, no. 7644, 3 March.

Edin, P-A. and Holmlund, B. (1992), 'The Swedish wage structure: the rise and fall of solidarity wage structure', *mimeo*, Uppsala University.

Eichengreen, B. (1990), 'Currency union', *Economic Policy*, no. 10, April.

Epstein, G.A. (1992), 'Political economy and comparative central banking', *Review of Radical Political Economics*, vol. 24, no. 1,

Spring.

Epstein, G.A. and Schor, J.B. (1990), 'Macropolicy in the rise and fall of the Golden Age', in Marglin and Schor (1990).

Esping-Andersen, G. (1985), *Politics against Markets: The Social Democratic Road to Power*, Princeton University Press, Princeton, New Jersey.

Esping-Andersen, G. (1990), *The Three Worlds of Welfare Capitalism*, Polity Press, Cambridge.

Esping-Andersen, G. and Korpi, W. (1984), 'Social policy as class politics in post-war capitalism: Scandinavia, Austria, and Germany', in Goldthorpe (1984).

European Industrial Relations Report (EIRR) (1991) 'Portugal: the economic and social agreement', Number 208, May.

Fallick, J.I. and Elliott, R.F. (1981), *Incomes Policies, Inflation and Relative Pay*, George Allen and Unwin, London.

Faxen, K.-O. (1982), 'Incomes policy and centralized wage formation', in Boltho, A. (ed.), *The European Economy: Growth and Crisis*, Oxford University Press, Oxford.

Frey, B.J. and Schneider, F. (1975), 'On the modelling of politico-economic interdependence', *European Journal of Political Research*, vol. 3, no. 3, September.

Friedman, J.W. (1986), *Game Theory with Applications to Economics*, Oxford University Press, Oxford.

Friedman, M. (1968), 'The role of monetary policy', *American Economic Review*, vol. 58, no. 1, March.

Gamble, A. (1993), 'The decline of corporatism', in Crabtree, D. and Thirlwall, A.P. (eds), *Keynes and the Role of the State*, Macmillan, London.

Garrett, G. and Lange, P. (1989), 'Government partisanship and economic performance: when and how does "who governs" matter?', *Journal of Politics*, vol. 51, no. 3, August.

Geer, H. de (1993), *The Rise and Fall of the Swedish Model*, Carden Publications, London.

Geroski, P. (1989), '1992 and European industrial structure', in McKenzie, G. and Venables, A.J. (eds), *The Economics of the Single European Act*, Macmillan, London.

Giavazzi, F. (1988), 'Discussion', *Economic Policy*, no. 6, April.

Gibson, H.D. and Tsakalotos E. (1991), 'European monetary union and macroeconomic policy in southern Europe: the case for positive integration', *Journal of Public Policy*, vol. 11, no. 3, July/September.

Giersch, H. (1985), 'Eurosclerosis', *Discussion Paper* no. 112, Kiel Institute for World Economics, October.

Glyn, A. (1991), 'Stability, egalitarianism and dynamism: an overview of the advanced capitalist countries in the 1980s', *mimeo*, Corpus Christi College, Oxford.

Glyn, A. (1992), 'Corporatism, patterns of employment and access to consumption', in Pekkarinen *et al.* (1992).

Glyn, A. and Rowthorn, B. (1988), 'West European unemployment: corporatism and structural change', *American Economic Review, Papers and Proceedings*, vol. 78, no. 2, May.

Glyn, A., Hughes, A., Lipietz, A. and Singh, A. (1990), 'The rise and fall of the Golden Age', in Marglin and Schor (1990).

Goldthorpe, J.H. (ed.) (1984), *Order and Conflict in Contemporary Capitalism*, Clarendon Press, Oxford.

Goldthorpe, J.H. (1984a), 'The end of convergence: corporatist and dualist tendencies in modern Western societies', in Goldthorpe (1984).

Goldthorpe, J.H. (1987), 'Problems of political economy after the post-war period', in Maier, C. S. (ed.), *Changing Boundaries of the Political: essays on the evolving balance between the state and society, public and private in Europe*, Cambridge University Press, Cambridge.

Goodhart, C.A.E. (1989), *Money, Information and Uncertainty*, 2nd edn., Macmillan, London.

Goodhart, C.A.E. (1990), 'Fiscal policy and EMU', in Pohl, K.-O., *et al.*, *Britain and EMU*, Centre for Economic Performance, London School of Economics.

Gordon, D.M. (1991), 'Comment: institutions for the transition to the free market', in Atkinson, A.B. and Brunetta, R. (eds), *Economics for the New Europe*, Macmillan, London.

Grahl, J. and Teague, P.T. (1990), *1992 – the Big Market: the future of the European Community*, Lawrence and Wishart, London.

Green, F., Henley, A. and Tsakalotos, E. (1992), 'Income inequality in corporatist and liberal economies: a comparison of trends within OECD countries', *Studies in Economics*, no. 92/13, University of Kent at Canterbury.

Grossman, H. and Stiglitz, J. E. (1976), 'Information and competitive price systems', *American Economic Review*, vol. 66, no. 2, May.

Grout, P. A. (1984), 'Investment and wages in the absence of legally binding labour contracts', *Econometrica*, vol. 52, no. 2, March.

Grubb, D. (1986), 'Topics in the OECD Phillips curve', *Economic Journal*, vol. 96, no. 381, March.

Grubb, D., Jackman, R. and Layard, P.R.G. (1983), 'Wage rigidity and unemployment in OECD countries', *European Economic Review*, vol. 21, no. 1, January.

Guger, A. (1989), 'Einkommensverteilung und Verteilungspolitik in Osterreich', in Abele, A., Nowotny, E., Schleicher, S. and Winckler, G. (eds), *Handbuch der osterreichischen Wirtschafts-politik*, Manzsche Verlags- und Universitatsbuchhandlung, Vienna.

Guger, A. (1992), 'Corporatism: success or failure? Austrian experiences', in Pekkarinen *et al.* (1992).

Gustafsson, B. and Uusitalo, H. (1990), 'Income distribution and redistribution during two decades: experiences from Finland and Sweden', in Persson, I. (ed.), *Generating Equality in the Welfare State: The Swedish Experience*, Norwegian University Press, Oslo.

Hahn, F. (1984), *Equilibrium and Macroeconomics*, Basil Blackwell, Oxford.

Hahn, F. (1985), 'Recognizing the limits', *The Times Literary Supplement*, 6 December.

Hall, M. (1992), 'Behind the European works councils directive: the European Commission's legislative strategy', *British Journal of Industrial Relations*, vol. 30, no. 4, December.

Hall, P. (1986), *Governing the Economy: The Politics of State Intervention in Britain and France*, Polity Press, Cambridge.

Henley, A. (1990), *Wages and Profits in the Capitalist Economy*, Edward Elgar, Aldershot.

Henley, A. and Tsakalotos, E. (1991), 'Corporatism, profit squeeze and investment', *Cambridge Journal of Economics*, vol. 15, no. 4, December.

Henley, A. and Tsakalotos, E. (1992), 'Corporatism and the European labour market after 1992', *British Journal of Industrial Relations*, vol. 30, no. 4, December.

Hibbs, D.A. (1977), 'Political parties and macroeconomic policy', *American Political Science Review*, vol. 71, no. 4, December.

Hibbs, D.A. (1978), 'On the political economy of long run trends in strike activity', *British Journal of Political Science*, vol. 8, no. 2,

April.

Hibbs, D.A. (1979), 'Rejoinder', *American Political Science Review*, vo. 73, no. 1, March.

Hicks, A. (1988), 'Social democratic corporatism and economic growth', *Journal of Politics*, vol. 50, no. 3, March.

Hicks, A. and Patterson W.D. (1989), 'On the robustness of the left corporatist model of economic growth', *Journal of Politics*, vol. 51, no. 3, August.

Higgins, W. and Apple, N. (1983), 'How limited is reformism? A critique of Przeworski and Panitch', *Theory and Society*, vol. 12, no. 5, September.

Hirsch, P., Michaels, S. and Friedman, R. (1990), 'Clean models vs. dirty hands: why economics is different from sociology', in Zukin and DiMaggio (1990).

Hodgson, G. (1984), *The Democratic Economy*, Penguin, Harmondsworth.

Hodgson, G. (1988), *Economics and Institutions*, Polity Press, Cambridge.

Hodgson, G. (1989), 'Institutional economic theory: the old versus the new', *Review of Political Economy*, vol. 1, no. 3, September.

Holden, S. (1989), 'Wage drift and bargaining: evidence from Norway', *Economica*, vol. 56, no. 244, November.

Holden, S. (1990), 'Wage drift in Norway: a bargaining approach', in Calmfors (1990).

Holmlund, B. (1986), 'Centralized wage setting, wage drift and stabilization policies under trade unionism', *Oxford Economic Papers*, vol. 38, no. 3, July.

Holmlund, B. and Skedinger, P. (1990), 'Wage bargaining and wage drift: evidence from the Swedish wood industry', in Calmfors (1990).

Holmlund, B. and Zetterberg, J. (1991), 'Insider effects in wage determination: evidence from five countries', *European Economic Review*, vol. 35, no. 5, July.

Honkapohja, S. (1988), 'Discussion', *Economic Policy*, no. 6, April.

Hoover, K.D. (1988), *The New Classical Macroeconomics: A Sceptical Inquiry*, Basil Blackwell, Oxford.

Industrial Relations Review and Report (IRRR) (1990), 'Developments in European collective bargaining: 2', *IRS Employment Trends*, no. 465, 6 June.

Ingham, G. (1984), *Capitalism Divided: City and Industry in British Social Development*, Macmillan, London.

Jackman, R. (1990), 'Wage formation in the Nordic countries viewed from an international perspective', in Calmfors (1990).

Jackman, R., Pissarides, C. and Savouri, S. (1990), 'Labour market policies and unemployment in the OECD', *Economic Policy*, no. 11, October.

Jackman, R.W. (1987), 'The politics of economic growth in the industrial democracies, 1974–80: leftist strength or North Sea oil?', *Journal of Politics*, vol. 49, no. 1, February.

Jackman, R.W. (1989), 'The politics of economic growth, once again', *Journal of Politics*, vol. 51, no. 3, August.

Johansons, J. and Mattson, L.-G. (1991), 'Interorganizational relations in industrial systems: a network approach compared with the transactions-cost approach', in Thompson *et al.* (1991).

Johnson, P. and Webb, S. (1993), 'Explaining the growth in UK income inequality: 1979–1988', *Economic Journal*, vol. 103, no. 417, March.

Kalecki, M. (1938), 'The determinants of the distribution of national income', *Econometrica*, vol. 6, no. 2, April.

Kalecki, M. (1943), 'Political aspects of full employment', *The Political Quarterly*, vol. 14, no. 4, October/December.

Katzenstein, P.J. (1985), *Small States in World Markets*, Cornell University Press, Ithaca.

Kay, J. (1993), *Foundations of Corporate Success: How Business Strategies Add Value*, Oxford University Press, Oxford.

Kenworthy, L. (1990), 'Are industrial policy and corporatism compatible?', *Journal of Public Policy*, vol. 10, no 3, July/September.

Kerr, C. (1950), 'Labor markets: their character and consequences', *American Economic Review*, vol. 40, no. 2, May.

Kerr, C. (1954), 'The Balkanization of labor markets', in Bakke, E.W. (ed.), *Labor Mobility and Economic Opportunity*, John Wiley, New York.

Keynes, J. M. (1936), *The General Theory of Employment, Interest and Money*, Macmillan, London.

Korkman, S. (1992), 'Exchange rate policy and employment in small open economies', in Pekkarinen *et al.* (1992).

Korpi, W. (1991), 'Political and economic explanations for

unemployment: a cross-national and long-term analysis', *British Journal of Political Science*, vol. 21, no. 3, July.

Korpi, W. and Shalev, M. (1979), 'Strikes, industrial relations and class conflict in capitalist societies', *British Journal of Sociology*, vol. 30, no. 2, June.

Korpi, W. and Shalev, M. (1980), 'Strikes, power and politics in western nations, 1900–1976', *Political Power and Social Theory*, vol. 1.

Kritsantonis, N.D. (1992), 'Greece: from state authoritarianism to modernization', in Ferner, A. and Hyman, R. (eds.) *Industrial Relations in the New Europe*, Basil Blackwell, Oxford

Krugman, P. (1990), *The Age of Diminished Expectations*, MIT Press, Cambridge, MA.

Kurzer, P. (1988), 'The politics of central banks: austerity and unemployment in Europe', *Journal of Public Policy*, vol. 8, no. 1, Jan/March.

Kydland, F. and Prescott, E.C. (1977), 'Rules rather than discretion: the inconsistency of optimal plans', *Journal of Political Economy*, vol. 85, no. 3, June.

Lancaster, K. (1973), 'The dynamic inefficiency of capitalism', *Journal of Political Economy*, vol. 81, no. 5, September/October.

Landesmann, M. (1992), 'Industrial policies and social corporatism', in Pekkarinen *et al.* (1992).

Landesmann, M. and Vartiainen, J. (1992), 'Social corporatism and long-term economic performance', in Pekkarinen *et al.* (1992).

Lange, O. (1935), 'Marxian economics and modern economic theory', *Review of Economic Studies*, vol. 2, no. 3.

Lange, P. (1984), 'Unions, workers, and wage regulation: the rational bases on consent', in Goldthorpe (1984).

Lange, P. and Garrett, G. (1985), 'The politics of growth: strategic interaction and economic performance in the advanced industrial democracies, 1974–1980', *Journal of Politics*, vol. 47, no. 3, August.

Lange, P. and Garrett, G. (1987), 'The politics of growth reconsidered', *Journal of Politics*, vol. 49, no. 1, February.

Lash, S. (1985), 'The end of neo-corporatism? The breakdown of centralized bargaining in Sweden', *British Journal of Industrial Relations*, vol. 23, no. 2, July.

Layard, P.R.G. (1990), 'Wage bargaining and EMU', in Pohl K.-O. *et al.*, *Britain and the EMS*, Centre for Economic Performance, London School of Economics.

Layard, P.R.G. and Nickell, S.J. (1986), 'Unemployment in Britain', *Economica*, vol. 53, no. 210, supplement.

Layard, P.R.G. and Philpott, J. (1991), *Stopping Unemployment*, Employment Institute, London.

Layard, P.R.G., Nickell, S.J. and Jackman, R. (1991), *Unemployment: Macroeconomic Performance and the Labour Market*, Oxford University Press, Oxford.

Lazonick, W. (1991), *Business Organization and the Myth of the Market Economy*, Cambridge University Press, Cambridge.

Lehmbruch, G. (1984), 'Concertation and the structure of corporatist networks', in Goldthorpe (1984).

Lehmbruch, G. and Schmitter, P.C. (eds) (1982), *Patterns of Corporatist Policy Making*, Sage Publications, London.

Levy, F. (1987), *Dollars and Dreams: The Changing American Income Distribution*, Basic Books, New York.

Leys, C. (1985), 'Thatcherism and British manufacturing', *New Left Review*, no. 151, May/June.

Lijphart, A. and Crepaz, M.M.L. (1991), 'Corporatism and consensus democracy in eighteen countries: conceptual and empirical linkages', *British Journal of Political Science*, vol. 21, no. 2, April.

Lindbeck, A. (1985), 'What is wrong with the West European economies?', *World Economy*, vol. 8, June.

Lindbeck, A, and Snower, D.J. (1989), *The Insider–Outsider Theory of Employment and Unemployment*, MIT Press, Cambridge MA.

Lipietz, A. (1986), 'Behind the crisis: the exhaustion of a regime of accumulation', *Review of Radical Political Economics*, vol. 18, nos 1–2, Spring/Summer.

Locksley, G. (1980), 'The political business cycle: alternative explanations', in Whiteley, P. (ed.), *Models of Political Economy*, Sage Publications, London.

Lorenz, E.H. (1991), 'Neither friends nor strangers: informal networks of subcontracting in French industry', in Thompson *et al.* (1991).

MacDonald, R. and Milbourne, R. (1990), 'Recent developments in monetary theory', *Discussion Paper*, Department of Economics, University of Dundee, April.

Macrae, C.D. (1977), 'A political model of the business cycle', *Journal of Political Economy*, vol. 85, no. 2, April.

Maier, C.S. (1984), 'Preconditions for corporatism', in Goldthorpe (1984).

Maier, C.S. and Lindberg, L.N. (1985), 'Alternatives for future crises', in Lindberg, L.N. and Maier, C.S. (eds), *The Politics of Inflation and Economic Stagnation*, Brookings Institution, Washington DC.

Mankiw, N.G. (1990), 'A quick refresher course in macroeconomics', *Journal of Economic Literature*, vol. 28, no. 4, December.

Manning, A. (1987), 'An integration of trade union models in a sequential bargaining framework', *Economic Journal*, vol. 97, no. 385, March.

Manning, A. (1993), 'Wage bargaining and the Phillips curve: the identification and specification of aggregate wage equations', *Economic Journal*, vol. 103, no. 416, January.

Manoilescu, M. (1938), *La Siècle du Corporatisme: Doctrine du Corporatisme Intégral et Pur*, Alcan, Paris.

Marglin, S. (1990), 'Lessons of the Golden Age: an overview', in Marglin and Schor (1990).

Marglin, S. and Bhaduri, A. (1990), 'Profit squeeze and Keynesian theory', in Marglin and Schor (1990).

Marglin, S. and Schor, J.B. (eds) (1990), *The Golden Age of Capitalism: Lessons for the 1990s*, Clarendon Press, Oxford.

Marquand, D. (1988), *The Unprincipled Society: New Demands and Old Politics*, Fontana Press, London.

Martin, A. (1979), 'The dynamics of change in a Keynesian political economy: the Swedish case and its implications', in Crouch (1979).

Martinez Lucio, M. (1992), 'Spain: constructing institutions and actors in a context of change', in Ferner, A. and Hyman, R. (eds), *Industrial Relations in the New Europe*, Basil Blackwell, Oxford.

Matthews, R.C.O. (1986), 'The economics of institutions and the sources of growth', *Economic Journal*, vol. 96, no. 384, December.

McCallum, J. (1986), 'Unemployment in OECD countries in the 1980s', *Economic Journal*, vol. 96, no. 384, December.

Moohkerjee, D. and Shorrocks, A. (1982), 'A decomposition analysis of the trend in UK income inequality', *Economic Journal*, vol. 92, no. 368, December.

Mullard, M. (1992), *Understanding Economic Policy*, Routledge, London.

Newell, A. and Symons, J.S.V. (1985), 'Wages and employment in OECD countries', *Discussion Paper*, no. 219, Centre for Labour

Economics, London School of Economics.

Newell, A. and Symons, J.S.V. (1987), 'Corporatism, laissez-faire and the rise in unemployment', *European Economic Review*, vol. 31, no. 3, March.

Nickell, S.J. (1990), 'Unemployment: a survey', *Economic Journal*, vol. 100, no. 401, June.

Nickell, S.J. and Andrews, M. (1983), 'Unions, real wages and employment in Britain 1951–79', *Oxford Economic Papers*, vol. 35, supplement, November.

Nordhaus, W. (1975), 'The political business cycle', *Review of Economic Studies*, vol. 42, no. 2, April.

North, D.C. (1990), *Institutions, Institutional Change and Economic Performance*, Cambridge University Press, Cambridge.

Northrup, H.R., Campbell, D.C. and Slowinski, B.J. (1988), 'Multinational union–management consultation in Europe and resurgence in the 1980s?', *International Labour Review*, vol. 127, no. 3, September.

O'Brien, D.J. and Shannon, T.A. (1992), *Catholic Social Thought: The Documentary Heritage*, Orbis, New York.

OECD (1988), 'Profiles of labour market budgets', *OECD Employment Outlook*, September.

OECD (1991), 'Trends in trade union membership', *OECD Employment Outlook*, July.

Offe, C. (1985), 'The two logics of collective action', in Offe, C., *Disorganized Capitalism*, Polity Press, Cambridge.

Okun, A.M. (1981), *Prices and Quantities: A Macroeconomic Analysis*, Brookings Institution, Washington DC.

Olson, M. (1965), *The Logic of Collective Action*, Harvard University Press, Cambridge, MA.

Olson, M. (1982), *The Rise and Decline of Nations*, Yale University Press, New Haven, Conn.

Oswald, A.J. (1985), 'The economic theory of trades unions: a introductory survey', *Scandinavian Journal of Economics*, vol. 87, no. 2, June.

Oswald, A.J. (1987), 'Efficient contracts are on the labour demand curve: theory and facts', *Discussion Paper* no. 284, Centre for Labour Economics, London School of Economics.

Oswald, A.J. and Turnbull, P.J. (1985), 'Pay and employment determination in Britain: what are labour "contracts" really like?',

Oxford Review of Economic Policy, vol. 1, no. 2, Summer.

Panitch, L. (1980), 'Recent theorisations of corporatism: reflections on a growth industry', *British Journal of Sociology*, vol. 31, no. 2, June.

Payne, J. (1979), 'Communication', *American Political Science Review*, vol. 73, no. 1, March.

Pekkarinen, J. (1992), 'Corporatism and economic performance in Sweden, Norway and Finland', in Pekkarinen *et al.* (1992).

Pekkarinen, J., Pohjula, M. and Rowthorn, R.E. (eds.) (1992), *Social Corporatism: A Superior Economic System?*, Clarendon Press, Oxford.

Perrow, C. (1990), 'Economic theories of organization', in Zukin and DiMaggio (1990).

Pimlott, B. (1992), *Harold Wilson*, Harper Collins, London.

Pissarides, C.A. and Moghadam, R. (1990), 'Relative wage flexibility in four countries', in Calmfors (1990).

Pizzorno, A (1978), 'Political exchange and collective identity in industrial conflict', in Crouch, C. and Pizzorno, A. (eds), *The Resurgence of Class Conflict in Western Europe since 1968*, Macmillan, London.

Ploeg, F. van der (1987), 'Trade unions, investment and employment: a non-cooperative approach', *European Economic Review*, vol. 31, no. 8, October.

Pohjula, M. (1992), 'Corporatism and wage bargaining', in Pekkarinen *et al.* (1992).

Pontusson, J. (1984), 'Behind and beyond social democracy in Sweden', *New Left Review*, no. 143, January/February.

Pontusson, J. (1991), 'Labor, corporatism and industrial policy: the Swedish case in comparative perspective', *Comparative Politics*, vol. 23, no. 2, January.

Pontusson, J. (1992a), *The Limits of Social Democracy: Investment Politics in Sweden*, Cornell University Press, Ithaca, N.Y.

Pontusson, J. (1992b), 'At the end of the third road: Swedish social democracy in crisis', *Politics and Society*, vol. 20, no. 3, September.

Powell, W.W. (1991), 'Neither market nor hierarchy: network forms of organization', in Thompson *et al.* (1991).

Pryor, F.L. (1988), 'Corporatism as an economic system: a review essay', *Journal of Comparative Economics*, vol. 12, no. 3, September.

Pryor, F.L. (1993), 'A Roman Catholic approach toward an ideal economic system', *Journal of Comparative Economics*, vol. 17, no. 1, March.

Przeworski, A. and Wallerstein, M. (1982), 'The structure of class conflict in democratic capitalist societies', *American Political Science Review*, vol. 76, no. 2, June.

Quiggin, J. (1992), 'Testing the implications of the Olson hypothesis', *Economica*, vol. 59, no. 235, August.

Regini, M. (1984), 'The conditions for political exchange: how concertation emerged and collapsed in Italy and Great Britain', in Goldthorpe (1984).

Reid, G. (1987), *Theories of Industrial Organization*, Basil Blackwell, Oxford.

Ringen, S. (1991), 'Households, standards of living and inequality', *Review of Income and Wealth*, series 37, no. 1, March.

Robinson, P. (1989), *What can Britain Learn from Sweden's Commitment to Full Employment?*, Campaign for Work, London.

Rødseth, A. and Holden, S. (1990), 'Wage formation in Norway', in Calmfors (1990).

Rogoff, K. (1985), 'The optimal degree of commitment to a intermediate monetary target', *Quarterly Journal of Economics*, vol. 100, no. 4, November.

Rotemberg, J. and Saloner, G. (1986), 'A super-game-theoretic model of price wars during booms', *American Economic Review*, vol. 76, no. 3, June.

Rowthorn, B. (1977), 'Conflict, inflation and money', *Cambridge Journal of Economics*, vol. 1, no. 3, September, reprinted in Rowthorn (1980).

Rowthorn, B. (1980), *Capitalism, Conflict and Inflation*, Lawrence and Wishart, London.

Rowthorn, B. (1983), 'The past strikes back', in Hall, S. and Jacques, M. (eds), *The Politics of Thatcherism*, Lawrence and Wishart, London.

Rowthorn, B. (1992a), 'Corporatism and labour market performance', in Pekkarinen *et al.* (1992).

Rowthorn, B. (1992b), 'Centralization, employment and wage dispersion', *Economic Journal*, vol. 102, no. 412, May.

Rowthorn, B. and Glyn, A. (1990), 'The diversity of unemployment experience', in Marglin and Schor (1990).

Rubery, J. and Wilkinson, F. (1986), 'Inflation and income distribution' in Nolan, P. and Paine, S. (eds), *Rethinking Socialist Economics*, Polity Press, Cambridge.

Sachs, J. (1979), 'Wages, profits and macroeconomic adjustment: a comparative study', *Brookings Papers on Economic Activity*, no. 2.

Samuels, W.J. (1987), 'Institutional economics', in Eatwell, J., Milgate, M. and Newman, P. (eds), *New Palgrave Dictionary of Economics*, Macmillan, London.

Sargent, T.J. and Wallace, N. (1975), 'Rational expectations, the optimal monetary instrument and the optimal money supply rule', *Journal of Political Economy*, vol. 83, no. 2, April.

Sawyer, M.C. (1989), *The Challenge of Radical Political Economy: An Introduction to the Alternatives to Neo-Classical Economics*, Harvester Wheatsheaf, London.

Sawyer, M.C. (1992), 'Unemployment and the dismal science', *Discussion Paper* no. G92/15, University of Leeds, School of Business and Economic Studies.

Scharpf, F.W. (1984), 'Economic and institutional constraints of full employment strategies: Sweden, Austria, and West Germany, 1973–1982', in Goldthorpe (1984).

Scharpf, F.W. (1991), *Crisis and Choice in European Social Democracy*, Cornell University Press, Ithaca, N.Y.

Schmidt, G. and Reissart, B. (1988), 'Do institutions make a difference? Financing systems of labour market policy', *Journal of Public Policy*, vol. 8, no 2, April/June.

Schmidt, M.G. (1982), 'Does corporatism matter? Economic crisis, politics and rates of unemployment in capitalist democracies in the 1970s', in Lehmbruch and Schmitter (1982).

Schmitter, P.C. (1974), 'Still the century of corporatism', *Review of Politics*, vol. 36, no. 1, January.

Schmitter, P.C. (1982), 'Reflections on where the theory of neo-corporatism has gone and where the praxis of neo-corporatism may be going', in Lehmbruch and Schmitter (1982).

Schmitter, P.C. (1991), 'Social concertation in comparative perspective', in Espina, A. (ed.), *Social Concertation, Neocorporatism and Democracy*, Centro de Publicaciones, Ministerio de Tradajo y Seguridad Social, Madrid.

Schott, K. (1984), 'Investment, order, and conflict in a simple dynamic model of capitalism', in Goldthorpe (1984).

Schotter, A. (1981), *The Economic Theory of Social Institutions*, Cambridge University Press, Cambridge.

Schwerin, D.S. (1984), 'Historic compromise and pluralist decline? Profits and capital in the Nordic countries', in Goldthorpe (1984).

Shalev, M. (1978), 'Strikers and the state: a comment', *British Journal of Political Science*, vol. 8, no. 4, October.

Shonfield, A. (1965), *Modern Capitalism*, Oxford University Press, Oxford.

Sisson, K. (1987), *The Management of Collective Bargaining: An International Comparison*, Basil Blackwell, Oxford.

Sisson, K. (1991), 'Employers' organizations and industrial relations: the significance of the strategies of large companies', *mimeo*, Industrial Relations Research Unit, University of Warwick.

Slichter, S.H. (1954), 'Do the wage-fixing arrangements in the American labor market have an inflationary bias?', *American Economic Review*, Papers and Proceedings, vol. 44, no. 2, May.

Solo, R.A. (1989), 'Institutional economics', in Hey, J. D. (ed.), *Current Issues in Microeconomics*, Macmillan, London.

Solow, R.M. (1990), *The Labour Market as a Social Institution*, Basil Blackwell, Oxford.

Soskice, D. (1990), 'Wage determination: the changing role of institutions in advanced industrialized countries', *Oxford Review of Economic Policy*, vol. 6, no. 4, Winter.

Soskice, D. (1991), 'The institutional infrastructure for international competitiveness: a comparative analysis of the UK and Germany', in Atkinson, A. B. and Brunetta, R. (eds), *Economics for the New Europe*, Macmillan, London.

Standing, G. (1988), 'Training, flexibility and Swedish full employment', *Oxford Review of Economic Policy*, vol. 4, no. 3, Autumn.

Stephens, J. (1979), *The Transition from Capitalism to Socialism*, Macmillan, London.

Stiglitz, J.E. (1985), 'Information and economic analysis – a perspective' *Economic Journal*, vol. 95, no. 5, Supplement, March.

Stoneman, P. and Francis, N. (1992), 'Double deflation and the measurement of output and productivity in UK manufacturing 1979–89', *mimeo*, University of Warwick Business School.

Streeck, W. and Schmitter, P.C. (1991), 'Community, market, state – and associations? The prospective contribution of interest governance to social order', in Thompson *et al.* (1991).

Streeck, W. and Schmitter, P.C. (1992), 'From national corporatism to transnational pluralism: organized interests in the Single European Market', *Politics and Society*, vol. 19, no. 2, June.

Sugden, R. (1981), *The Political Economy of Public Choice*, Martin Robertson, Oxford.

Swenson, P. (1988), *Fair Shares: Unions, Pay and Politics in Sweden and West Germany*, Cornell University Press, Ithaca, N.Y.

Tabellini, G. (1987), 'The politics of inflation and economic stagflation', *Journal of Monetary Economics*, vol. 19, no. 4, November.

Taylor, G.W. and Pierson, F.C. (eds) (1957), *New Concepts in Wage Determination*, McGraw-Hill, New York.

Teague, P.T. and Grahl, J. (1992), *Industrial Relations and European Integration*, Lawrence and Wishart, London.

Therborn, G. (1986), 'The two-thirds, one-third society', in Hall, S. and Jacques, M. (eds), *New Times*, Lawrence and Wishart, London.

Therborn, G. (1992), 'Lessons from "corporatist" theorizations', in Pekkarinen *et al.* (1992).

Thompson, G., Frances, J., Levacic, R. and Mitchell, J. (1991), *Markets, Hierarchies and Networks: The Coordination of Social Life*, Sage Publications, London.

Tsakalotos, E. (1991), *Alternative Economic Strategies: The Case of Greece*, Avebury, Aldershot.

Ullman, L. and Flanagan, R.J. (1971), *Wage Restraint: A Study of Incomes Policy in Western Europe*, University of California Press, Berkeley and Los Angeles.

Vaillancourt, F. (1985), *Income Distribution and Economic Security in Canada*, University of Toronto Press, Toronto.

Vilrokx, J. and Van Leemput, J. (1992), 'Belgium: a new stability in industrial relations', in Ferner, A. and Hyman, R. (eds), *Industrial Relations in the New Europe*, Basil Blackwell, Oxford.

Visser, J. (1990), *In Search of Inclusive Unionism*, published as *Bulletin of Comparative Labour Relations*, no. 18.

Wagner, R.E. (1977), 'Economic manipulation for political profit: macroeconomic consequences and constitutional implication', *Kyklos*, vol. 30, no. 3, August.

Waterson, M. (1984), *Economic Theory of the Industry*, Cambridge University Press, Cambridge.

Weisskopf, T. (1987), 'The effect of unemployment on labour productivity: an international comparative analysis', *International Review of Applied Economics*, vol. 1, no. 2, July.

Williamson, O.E. (1975), *Markets and Hierarchies: Analysis and Antitrust Implications*, Free Press, New York.

Williamson, O.E. (1985), *The Economic Institutions of Capitalism*, Free Press, New York.

Williamson, P.J. (1989), *Corporatism in Perspective*, Sage Publications, London.

Zimbalist, A., Sherman, H.J. and Brown, S. (1989), *Comparing Economic Systems: A Politico-Economic Approach*, 2nd edn, Harcourt Brace Jovanovich, New York.

Zukin, S. and DiMaggio, P. (eds) (1990), *Structures of Capital: The Social Organization of the Economy*, Cambridge University Press, Cambridge.

Zysman, J. (1983), *Governments, Markets and Growth*, Cornell University Press, Ithaca, N.Y.

Author Index

Subject Index

214

New Directions in Modern Economics

Post-Keynesian Monetary Economics
New Approaches to Financial Modelling
Edited by Philip Arestis

Keynes' Principle of Effective Demand
Edward J. Amadeo

New Directions in Post-Keynesian Economics
Edited by John Pheby

Theory and Policy in Political Economy
Essays in Pricing, Distribution and Growth
Edited by Philip Arestis and Yiannis Kitromilides

Keynes' Third Alternative?
The Neo-Ricardian Keynesians and the Post Keynesians
Amitava Krishna Dutt and Edward J. Amadeo

Wages and Profits in the Capitalist Economy
The Impact of Monopolistic Power on Macroeconomic Performance
in the USA and UK
Andrew Henley

Prices, Profits and Financial Structures
A Post-Keynesian Approach to Competition
Gokhan Capoglu

International Perspectives on Profitability and Accumulation
Edited by Fred Moseley and Edward N. Wolff

Mr Keynes and the Post-Keynesians
Principles of Macroeconomics for a Monetary Production Economy
Fernando J. Cardim de Carvalho

The Economic Surplus in Advanced Economies
Edited by John B. Davis

Foundations of Post-Keynesian Economic Analysis
Marc Lavoie

The Post-Keynesian Approach to Economics
An Alternative Analysis of Economic Theory and Policy
Philip Arestis

Income Distribution in a Corporate Economy
Russell Rimmer

The Economics of the Profit Rate
Competition, Crises and Historical Tendencies in Capitalism
Gérard Duménil and Dominique Lévy

Corporatism and Economic Performance
A Comparative Analysis of Market Economies
Andrew Henley and Euclid Tsakalotos